Town Planning in Frontier America

Town Planning in Frontier America

BY

JOHN W. REPS

PRINCETON UNIVERSITY PRESS

PRINCETON, NEW JERSEY

This book is based closely on my longer and more complete study of city planning in the United States, *The Making of Urban America*, published in 1965. It is an attempt to make available to a wider audience the material first presented in that volume, which, because of its size and cost, was necessarily limited to an edition of modest numbers. The tradition of American urban planning is a long and interesting one and deserves to be more widely understood and appreciated. I hope that this version of the history of an important aspect of our country's development will prove as attractive to the general reader as my earlier effort apparently did to more specialized scholars.

I have limited the scope of this work to an examination of city plans prepared before the middle of the 19th century, beginning with the first permanent European settlement in 1565 at St. Augustine. In order to make this narrative as compact as possible I have selected for review and discussion only the more important events of urban planning. The reader who wishes additional information for the period covered or material on the later history of planned city development to the beginning of the modern era may wish to explore my earlier and longer study and to consult its more detailed bibliography.

This volume incorporates new material discovered since the publication of its parent book. Much of the original text has been rewritten or rearranged. In this task I have had the benefit of comments, suggestions, and reviews stimulated by *The Making of Urban America*. Many of these have proved helpful to me in editing some of the earlier material, in correcting errors, and in modifying my first interpretations. I wish to express my gratitude to those who have contributed in this way to the present study as well as to thank again those individuals and institutions who aided my original research.

CONTENTS

List of Illustrations

(Notes on the illustrations begin on page 431.)

Town Planning in Frontier America

From the beginning of American settlement the planning of towns played an important role in the development of colonial empires by the European powers contending for the prize of the New World. Whether as market centers, bases for exploration and exploitation of natural resources, military camps for the subjugation of a region, ports for fishing and trade, or havens from the religious persecutions of Europe, the founding of towns occupied a key position in colonial policy.

The forms these towns took varied with the purposes of settlement and the skills of their founders. Although in Europe most urban growth occurred by gradual extensions and enlargements of long-established towns and cities, the towns of America were planned on virgin land. Their original plans, aside from their intrinsic interest, furnish valuable clues to the character of frontier life and the development of distinctive American urban patterns.

The first settlers brought with them concepts of towns and cities derived from European experience. These ideas of the proper patterns of streets, building sites, and open spaces and the institutional arrangements of land tenure were transplanted to an environment that differed sharply from Europe. Here was a vast continent stretching almost endlessly, where land was the most abundant of all resources. Certainly no shortage of building sites compelled settlers to cluster closely together in nucleated settlement patterns. Town life became the basis of colonial development for two reasons: it afforded the best protection against possible hostile attack, and it represented a continuation of the established system of living with which most colonists were familiar.

By the beginning of the 17th century each of the European colonizing powers had accumulated a substantial body of domestic experience in the design of towns, both in the creation of entirely new communities and, more commonly, in the extension or improvement of older settlements. During the years of active exploration and colonization in the New World, additional urban planning projects were carried out in the Old. This quite substantial body of urban planning theory and practice was thus available for application on the American continent.

Physical environment, isolation, and inadequate resources all acted in different ways to prevent wholesale transplanting to the colonies of the newer techniques of city design which had evolved in Europe. The North Atlantic proved a formidable barrier, permitting only the barest of essentials to be sent to frontier outposts clinging precariously to the outer rim of the continent. A harsh environment and a hostile native population forced settlers to concentrate on those aspects of settlement which ensured mere survival and precluded much attention to many amenities of life, let alone more sophisticated approaches to settlement forms.

On the few occasions where elaborate urban forms were prescribed by some official in the comfortable surroundings of a European city, they were soon abandoned as impractical and beyond the limited resources of an infant colony struggling to maintain life itself. Thus the intricate instructions for city planning in New Amsterdam in 1624 drawn up in Holland had to be scrapped almost immediately. Only toward the end of the 17th century can one find examples of successful implementation of city plans that went beyond a tiny cluster of houses on a network of gridiron streets.

With the gradual easing of the Indian menace, the establishment of craft industry, and the development of regular trade with the mother countries, life became less bleak and attention could be diverted from activities aimed at survival and devoted to those aspects of settlement providing greater comfort and enjoyment. Among those was the planning of new towns in more sophisticated patterns and the extension or rearrangement of older communities on more spacious and attractive lines. At this stage of colonial development we can discern the influence of European ideas of city planning, modified to fit the environmental circumstances of America and further limited by the skills of technicians and the still restricted resources of colonial society.

The European city planning tradition on which our own was based exhibited a rich variety of elements and influences. A brief summary of this background of European planning is helpful for an understanding of how American city forms gradually emerged and in what ways they resembled and differed from their European counterparts. A number of distinct influences can be identified.

There was a series of architectural works dealing in part with the principles of planning, urban reconstruction, the extensions of towns, and the design of new cities. Of these the writings of Alberti and Palladio exerted the greatest influence on their contemporaries. Similar in many respects but forming a separate category were the various ideal city proposals put forward by utopian philosophers, economic reformers, and military engineers.

The European tradition also included a number of new towns, completely preplanned and built largely as designed. While most of these dated from the late middle ages, many came into existence during the Renaissance and Baroque periods just before or during the era of American colonization. Urban extension projects for most of the major cities of Europe also provided experience in large-scale planning and construction and furnished possible examples for colonial urban growth.

An important aspect of European planning which had a major influence in many New World towns was the development of residential squares and public piazzas or *places*. Not so extensive in scale as new towns or additions to existing cities, the squares nevertheless provided a sense of geometric order in urban communities which had grown slowly and irregularly.

Finally, the European tradition included a history of evolution in garden and park design, which in turn strongly influenced the layout of cities and especially the alignment of major streets and boulevards. The similarity in both scale and form between the gardens of Versailles and the plan of Washington, D.C., was no mere coincidence.

We now turn to an examination of these several related aspects of the European planning tradition.

The Theoretical Basis for European
Town Planning

The Renaissance in Europe witnessed the publication of numerous books on architectural theory and practice. Most of these works contained at least some reference to the ideal layout of cities. In this, Renaissance authors followed the model of Vitruvius, who wrote in the first century B.C. and whose rediscovery in the 15th century stimulated a long series of similar theoretical works.

The first important treatise of this type to appear was Leon Battista Alberti's *De Re Aedificatoria*, published posthumously in 1485. He was one of the acknowledged masters of the early Renaissance, having designed important buildings in Mantua, Rimini, Florence, and other Italian cities. Alberti, like Vitruvius, began by considering the ideal site for cities, then turned to such matters as the shape of towns, their walls and fortifications, and water supply. He gave particular attention to the system of streets and open spaces. For large and important towns Alberti felt the streets should be wide and straight. Smaller and less fortified towns should be planned with winding streets to increase their beauty and to give the impression of greater size. He singled out other streets leading to public places as requiring special architectural treatment for the buildings along their path. He advocated the development of piazzas and recreational areas for each district of the city. Finally, he suggested that certain industrial activities, offensive because of odor or noise, be prohibited from towns altogether and that the various crafts and industries be grouped together in districts set aside for that purpose.

A century later, in 1570, Andrea Palladio published a similar work. His *I Quattro Libri dell' Architettura* bulged with sumptuous views and plans of magnificent palaces and public buildings. The relative simplicity and restraint of Alberti's day had given way to the elaborate devices of the Baroque. Palladio's chief concern lay in the city as a visual experience. Mundane problems of water supply and sewage disposal he dismissed in a few short lines. Broad streets lined with imposing buildings leading to great squares embellished with fountains and statues are admiringly described. The image of the Baroque city of pomp and pageant appears in these pages—and it soon began to take shape as powerful princes, both secular and spiritual, began to remake European cities into these new patterns.

Every European country produced architectural theoreticians of the Vitruvian mold, although the Italians remained best known. The works of both Alberti and Palladio were translated into other languages, and these books and others of similar character exerted a powerful influence on the design of new towns, urban extension projects, the layout of squares and plazas, and the character of new streets and boulevards.

The theoretical basis for town planning also became a major consideration of military engineers. The introduction of gunpowder into Europe in the 14th century made traditional types of fortification obsolete. Castle walls which had served so well as a defense against more primitive weapons now were vulnerable to the breaching fire from cannon. Clearly some way was needed to keep artillery at bay. The method finally devised involved the construction of various types of outworks, either as separate strongpoints or as projections from the main wall. These outworks or bastions were usually flat, thus presenting a small target area, and so laid out that the flanks of salients received protection from adjoining points.

Such new methods of fortifying cities gave rise to a host of theories and proposals. Francesco Martini was one of the earliest and most prolific theoreticians, the designer of several ideal military city plans dating from the late 15th century. It was not long before these theories were given practical application. One of the first towns of this type was Vitry-le-François, designed in 1545, by order of Francis I, by the Italian engineer Hieronimo Marino for a site on the Marne River in eastern France (Fig. 1). Here a gridiron street system was employed within the fortified perimeter. At the center of the town the designer placed an open space at the intersection of the four main streets which served as both market square and military mustering ground.

A somewhat later and quite different plan resulted from the studies of Vincenzo Scamozzi for Palma Nova, built in 1593 as a military strongpoint north of Venice (Fig. 2). Here the walls and bastions enclosed a nine-sided town with a system of radial streets focusing on a great central place, hexagonal in shape, in the middle of which stood the tower or keep. Six subsidiary squares midway between the center and the perimeter provided open spaces for the several quarters of the town, and smaller squares before the gates and the bastions also appear.

VITRY·LE·FRANÇOIS

Figure 1. View of Vitry-le-François, France: 1634

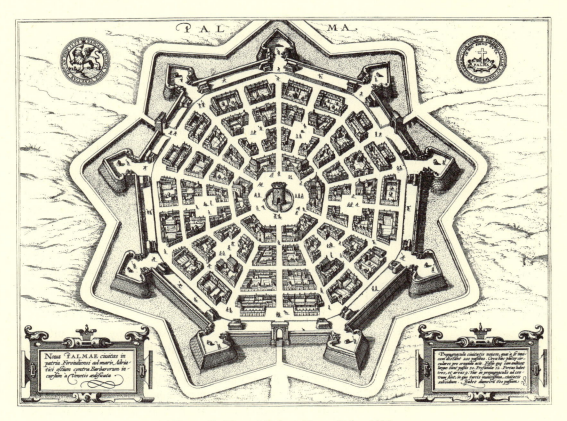

Figure 2. Plan of Palma Nova, Italy: 1598

Another group of treatises influenced the layout of cities. These were works dealing with the art of castrametation, that is, the design of military camps. Castrametation books were based largely on Roman writings. Niccolo Machiavelli's *Arte della Guerra*, which appeared in 1521, was one of the earliest of a long list of such works. Most of them contained illustrations and diagrams of camp layouts, and there are certain similarities between some of these illustrations and the plans used in a few American colonial settlements.

Other theoretical sources for Renaissance town planning came from the utopian philosophers, chiefly Thomas More, Tomasso Campanella, Eximenic, Johann Valentin Andreae, and Francis Bacon. The utopian tradition, as well as the word itself, began with More. His *Utopia* appeared in 1516 and described an imaginary island containing fifty-four cities, each the center of a little city-state. Amaurot, the capital, like the others was limited in size to 6,000 families. More's cities had three-story row houses "so uniform, that a whole side of a street looks like one house." Each city contained four neighborhoods grouped around market squares. Like Alberti, More suggested that offensive uses be banned from the city proper and located nearby in the countryside.

The contribution to European town planning by these utopian writers cannot be precisely measured. Their direct effects were negligible. Indeed the authors themselves scarcely hoped for practical results; the descriptions of communities in their writings were intended primarily to lend an air of realism to programs for social and political reform. Indirectly, however, these writers may well have stimulated further thinking about the function of cities and how they could be planned.

New Cities for a New Era

Completely new towns built on virgin sites and completed within a brief span of years were also part of the European planning tradition. Many of these date from the 13th century, when wholesale town planning took place in southwestern France by both the French and the English and, to a lesser extent, in northern Spain and in England and Wales. These so-called *bastide* communities were small, more or less rectilinear in outline, and generally exhibited a checkerboard or gridiron street pattern, often modified somewhat to conform to irregularities of the site.

The best known of the French *bastides* is Monpazier (Fig. 3). It is a model of geometric precision, although there are subtle differences in the size of its blocks and the manner in which individual lots are arranged. Other *bastides* of this region show some of the influences of topography in their modifications of strict rectilinear order to fit sites of restricted area or with steep slopes. At least one American town partly resembled these 13th-century French settlements. Detroit, founded in 1701, had the same tight organization of gridiron streets within a limited perimeter. Its planner, Cadillac, was born in one of the *bastides*, spent his youth in another, and took his name from still a third. This suggests a direct connection between the plan forms of southwestern France and the original design of Detroit, although no documentary proof of this has been discovered.

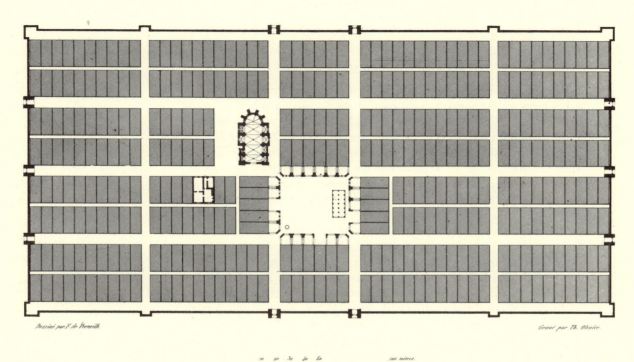

10   20   30   40   50   100 mètres.

Figure 3. Plan of Monpazier, France: 1284

new town of Nancy, planned in 1588 by the Italian Citoni, sprang into existence adjacent to the older settlement of the same name.

Nearby, also in eastern France, Charles of Gonzaga founded in 1608 one of the most elaborate of Baroque new towns. This was Charleville, whose plan incorporated virtually all of the devices of formal planning advocated by the architectural theorists of the time (Fig. 4). Generally rectangular in its street pattern, the plan included several squares and *places* where minor streets terminated. The noble ducal palace fronted the central square, which was surrounded by continuous buildings with uniform façades rising above arcaded sidewalks. Three major streets, one from the river and two from land gates standing behind the moat and surrounding fortifications, led directly to this central *place*. A fourth street from the western gate ended at the rear of the palace. No more consistent expression of Palladian principles can be found. The clear differentiation of major and minor streets, the subsidiary squares, the Place Ducale, the careful attention to street façades, and the skillful placement of important buildings on axis with approaching streets, all demonstrate an understanding of the principles of Baroque town planning.

The one new town in Spain that undoubtedly influenced subsequent colonization efforts dates from 1492, the very year that Spanish exploration led to the discovery of a new and unsuspected continent. Ferdinand and Isabella, by their marriage in 1469, brought together the separate kingdoms of Aragon, Castile, and Leon. When Columbus departed on his first voyage the new Spanish nation was engaged in the last efforts to drive the Moors from the Iberian peninsula. Near

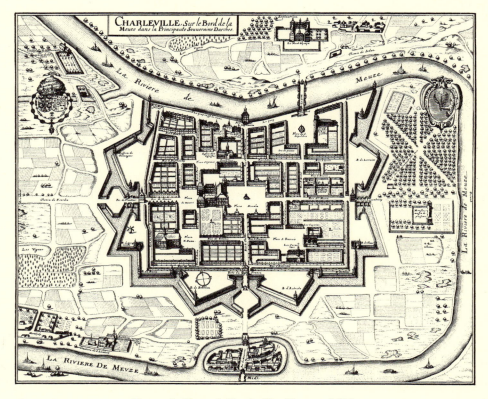

Figure 4. Plan of Charleville, France: 1656

Figure 5. Vertical Aerial View of Santa Fé, Spain: 1958

Granada, the remaining Moorish stronghold, the Spanish rulers established the siege town of Santa Fé (Fig. 5). More than a temporary camp, the town even then had the appearance of a permanent community, and its plan remains little changed in the almost five centuries that have intervened.

Santa Fé, in its scale and regular street plan, follows the familiar *bastide* pattern. The central square differs somewhat in form from that of Monpazier and the other *bastides*. On one side it is bordered by the main street of the town running from gate to gate. A short cross street enters the sides of the square near their midpoints, thus conforming in part to the canons of Renaissance planning. Here at Santa Fé may be the genesis of the remarkable Laws of the Indies that were to guide the planning of hundreds of Spanish colonial towns during the coming centuries. The close royal connection with Santa Fé and the planning of a number of colonial towns during the remaining years of the king and queen suggest that the Spanish-American towns owe their form in part to this specialized military community.

In turning to England we are struck by the almost complete absence of new town planning at the time such activities were at their height in France and also, in a more limited way, in the Low Countries, where such new communities as Philippeville, Willemstad, Coeworden, Naarden, Elburg, and Klundert had been established. The Renaissance came to insular England later than to other European countries, and its effect on town planning was rather different. Yet in the 17th century two examples, widely separated in space, scale, and design, must be mentioned. The first occurred early and resulted in the creation of several small new towns in northern Ireland. The second resulted from the famous London fire of 1666 and consisted of no less than eight separate plans for rebuilding the city. These were essentially new town schemes and properly belong in the group of plans we have been describing.

The province of Ulster in northern Ireland came under the jurisdiction of the English Crown at the beginning of the 17th century following the flight of the Irish earls. Their lands were declared forfeit and were disposed of by the Crown to the Irish Society, a colonizing company created by the common council of the City of London. In turn the society reached agreements with certain of the London companies for the settlement and development of designated portions of the area, retaining as its own responsibility the building of the towns of Derry and Coleraine.

Both plans date from about 1611 and are similar in that each had a gridiron layout with straight streets crossing at right angles. Each had a central square. That of Coleraine was about twice as long as it was broad and the streets entering the narrow sides intersected the square at the midpoints of the sides. Londonderry had a more regular design (Fig. 6). Its central square had sides of equal length, and all four streets providing access to the square entered at the midpoints of its sides. Uniform rows of attached houses lined the four approach streets to the square and continued around its boundaries. In the center stood the most imposing building of the town, housing a market, a prison, and the town hall.

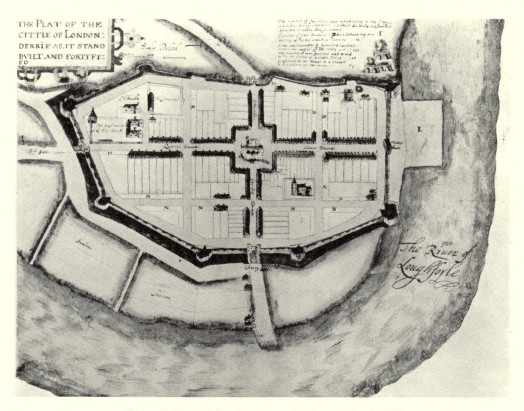

Figure 6. Plan of Londonderry, Northern Ireland: 1622

Other Irish town plans, including those of Bangor, Holywood, Comber, Killyleagh, and Bellaghy, were less sophisticated. Some were simple grids lacking any central open space; others were merely linear settlements along a single street. These same forms were to appear within a few years in New England and Virginia, but it was in Ulster, the first frontier of English 17-century colonization, that these simple village and town patterns had their beginnings. Many of the participants in the Irish colonization enterprise were also active in the settlement of Virginia and New England, and it is only logical to assume that some of the experience gained in town building in northern Ireland under English direction found application in the more distant colonies of the New World.

Too late to influence the design of the earliest English colonial towns but of considerable importance to later communities, the eight plans for rebuilding London after the great fire reveal the diversity of English planning toward the end of the 17th century. The widely known three plans by John Evelyn and the one by Christopher Wren illustrate the attractions of continental Baroque urban patterns to the more sophisticated and artistic of Englishmen (Fig. 7). Great diagonal avenues, *rond-points*, ovals, and squares appear in these schemes as though sketched by Palladio himself. Both Wren and Evelyn combined radial with rectilinear street patterns and accented the importance of major building sites by converging on them as many streets as possible.

The four other known plans demonstrated the force which simpler and more orthodox grid systems still exerted on more traditional

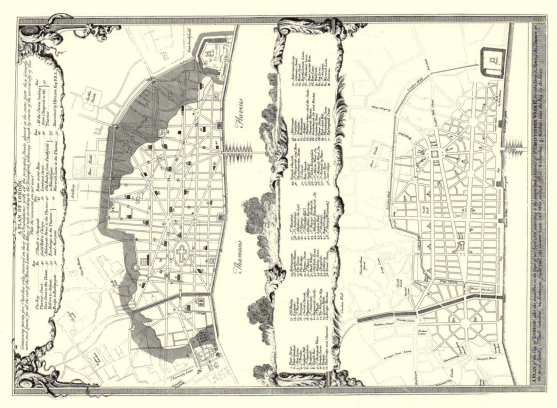

Figure 7. Plans for rebuilding London by Christopher Wren and John Evelyn: 1666

minds. That of Captain Valentine Knight provided for twenty-four east-west streets and twelve cross streets to run north and south. The plan attributed to Robert Hooke was a more regular checkerboard with square blocks and four open squares. Two other grid schemes came from Richard Newcourt. Both called for a series of square blocks each containing a parish church in the center. Newcourt's plans also showed five open spaces, one larger than the others as a great civic square. His two plans differed only in the number and size of the blocks to be used for building.

As it turned out, London adopted none of these various proposals. But from the discussion of the plans surely came a wider understanding of the problems involved in laying out cities. The effects on colonial town planning were indirect and, as is often the case with elements of European planning, cannot be measured with precision. The new style of Baroque layout put forward by Wren and Evelyn for the capital of the Empire may well have had its first tentative application in the tiny capital city of Maryland some thirty years later. In 1682, William Penn or his surveyor Thomas Holme may have recalled Newcourt's plan when they came to lay out the streets and squares in Philadelphia, which also had a large central square and four subsidiary open spaces. But the London plans of 1666 probably had an impact first on the design of individual urban improvement and extension projects in England and, through them, on the form of similar elements in the American colonial towns.

In no other aspect of city planning did the Renaissance produce such numerous and magnificent results as in the development of great civic open spaces. As a practical matter, such projects were obviously less difficult to bring into reality than whole towns. First in Italy and then later throughout Europe, kings and popes, cardinals and princes sponsored the creation of planned urban spaces as settings for palaces, churches, and monumental groups of buildings. Many of Europe's greatest architectural glories date from this era.

Two general types of squares can be distinguished. The first to appear were the public squares—those conceived as settings for major buildings or as gathering places for religious, royal, or civic pageants and festivals. The Piazza di San Pietro, Bernini's masterpiece in the Vatican, is an example of this type of urban embellishment. In France the great civic squares date mainly from the 18th century. Pierre Patte's composite drawing in 1765 of the competition designs submitted for a monument to Louis XV illustrate the variety of forms which were then proposed (Fig. 8).

A second type of square, more influential in American colonial planning, developed mainly in France and England. This was the enclosed residential square, the first important example of which is the Place Royale (now the Place des Vosges), begun in 1605 by Henry IV as one of the many improvements carried out by this energetic monarch in Paris (Fig. 9). The Place Royale was square. Houses were built by individuals to designs established at the outset. Entrances

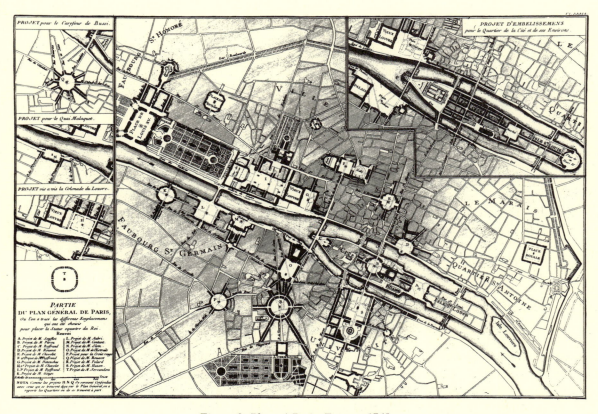

Figure 8. Plan of Paris, France: 1765

Liure de diuerses Veuës, Perspectiues, et Paysages faicts sur le naturel.
DEDIEZ AV ROY, *par Israel auec Priuilege de* **SA MAIESTE**.
A Paris Chez Israel Henriet, rue de larbre sec au logis de Monsieur le Mercier Orfeure de la Reyne proche la croix du Tiroir.1651.

Figure 9. View of the Place Royale in Paris, France: 1652

opened off an arcaded sidewalk on the four sides. The center of the square was at first left in sand and for several years was used for tournaments. Then it was covered with turf; only in relatively recent times has it been planted with trees and decorative flower gardens.

Henry also created another residential precinct of similar scale and character in the Place Dauphine, which encloses a triangular space at the point of the Île de la Cité. Both these developments represented significant innovations. The domesticity, the quiet, the privacy, all contrast with the imposing monumentality and bustle of the civic squares previously described. This device for organizing the residential environment soon found its way into town planning practice in other cities.

It was in fact in London that the residential square achieved its highest order of development. The first London square was a frank imitation of continental models. Inigo Jones, retained by the Earl of Bedford in 1630 to design a residential development on his estate which was then on the outskirts of London, produced a neat arcaded rectangle of houses with the Tuscan church of St. Paul's at the south end. This project came at a time when the great estates on London's fringe offered financially attractive opportunities for land development. In rapid sequence new squares appeared. They differed from models such as the Place Royale in their more restrained architecture and in the grassed or tree-shaded circles, ovals, or rectangles at their centers. Often the building façades were not exactly uniform, but they were almost always harmonious in scale, material, color, and general proportion.

By the middle of the 18th century the western portion of London had a dozen or more such major squares, giving to the city a unique quality of urbanity which has never been rivaled. And it was not only in London but in towns throughout the British Isles that this pattern came to be employed. It is little wonder, therefore, that in the English colonial cities we shall see evidences of the influence of this popular plan.

Planned Urban Extension

In addition to the planning of completely new towns and the development of civic and residential squares, the European tradition included experience with guided and directed urban growth. In Rome, for example, several of the 15th- and 16th-century popes changed the face of the city, cutting new streets, building bridges, and constructing new piazzas. Early in the 17th century Paris began to experience a period of growth aided by the vigorous policies of Henry IV. His Place Royale served as a node around which many new houses were constructed. New streets in this quarter generally followed rectangular alignments, although they deviated somewhat from a completely regular grid. Similar growth occurred in the Faubourg St. Germain across the Seine from the Tuileries Gardens. Here, too, the street pattern took rectangular form.

In Holland the art of planned town expansion reached a level of skill and perfection that has seldom been equaled. Amsterdam's history is best known, but it is only one example among many. Here early in the 17th century the city determined on a basic plan for expansion around the older medieval core (Fig. 10). A series of ring canals was planned, most of the land was acquired by the municipality, and there was filling of land to create building sites in the low-lying area. The city then established a series of regulations governing the buildings that could be constructed and proceeded to dispose of the land under these terms. The result was one of the greatest achievements of all time in planned urban development.

It was only to be expected that when the time came for the Dutch to begin colonial town development something of this experience would find its way into early attempts to establish settlements in America. It was unfortunate for our later history that these efforts were unsuccessful and that little of the urban order and beauty of Amsterdam was ever to be duplicated in its namesake at the mouth of the Hudson.

Gardens, Parks, and the Design of Towns

We come now to the final element of the European planning tradition that influenced the design of American towns, both in colonial times and in the years following independence. For our exploration of this subject we must go back to the earliest years of the Renaissance in Italy and the development of ducal palaces, villas, and estates. Following medieval monastic herbal garden design and the descriptions of Roman gardens in such works as Pliny's, designers of early Renaissance villas included garden design as an integral part of the whole composition. The gardens commonly were divided into

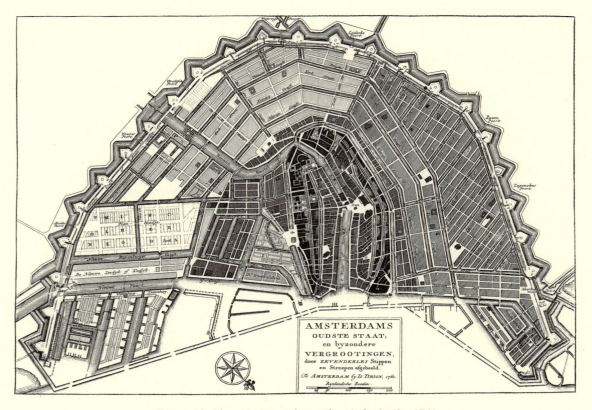

Figure 10. Plan of Amsterdam, The Netherlands: 1760

many groups of plant materials separated by paths. Geometric arrangements prevailed. Major paths normally divided the entire garden into some kind of grid pattern, although the resulting beds or *parterres* did not all have the same dimensions. Minor paths further subdivided the *parterres* into smaller planting groups. At first these too were rectilinear in pattern.

These gardens were designed to be seen from above, from the terraces, the porches, and balconies of the villa or palace. To dazzle the eye of the beholder designers turned to more intricate and elaborate patterns. Within individual *parterres* the paths and planted beds were now laid out with diagonal and circular lines. Within the basic grid pattern of the major garden paths an almost bewildering variety of *parterre* design could be seen.

Garden design reached its height in France during the last half of the 17th century under André Le Nôtre. First at Vaux-le-Vicomte for Fouquet and then at Versailles for Louis XIV, Le Nôtre elaborated on and vastly extended the Italian garden concept. At Versailles beyond the garden proper with its intricate *parterres* stretched the great royal park (Fig. 11). Here Le Nôtre ran tree-lined *allées* radiating outward from *rond-points* in bold diagonal lines. These were echoed on the opposite side of the chateau by two diagonal streets running through the planned town, the layout of which included a number of squares and *places*.

This new scale of design was soon to be employed in Paris itself. The Avenue de Champs-Élysées and the streets radiating from the Place de l'Etoile repeat Versailles in an urban setting. While these

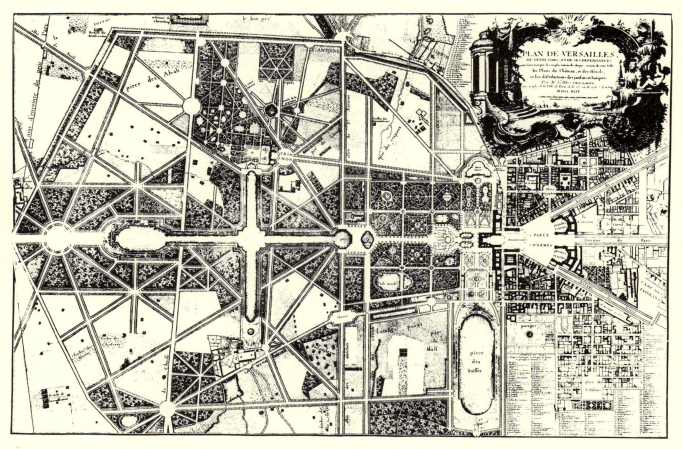

Figure 11. Plan of Versailles, France: 1746

planning projects in Paris occurred after the pattern of French colonial towns had already been established, they affected strongly the subsequent course of American city planning.

Enough has now been said to provide the reader with some understanding of the state of European town planning just prior to and during American colonization and urban settlement. We are now ready to examine the planning of towns in the New World and to appreciate the ways in which these European devices for bringing order to urban settlements were applied in a new environment and under different economic, social, and political institutions.

II · *Pueblo and Presidio:*
Spanish Planning in Colonial America

To a far greater degree than any of the other colonizing powers in the New World the Spanish followed a system of land settlement and town planning formalized in written rules and regulations. Although time and man have succeeded in obliterating many of the results of this period of American city building, much still remains. In a great arc from the Gulf States to New Mexico and up through California to the Golden Gate stretches the vast domain once subject to Spanish rule. Here and there, now almost hidden by later urban accretions, may still be seen the precious heritage of this era in our urban history.

For an understanding of the urban pattern established by the Spanish we must go back to the very discovery of the land itself—to the end of the 15th century, when the voyages of Columbus revealed a new continent and the way was opened for white settlement in America.

Española and its Colonial Towns

When, in December of 1492, Christopher Columbus built a crude fortress from the timbers of the wrecked *Santa Maria* on the northern coast of the island of Española (the modern Santo Domingo) he began an era of city planning in the Americas. La Navidad, that first primitive military outpost of Europeans in the New World, did not survive, nor did Isabela, the town laid out some miles to the east on Columbus's second voyage the following year. It was not until 1496 that the Spanish finally succeeded in establishing a permanent settlement. This was Santo Domingo on the southern side of the island, the oldest existing city founded by Europeans in America.

No plan of the first city of Santo Domingo has apparently survived. In 1502, following a storm which destroyed the settlement, Nicolás de Ovando, the governor recently arrived from Spain, moved the location of the city across the river to the west. Under Ovando's direction the town was planned with a rectangular street system which was to establish a pattern widely employed by the Spanish throughout the New World. The city quickly developed as an important base for further explorations and became an administrative and military center.

As early as 1526 Gonzalo Fernández de Oviedo y Valdés, one of the earliest Spanish historians of the first years of colonization and himself intimately familiar with Santo Domingo, could describe the city in these words:

"Concerning Santo Domingo . . . I wish to point out that with regard to the buildings, no town in Spain—unless it is Barcelona, which I have seen many times—is superior in general. The houses in Santo Domingo are for the most part of stone like those in Barcelona, and the walls are strong and beautiful, constructed of wonderful masonry. The general layout of the city is much better than that of Barcelona, because the many streets are more level and wide and incomparably straighter. Since the city was founded in our own time, there was opportunity to plan the whole thing from the beginning. It was laid out with ruler and compass, with all the streets being carefully measured. Because of this, Santo Domingo is better planned than any town I have seen. . . .

"There must be some seven hundred citizens in this city, living in such houses as I have already described. Some of the private homes are so luxurious that any grandee in Spain would find himself most comfortable there. . . .

"A cathedral is now being constructed, and the Bishop and other dignitaries and canons are well provided for. Since there is an abundance of materials and labor, it should be completed soon. From what I have already seen, I believe it will be a magnificent building of good proportions.

"There are also three monasteries (Dominican, Franciscan, and Saint Mary of Mercy) which have handsome but modest buildings which are not so grotesque as some of those in Spain. . . .

"Day by day the city is growing larger and becoming more noble, and this is certain to continue since the Viceroy and your Majesty's high court of justice and Royal Chancellery are located there. . . ."[1]

The famous view of Santo Domingo engraved by Arnoldus Montanus in 1671 is based on earlier plans and sketches of the later 16th

[1] Gonzalo Fernández de Oviedo, *Natural History of the West Indies* (Toledo, 1526), translated and edited by Sterling A. Stoudemire, Chapel Hill, 1959, pp. 11-13.

century and reveals the rather impressive settlement described by Oviedo centered around its plaza and cathedral (Fig. 12). Straight, wide streets divided the town into rectangular blocks containing the homes of the settlers, warehouses, barracks, and buildings for religious orders. Virtually all buildings were constructed on the street lines, with the interiors of the blocks devoted to gardens, cloisters, or mustering grounds.

The development within a few decades of Santo Domingo and other equally impressive towns elsewhere on this island and on the mainland of the Americas was a remarkable achievement in city planning. Nothing of this sort had been visualized by the Spanish Crown when it dispatched Columbus and other early voyagers to open up trade routes to China and Japan. During the early years of exploration everyone was under the impression that the land was some part of fabulous Cathay. The Spanish were totally unprepared for the task of exploring an unknown continent, selecting sites for cities, bringing in colonists, distributing land, and administering the affairs of an enterprise based on farming and mining rather than trade and plunder. Only gradually did it become apparent that a new empire lay before them, one which must be settled and subjugated before it could yield the riches that were so confidently expected.

Further exploration soon revealed the immense dimensions of the new discovery. Port towns were needed first to serve as outfitting points for expeditions and as bases for supplies and anticipated trade. At first the leaders of expeditions setting out from Spain were given considerable latitude in deciding on the location and layout of

Figure 12. Plan of Santo Domingo, Dominican Republic: 1671

these settlements. In 1501, for example, Ferdinand issued the following instructions to Nicolás de Ovando: "As it is necessary in the island of Española to make settlements and from here it is not possible to give precise instructions, investigate the possible sites, and in conformity with the quality of the land and sites as well as with the present population outside present settlements establish settlements in the numbers and in the places that seem proper to you."[2]

Within a few years, however, much more precise directives were being provided. The instructions to Pedrarias Davila in 1513 indicate that the first two decades of town planning experience had been carefully reviewed and that much closer central control over colonial city development had been adopted as a general policy:

"One of the most important things to observe is that . . . the places chosen for settlement . . . be healthy and not swampy, good for unloading goods; if inland to be on a river if possible . . . good water and air, close to arable land. . . .

"In view of these things necessary for settlements, and seeking the best site in these terms for the town, then divide the plots for houses, these to be according to the status of the persons, and from the beginning it should be according to a definite arrangement; for the manner of setting up the *solares* [building sites] will determine the pattern of the town, both in the position of the plaza and the church and in the pattern of streets, for towns newly founded may be estab-

[2] As quoted by Dan Stanislawski, "Early Spanish Town Planning in the New World," *Geographical Review*, Vol. 37 (January 1947), p. 95.

lished according to plan without difficulty. If not started with form, they will never attain it."[3]

The Laws of the Indies: America's First
Planning Legislation

As the Spanish extended their settlements throughout the Caribbean islands and to Mexico and Central and South America, and as the pace of colonization accelerated, the issuance of individual orders and directives for each expedition became inefficient and unnecessary. In 1573 Philip II proclaimed the Laws of the Indies to establish uniform standards and procedures for planning of towns and their surrounding lands as well as for all the other details of colonial settlement. While parts of these royal ordinances established new requirements and regulations, virtually all of the sections governing town planning represented a mere codification of practices that had become fairly standardized some years earlier. This conclusion is supported by an examination of plans of cities founded before 1573, which appear to coincide in all essential features with the prescriptions of the Laws of the Indies.

Because of the relative inflexibility of Spanish colonial policy, the regulations of 1573 remained virtually unchanged throughout the entire period of Spanish rule in the Western Hemisphere. Literally hundreds of communities were planned in conformity to their specifications—a phenomenon unique in modern history. A brief review of some of the more important town planning aspects of the Laws of the

[3] *ibid.*, p. 96.

Indies is essential for an understanding of the urban forms which were to be used by the Spanish settlers in the area of the United States.[4]

The Laws begin with the selection of a suitable site for a town, indicating that if possible it should be on an elevation surrounded by good farming land, possessing an ample supply of water, and with fuel and timber available. The site was to be generous in area, and a plan was to be decided upon before beginning any construction. As the Laws stated: "The plan of the place, with its squares, streets and building lots is to be outlined by means of measuring by cord and ruler, beginning with the main square from which streets are to run to the gates and principle roads and leaving sufficient open space so that even if the town grows it can always spread in a symmetrical manner."

Several paragraphs of the regulations dealt with the plaza, that distinctive element in all Spanish-American towns. For coastal cities the regulations prescribed a location for the plaza near the shore; for inland cities, in the center of the town. As to shape, the regulations specified that the length should be at least one and a half times the width since "this proportion is the best for festivals in which horses are used. . . ." Planners were instructed to consider the eventual size of the town in deciding on the dimensions of the main plaza. Here the regulations were quite specific: "It shall not be smaller than two hundred feet wide and three hundred feet long nor larger than eight

[4] Quotations from the Laws of the Indies are from the translation by Zelia Nuttall, "Royal Ordinances Concerning the Laying Out of New Towns," *Hispanic American Historical Review*, Vol. 5 (1922), pp. 249-54.

hundred feet long and three hundred feet wide. A well proportioned medium size plaza is one six hundred feet long and four hundred feet wide."

The main plaza was to be oriented so that its four corners pointed to the four cardinal points of the compass. This feature was designed to prevent exposure "to the four principal winds" which would otherwise result in "much inconvenience." In other parts of the towns smaller, "well proportioned" open spaces were to be provided as sites for churches and other religious buildings.

From the main plaza principal streets were to lead from the middle of each side, with two minor streets also diverging from each corner. The regulations called for another distinctive aspect of Spanish colonial towns: "The whole plaza and the four main streets diverging from it shall have arcades, for these are a great convenience for those who resort thither for trade. The eight streets which run into the plaza at its four corners are to do so freely without being obstructed by the arcades of the plaza. These arcades are to end at the corners in such a way that the sidewalks of the streets can evenly join those of the plaza." Other streets were to be located "consecutively around the plaza." Although nowhere do the Laws so state, it is obvious that they envisaged a gridiron or checkerboard pattern of straight streets with intersections at right angles.

The Laws provided precise guides for the location of important buildings of the town. The principal church of coastal cities was to face the plaza near the harbor and be so constructed that it might be used as a fortified strong point in the event of attack. In inland towns, however, the church was to be located at a distance from the plaza, standing apart from other buildings and, if possible, on an elevation. Other sites around the plaza were to be assigned for the town hall, the customs house, the arsenal, a hospital, and other public buildings. Remaining sites fronting the plaza were to be set aside for shops and dwellings of merchants.

The regulations specified that the settlers should draw lots for their house sites and after erecting tents or temporary huts they were to join in the construction of a palisade around the plaza for immediate safety against Indian attack. The town itself was but one element in the settlement unit prescribed by the Laws. Surrounding it was to be a common "of adequate size so that even though it should grow greatly there would always be sufficient space for its inhabitants to find recreation and for cattle to pasture without encroaching upon private property."

Beyond the common were to be the agricultural lands, with as many farm parcels as there were house sites in the town and also to be distributed by the drawing of lots. If within the community territory there were lands capable of being irrigated, these were also to be subdivided into farming tracts and assigned to the settlers by lot. Remaining farm land was reserved to the Crown for distribution to settlers who might come at a later time.

The Laws contained many additional regulations governing such matters as construction of houses, planting of seeds, cattle breeding, and other details important in establishing a self-sufficient colony with efficiency and dispatch. One brief regulation covered the appearance of the community: "Settlers are to endeavor, as far as possible, to make all structures uniform, for the sake of the beauty of the town."

Finally, the Laws admonished the town founders not to permit any natives to enter the community during its construction until the fortifications and the houses were complete, "so that when the Indians see them they will be filled with wonder and will realize that the Spaniards are settling there permanently and not temporarily. They will consequently fear the Spaniards so much that they will not dare to offend them and will respect them and desire their friendship."

These remarkable regulations stand out as one of the most important documents in the history of city planning. Almost without exception they were followed throughout the subsequent period of Spanish colonization. Because this study is concerned with tracing the sources of ideas that have contributed to urban forms in America, the origins of the town planning principles embodied in the Laws of the Indies must be explored.

Certainly the trial-and-error experience gained in the colonies during the early years of the 16th century proved helpful in the framing of these regulations. Yet there were other sources of city planning experience and theory from which their compilers could and probably did draw. The works of the Roman architect Vitruvius, dating from about 30 B.C., contain many passages similar to those of the Laws of the Indies. Another possible source, and one much closer in time to the period of Spanish colonization, was the great treatise on architecture and planning by Leon Battista Alberti published posthumously in 1485.

In Spain itself, there were models from which lessons could be learned. Santa Fé, the siege town laid out in 1492 by Ferdinand and Isabella near Granada, had an orthogonal street system and a central plaza. It is significant that Ovando, the planner of Santo Domingo, had been in Santa Fé during the battle with the Moors. Similar planned fortress towns dating from the middle ages existed in northern Spain and southern France, where hundreds of *bastide* towns had been founded in the 12th and 13th centuries, all with regular gridiron street patterns.

The more ancient Roman *castra* or military settlements in Spain had established a rectangular street pattern and central mustering place which in many cases had given the form to civil communities that gradually developed on their sites. The works of Guillaume du Choul describing Roman castrametation theories had been published in Italy as early as 1555 and were translated into Spanish in 1579, an indication that the subject had already stimulated interest in Spain. It seems likely that the Spanish would have known Machiavelli's *Arte della Guerra*, which appeared in 1521 and included an encampment plan with a central square, rectangular perimeter, and gridiron streets.

The history of ideas is never a simple matter, particularly when concerned with a series of events so far distant in time from our own and so meagerly documented. We can only conclude that the Laws of the Indies, presenting a hitherto unique combination of town planning doctrines, stemmed from a number of diverse European sources, modified by experience in the islands and on the mainland of Hispanic America.

Turning now to the application of the Laws of the Indies in actual town development our approach will be from east to west, coinciding roughly with the chronological development of Spanish cities in North America.

St. Augustine: the Oldest City in the United States

By the middle of the 16th century New Spain had become a rich source of treasure for the mother country. Twice each summer convoys of merchant ships guarded by men-of-war sailed northward from Havana between Florida and the Bahamas. In the vicinity of Bermuda they then set an eastward course for Seville. The Florida Straits were perilous waters for the clumsy, heavily laden treasure ships. A strong base on the eastern coast of Florida was needed to provide protection against pirates and privateers and as a source of aid for storm-wrecked vessels.

Spain was spurred to action by the unwelcome news that a French colony had been established near the mouth of the St. John's River in 1564. Philip II attempted to persuade the French to withdraw, and when these negotiations failed he ordered Don Pedro Menéndez de Avilés, an experienced soldier and skilled mariner, to remove the French and establish a Spanish base on the Florida coast.

The fleet commanded by Menéndez arrived off the Florida coast on St. Augustine's day, the 28th of August, although it was not until September 6 that the soldiers and settlers disembarked. The temporary settlement then constructed was later moved to another location some distance away, and not until 1570 was the present site occupied, but the year 1565 properly dates the beginning of Spanish colonization in the area of the United States.

One of the earliest views of the city shows St. Augustine at the time of Francis Drake's attack in 1586 (Fig. 13). It depicts the town as a little grid settlement of eleven blocks located some distance from the fort which guarded the entrance to the harbor. Later plans dating from the 18th century show a much larger settlement with a distinctly linear configuration stretching along the bay southward from the fort (Fig. 14). The street pattern is an irregular gridiron centered on the plaza. The entire town was surrounded by a stockade or wall with projecting bastions located at intervals along its perimeter. One feature that can be noticed immediately is the open character of the community. Houses fronted directly on the streets, leaving generous areas to the rear for gardens and patios. As in most Spanish colonial towns, houses were usually two stories high, topped by flat roofs. Balconies at the upper levels over entrance porticos added interest to the street façades.

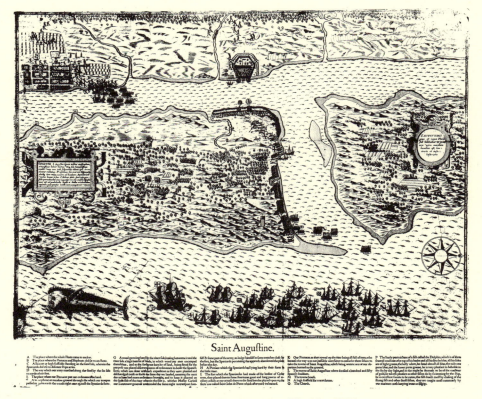

Figure 13. View of St. Augustine, Florida: 1588

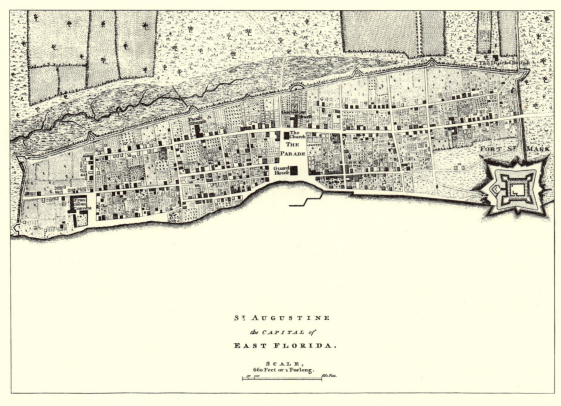

Figure 14. Plan of St. Augustine, Florida: 1763

At the time Menéndez founded the city the Laws of the Indies had not yet been established, and in many respects the plan of the town differs from the forms prescribed by those later regulations. Menéndez had apparently been given substantial discretion in determining the form of his city. Later Spanish colonial towns planned within the area of the United States were laid out in accordance with the royal regulations which were shortly to become effective.

St. Augustine combined in one community three distinct functions. The city was, first of all, a military post with its fort and military garrison. Secondly, it was designed as a civil settlement for trade, farming, and handicraft industry. And, finally, it was also intended as a center from which religious orders would begin the work of converting Indians to Christianity. Toward the end of the 16th century it became the policy of Spain to establish separate settlements for these three types of activities: missions, for religious orders and the Indians who were being converted; *présidios*, for military establishments and their ancillary activities; and *pueblos* or *villas,* as civil settlements for farming, trade, and town life.

There are two matters that should be made clear at this point. First, the Laws of the Indies applied to the *pueblo* type of settlement—that is, to civil communities. Second, the distinction between the three types of communities, clear enough in theory, often disappeared in practice. The mission communities, for example, were intended to be temporary arrangements for the "reduction" of the Indians to Christianity, while at the same time the natives were being instructed in self-government. At the end of the period of tutelage, the mission community was to become a civil *pueblo*. Nor did the *presidios* remain exclusively military in character. Married soldiers and other settlers not under military direction gave these fortress outposts something of the air of civil settlements. In many cases, too, *pueblos* were founded by groups of settlers that included soldiers who remained under military discipline. Finally, we find several instances where one or more missions, *presidios*, and *pueblos* were established in such close proximity to one another that the distinction became further blurred.

Towns of the Gulf and Southwest

Just such a mixture of civil, military, and religious settlements by the Spanish is part of the history of San Antonio, Texas. The *presidio* of San Antonio de Béjar had been founded by Martin de Alarcon, Governor of Coabuila, in 1718. Near it was the mission later to become famous as the Alamo, the Mission of San Antonio de Valero. Four other missions existed along a twelve-mile stretch of the San Antonio River. Yet this section of Texas remained far from secure, and Spanish authorities determined that a *pueblo* should also be established in the area. Families from the Canary Islands were recruited as the first settlers, and late in the fall of 1730 the group set out for their new home.

The original plan of the Pueblo of San Fernando, as it was called, showed a grid of rectangular blocks neatly arranged around the plaza, on which fronted the church and the royal house (Fig. 15). Some modifications were made when this plan came to be applied to

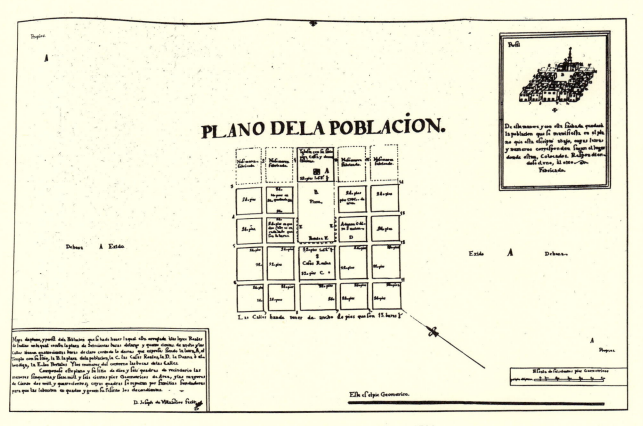

Figure 15. Plan of San Antonio, Texas: 1730

the site. The plaza was reduced in size, and the church was placed at one end. Around the perimeter only half blocks were laid out, but otherwise the original design, conforming in virtually all respects to the specifications of the Laws of the Indies, was followed.

The new *pueblo* was located immediately adjacent to the older *presidio*, separated only by the church. Across the river stood the mission of San Antonio. Further east lay the four additional mission communities. But while much effort had been expended, the results remained unimpressive. When Father Juan Agustín Morfi visited the settlement in 1777 he recorded this unflattering description: "The church building is spacious and has a vaulted roof, but the whole is so poorly constructed that it promises but a short life. The town consists of fifty-nine houses of stone and mud and seventy-nine of wood, but all poorly built . . . so that the whole resembles more a poor village than a villa, capital of so pleasing a province."[5]

The quality of building construction that so distressed Father Morfi typified at least the early years of Spanish colonization north of Mexico. This part of New Spain was full of such settlements, boldly conceived on an elaborate plan but carried out with little care or attention to details.

Galvez, Louisiana, serves as another example of some departures from the ideal city of the Laws of the Indies (Fig. 16). Here the planner, in 1778, made the plaza square instead of rectangular and provided for arcades along all of the streets instead of only along those

[5] Fray Juan Agustín Morfi, *History of Texas, 1673-1779*, translated by Carlos Eduardo Castañeda, Albuquerque, 1935, I, 92.

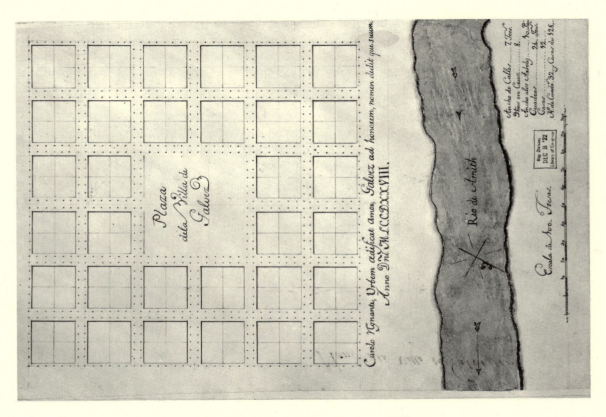

Figure 16. Plan of Galvez, Louisiana: 1778

entering the plaza. This town enjoyed but a brief life. The site was located on the border of Spanish Louisiana and English West Florida. With the fall of Florida to the Spanish, Galvez had no further reason for existence. From a peak population of 400 it quickly declined and within a few years lay virtually deserted.

Farther to the east along the Gulf of Mexico stands an earlier Spanish settlement, one that passed rapidly from Spanish to French to English hands with such bewildering frequency that its real character is difficult to classify. Yet the original plan of this town, Pensacola, was Spanish, and its later occupants merely modified and extended its original design.

The original settlement in Pensacola Bay dates from 1698, but this community was destroyed in 1754 by a hurricane. The residents then re-established the town on its present site, coming under British rule from 1763 to 1781. A detailed town plan from the British period shows a central fort, a reconstruction and enlargement of the Spanish defensive work that had previously existed (Fig. 17). Probably this town had been intended primarily as a garrison community and not as a civil settlement. This would explain the obvious departures from the Laws of the Indies.

Older than all of the Spanish towns in the United States except St. Augustine was Santa Fé, New Mexico. Originally La Villa Real de la Santa Fé de San Francisco, the city was founded by Don Pedro de Peralta in 1609 as the new capital of the most northerly of the provinces of New Spain, replacing the older capital of San Juan de los Caballeros first settled in 1598. Except for a period of Indian occupa-

Figure 17. Plan of Pensacola, Florida: 1778

tion from 1680 to 1698, Santa Fé has served continuously as the capital, first of the Spanish and then the Mexican province, then the territory, and now the state of New Mexico.

Virtually the only map showing the details of the city during the Spanish era dates from about 1766 (Fig. 18). It shows the rectangular street pattern and the plaza as prescribed by the Laws of the Indies, with the Governor's residence built along one side of the plaza. This was one of the first buildings erected in the town and still stands, although much altered and restored. Today's plaza is only a portion of the more generous area set aside in Peralta's original plan.

An 18th-century visitor, Father Francisco Atanasio Dominguez, found Santa Fé a disappointment, bearing little resemblance to the more prosperous Spanish cities in Mexico. Writing in 1776, he recorded this impression:

"The Villa of Santa Fé (for the most part) consists of many small ranchos at various distances from one another, with no plan as to their location, for each owner built as he was able, wished to, or found convenient.

"In spite of what has been said, there is a semblance of a street in this villa. It begins on the left facing north shortly after one leaves the . . . parish church and extends down about 400 or 500 varas. Indeed, I point out that this quasi-street not only lacks orderly rows, or blocks of houses, but at its very beginning, which faces north, it forms one side of a little plaza in front of our church. The other three sides are three houses of settlers with alleys between them. The

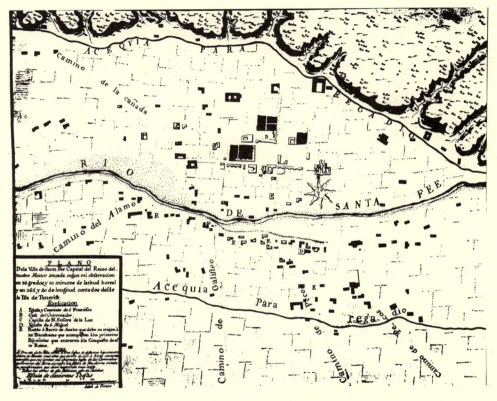

Figure 18. Plan of Santa Fé, New Mexico: ca. 1766

entrance to the main plaza is down through these. The sides, or borders, of the latter consist of the chapel of Our Lady of Light, which is to the left of the quasi-street mentioned. . . . The other side is the government palace. . . . The remaining two sides are houses of settlers, and since there is nothing worth noting about them, one can guess what they are like from what has been said. The government palace is like everything else there, and enough said."[6]

Even after making allowances for the differences that often arose between civil and religious authorities, which often colored their descriptions of the other activities, we can only conclude that Morfi's and Dominguez's opinions reflected actual conditions. The North American settlements of Spain's colonial empire were frontier outposts, far removed from the prosperity that characterized the cities at the heart of New Spain. Like frontier outposts at any period, conditions were primitive and unsophisticated. For all that the Laws of the Indies might prescribe about the details of land settlement, their administration, at least along the Gulf and in the southwest, appeared to be tempered with a measure of the casualness and carelessness that has often marked frontier government of other eras. Nor were these conditions to be substantially different in the last efforts by the Spanish to settle previously unoccupied portions of the continent.

[6] Fray Francisco Atanasio Dominguez, *The Missions of New Mexico, 1776*, translated by Eleanor B. Adams and Fray Angelico Chavez, Albuquerque, 1956, pp. 39-40.

A sustained attempt to settle California came only in 1769 when two expeditions, one by land and the other by sea, left Mexico to establish several missions and *presidios*. The first of the missions was founded that year at San Diego, the beginning of a chain of religious settlements that eventually extended northward beyond San Francisco Bay to Sonoma.

The missions of California, as was true elsewhere in Spanish America, were complexes of religious and secular buildings. The church and cloister formed the center. Clustered nearby were dormitories, shops, schoolrooms, the infirmary, quarters for the Indians, farm structures, and miscellaneous out-buildings. Usually the mission community included the houses of a few white settlers and a small garrison for the military guard. Many of these California mission buildings have been preserved, and the modern visitor can recapture the image of what life must have been like in these specialized religious and agricultural settlements.

The Spanish established four *presidios* or military communities in California: San Diego in 1769, Monterey in 1770, San Francisco in 1776 (Fig. 19), and Santa Barbara in 1782. These were stockaded or walled quadrangles containing the barracks, stores, shops, and stables of the military garrison, as well as the houses of a few settlers. With the passing of time, houses and farm buildings sprang up beyond the walls of the *presidio* proper. The military communities thus came to resemble the civil settlements of the *pueblos*.

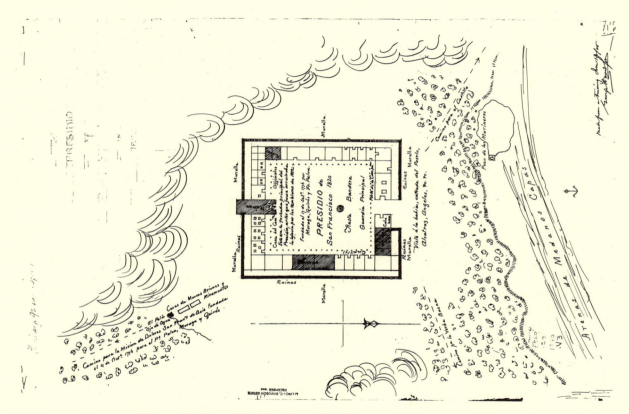

Figure 19. Plan of the Presidio of San Francisco, California: 1820

While the missions and *presidios* were numerically more important in California, the *pueblo* towns and their land system is of greater interest. These owe their founding to Philip de Neve, Governor of the province, who took up residence in Monterey in 1775. De Neve faced two problems: securing the province against encroachments by other powers, and increasing the supply of farm produce for the military garrisons which were then being supplied with wheat and other foodstuffs from Lower California and Mexico. He reasoned that further colonization of the province by Spaniards in civil communities would assist in solving both problems.

After a tour of the province he selected two sites for this purpose. Without waiting for approval from the viceroy or the king he chose nine soldiers from the Monterey *presidio* who had some farming experience and, with five other settlers, set out for one of the sites he had picked on the Guadalupe River. There, in 1777, he laid out the *pueblo* of San José and made preliminary allotments of land subject to later confirmation of his action by his superiors.

Four years later he completed plans for the second new community and in August, 1781 issued the following order for its planning and founding:

"For the establishment of the Pueblo of Los Angeles . . . there shall be included all the lands that may be benefitted by irrigation. . . .

"The site where the pueblo is to be established shall be marked out, on land slightly elevated, exposed to the north and south winds. Measures shall be taken to avoid the dangers of floods; the most immediate vicinity to the river . . . shall be preferred, taking care that from the pueblo the whole or greatest portion of the planting lands be seen.

"The plaza ought to be 200 feet wide by 300 long, from said plaza four main streets shall extend, two on each side, and besides these two other streets shall run by each corner. . . . For the purpose of building there shall be marked out as many building lots as there may be agricultural plots susceptible of irrigation. Also, a tract of land 600 feet wide between the planting lands and the pueblo shall be left vacant.

"Every building lot shall measure 60 feet wide by 120 feet long. . . .

"The front of the plaza looking towards the east shall be reserved to erect at the proper time the church and government buildings and other public offices, and the adjoining lots shall be allotted to settlers."[7]

Both San José and Los Angeles followed the arrangement of streets, plaza, and building sites specified by the Laws of the Indies, then beginning their third century as guides to town design. A redrawing of an early survey of Los Angeles shows the regular design of the plaza and the buildings around it in the town proper and, at a scale reduced to one-fifth that of the town, the checkerboard pattern of the farm fields beyond (Fig. 20).

[7] *Instrucción para la fundación de Los Angeles*, from a translation of the document in the Archives of California, State Papers, Missions and Colonization, Vol. I, used in evidence in the case of *Annis Merril v. J. S. Joerenhout, et al.*, filed in California Superior Court, Los Angeles County, May 10, 1869. Slightly edited for form by the author.

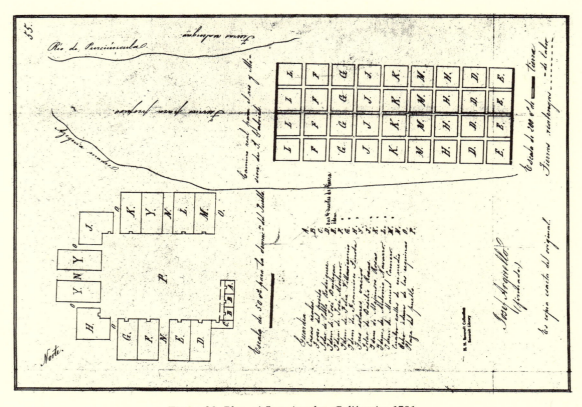

Figure 20. Plan of Los Angeles, California: 1781

Under Spanish and, later, Mexican rule, the *pueblos* remained small and relatively unimportant settlements. The first printed view of Los Angeles in 1856 shows the town as it may well have looked within two or three years after its founding (Fig. 21). It was from this unpromising nucleus that the present sprawling city has grown. The plaza has survived, but little else can be identified to suggest the humble but carefully planned origins of America's most disorderly metropolis.

The Spanish colonial *pueblo* was more than a town; it was intended as a self-contained urban-rural unit. In California, as elsewhere under Spanish rule, an intricate pattern of land distribution developed. A detailed description of this land system is of value not only for its intrinsic interest as an example of small scale regional planning, but also because it provides a basis for comparison with the methods of land settlement employed later by the French and English in North America.

The *pueblo* land tracts generally were square, ten thousand *varas,* or five and a quarter miles, on each side. The town proper occupied a site in or near the middle of this tract. Here each of the original settlers, or *pobladores*, had a house lot, or *solar*. Farming plots, or *suertes*, were laid out in rectangular fields beyond the town proper and were allotted to each settler. Apparently settlers did not receive absolute title to their lands, holding them instead in perpetuity subject to prescribed duties of cultivation. Nor could lands be sold. In this respect, the *suertes* closely resembled the common fields of the early New England communities.

Figure 21. View of Los Angeles, California: 1853

Certain farm tracts were reserved to the king, the *realengas*, and were to be used in making grants to settlers who might come later. Other farm tracts, called *propios*, remained as *pueblo* property to be rented, the income being devoted to community purposes. Common pasture lands and common woodlands were also set aside for general community purposes and not allotted to individuals. Finally, on one or more sides of the town, or completely surrounding it, were the *ejidos*. These also were common lands not under individual jurisdiction and were apparently for the purpose of permitting the enlargement of the town should additional streets and *solares* be needed.

The Spanish *pueblo* pattern of land division closely resembles that of the early New England towns. In the case of the English colonies this system of land distribution clearly stemmed from the conditions of land tenure in rural England at the time of American colonization. This in turn had slowly evolved from feudal land law. It seems a justifiable hypothesis that the Spanish *pueblo* land system similarly owed its origins to the pattern of feudal landholding in Spain. Indeed, throughout most of Western Europe these feudal patterns were common. In America the municipality—Spanish *pueblo* or New England town—replaced the feudal lord. It was, in fact, a fairly sophisticated concept of collective ownership and communal land management that guided the early years of these relatively simple communities.

Despite the more than two and a half centuries of Spanish town planning in North America the influences and tangible remains of the Laws of the Indies were slight. Within the present area of the United States, Spanish colonial efforts rarely were regarded in the home country as more than marginal activities. Because of undermanning and underfinancing, the Spanish reach always exceeded its grasp, and the results were meagre. In our efforts to explore our urban traditions and in our attempts to preserve representative examples of our architectural and planning heritage, an awareness of this dearth of our Spanish legacy should warn us against squandering what little is left of the inheritance from the past.

Along the great valleys of the St. Lawrence and Mississippi rivers the French established a string of trading posts, missions, and towns on the northern and western boundaries of colonial America. Unlike the Spanish communities to the south, the settlements of the French were not regulated by any Gallic equivalent to the Laws of the Indies. French colonial policy was less consistent than that of Spain, and much of the responsibility for town planning was delegated to individuals and companies who had been granted trading and settlement rights in New France.

Each settlement was thus planned according to the circumstances prevailing at the time and the skills and knowledge of its founder. Variety of urban form and pattern was the outcome, although certain common elements identify these towns as springing from the same culture and in response to similar conditions. The influence of French planning was substantial. Indeed, in such cities as Quebec and Montreal, where the original French character can still be perceived, the quality of the urban scene or townscape surpasses virtually anything else of its kind in North America.

French influence on American planning extended beyond the period of colonial activities. The plan of Washington, D.C., prepared by the French artist Pierre Charles L'Enfant, was later to furnish the model for many other neo-baroque city designs. Still later, Haussmann's bold reconstruction of Paris in the last century provided an example for Daniel Burnham as he set about the remaking of such cities as San Francisco and Chicago. In a variety of ways, therefore, French planning has helped shape the pattern of urban America.

Champlain and the Beginnings of Settlement in New France

French colonization of North America lagged more than a century behind that of Spain. The early explorations of Jacques Cartier and others failed to produce permanent settlements. Serious efforts at colonization began only in 1604 when Pierre du Guast, Sieur de Monts, obtained exclusive fur trading rights in Canada from his fellow Huguenot Henry IV. De Monts secured the services of Samuel de Champlain as geographer and navigator for an expedition that set out from France to explore the lands included in this patent and to establish one or more settlements to serve as trading centers.

Champlain also became the town planner, a role for which he was well qualified. From 1599 to 1601 he had served as commander of a Spanish merchant ship on a voyage to the Americas. During this trip he visited virtually all the important seaports as well as many major inland towns founded by the Spanish in the Caribbean and Central America. He undoubtedly knew the provisions of the Laws of the Indies and perhaps had already formulated his own concepts of town planning. Champlain was also a superb cartographer, and most of his maps, including several showing the details of the settlements he helped to found, have survived. Moreover, in his written works we have available an authoritative account of the country and unusually detailed descriptions of the towns he planned.

The expedition established its first settlement in 1604 on the island of Douchet, now part of the State of Maine, which de Monts named Île de Sainte Croix. There Champlain designed a small town consisting of a central square on which fronted the houses of the settlers, a storehouse, blacksmith and carpentry shops, a cook-house, and other structures. The perspective view drawn by Champlain also shows garden and farm plots surrounding this ordered grouping of buildings (Fig. 22).

It seems unlikely that the actual settlement ever bore much resemblance to this plan. The location proved so inhospitable because of the exposed site and the severe winter climate that in the following year de Monts decided to abandon it and seek another location. The site of this second settlement, named Port Royal, was on the western coast of Nova Scotia at a sheltered harbor off the Bay of Fundy. Champlain's description of this second and more compact settlement is of considerable interest: "The plan of the settlement was ten fathoms in length and eight in breadth. . . . On the eastern side is a storehouse of the full width. . . . On the north side is the Sieur de Mont's dwelling, constructed of fairly good woodwork. Around the courtyard are the quarters of the workmen. At one corner on the western side is a platform whereon were placed four pieces of cannon; and at the other corner, towards the east, is a palisade fashioned like a platform. . . ."[1]

[1] Samuel de Champlain, *The Voyages of the Sieur de Champlain* (Paris, 1613), in H. P. Biggar, ed., *The Works of Samuel de Champlain*, Toronto, 1922, I, 373.

A Logis du sieur de Mons.
B Maison publique ou l'on passoit le temps durant la pluie.
C Le magasin.
D Logement des suisses.
E La forge.
F Logement des charpentiers
G Le puis.
H Le four ou l'on faisoit le pain.

I La cuisine.
L Iardinages.
M Autres Iardins.
N La place où au milieu y a vn arbre.
O Palissade.
P Logis des sieurs d'Oruille, Champlain & Chandore.
Q Logis du sieur Boulay, & autres artisans.

R Logis ou logeoit les sieurs de Geneston, Sourin & autres artisans.
T Logis des sieurs de Beaumont, la Motte Bourioli & Fougeray.
V Logement de nostre curé.
X Autres iardinages.
Y La riviere qui entoure l'isle.

Figure 22. View of Ste. Croix (Douchet) Island, Maine: 1604

Champlain also relates how the forty-five persons making up the tiny colony soon began to plant gardens and make other preparations for a permanent settlement. He continued to explore much of the coast of northeastern America and then returned to France to report to de Monts, who had left the expedition after the founding of Port Royal.

In 1608 Champlain returned to Canada on a new expedition to establish a trading post well inland on the St. Lawrence River. In July he reached the site of Quebec, which he had noted on his earlier travels. There he constructed his famous "Habitation," a single, massive, fortified wooden structure on a narrow shelf of land by the river (Fig. 23). Around this almost medieval fortress the old lower town of Quebec began its slow growth. The arrival of Recollect missionaries in 1615 helped to establish the basis for true colonization. Their little chapel and living quarters and the first houses for settlers provided a beginning of town life.

Such were the origins of French colonization in Canada. But the policy of promoting colonization through the granting of trading concessions proved an ineffective device. Although these grants frequently obligated the recipient to settle a specified number of Frenchmen in the new country, in practice these conditions were often ignored or followed only in token fashion. English occupation of Quebec from 1629 to 1632 still further slowed the pace of French colonization.

Champlain at last persuaded Richelieu to modify colonial policy. Under the Cardinal's leadership the Company of the One Hundred Associates took over the activities of the old trading companies. This group was to settle four thousand persons in New France during a

ABITATION. DE QVEBECQ.

A Le magazin.
B Colombier.
C Corps de logis où sont nos armes, & pour loger les ouuriers.
D Autre corps de logis pour les ouuriers.
E Cadran.
F Autre corps de logis où est la forge, & artisans logez.
G Galleries tout au tour des logemens.
H Logis du sieur de Champlain.
I La porte de l'habitation, où il y a Pont-leuis.
L Promenoir autour de l'habitation contenant 10. pieds de large iusques sur le bort du fossé.
M Fossés tout autour de l'habitation.
N Plattes formes, en façon de tenailles pour mettre le canon.
O Iardin du sieur de Champlain.
P La cuisine.
Q Place deuant l'habitation sur le bort de la riuiere.
R La grande riuiere de sainct Lorens.

Figure 23. View of Champlain's Habitation at Quebec, Canada: 1608

fifteen-year period, a modest enough program but one far more vigorous than previously attempted. When, in the 1660's, rule by the Associates ended and Canada became a royal province, renewed and even more effective colonization measures developed.

By the end of French rule in Canada, Quebec had become an imposing city. A plan of the town drawn in 1759 shows the lower town as a tiny, rectangular grid of streets with a single open square that served as a market place, on which fronted the church (Fig. 24). While topography determined this linear pattern, it is obvious that this original part of Quebec was planned, doubtless by Champlain himself.

The upper town on the heights overlooking the river was much less restricted by topography. Moreover, its growth, while slow by contemporary standards, was relatively much more rapid than that of the settlement by the river. While it seems evident that no overall plan for the development of this part of Quebec was ever established, a study of the map reveals many sections in which regularity of streets and orientation of buildings indicate attempts at directing the growth of individual quarters. One of the most perceptive observers of the Quebec of this period was Father Pierre Charlevoix, who arrived in Canada in 1719. He has left this impression of the upper town, which was reached by a steep lane from the lower and older city:

"The first building worthy of notice you meet with . . . is the bishop's palace. . . . When you are got about twenty paces farther, you find yourself between two tolerably large squares; that towards the left is the place of arms, fronting which is the fort or citadel, where the

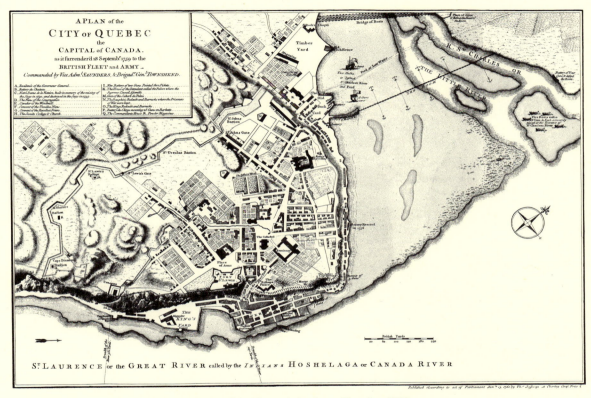

Figure 24. Plan of Quebec, Canada: 1759

governor-general resides; on the opposite side stands the convent of the Recollects, the other sides of the square being lined with handsome houses.

"In the square towards your right you come first of all to the cathedral, which serves also for a parish church to the whole city. Near this, and on the angle formed by the river St. Lawrence and that of St. Charles, stands the seminary. Opposite to the cathedral is the college of the Jesuits, and on the sides between them are some very handsome houses."[2]

Also to be seen on the map and described by Charlevoix are the Hospital and the convent of the Ursuline nuns. A substantial group of buildings stood on the lower elevation along the St. Charles river. Here were the principal docks, the residence of the Intendant, who was the commercial representative of the king, miscellaneous manufacturing establishments, and a number of residences backed against the steep escarpment.

The plan of the upper town of Quebec represents one type of urban form established by the French in North America. Here the general configuration of the community is compact and non-linear, thus resembling most European cities of the time. Another, and much more regular, example of this general type is Louisburg on Cape Breton Island, the site for which was selected in 1712. Louisburg was intended as the main French fortress town in Canada, and a plan of the town in 1758 shows the extent of the French commitment to this concept (Fig. 25). In all, thirty million francs were poured into the construc-

[2] Pierre François Xavier de Charlevoix, *Journal of a Voyage to North America* (London, 1761), Chicago, 1923, I, 105.

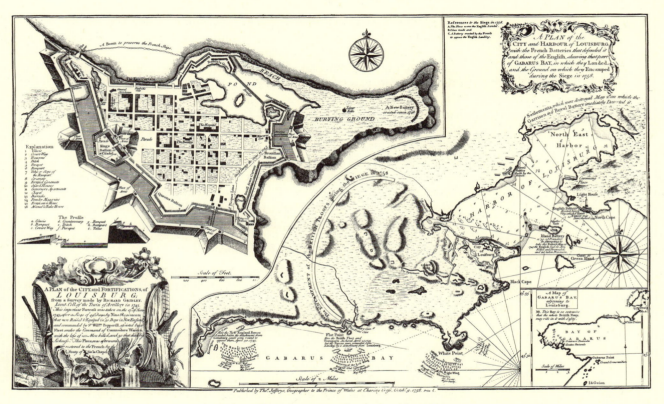

Figure 25. Plan of Louisburg, Canada: 1758

tion of this mighty fort, whose building occupied twenty years. The main ramparts extended for two miles, and in addition there were extensive outworks beyond the principal walls.

The plan of Louisburg followed the town and garrison layout theories and principles of the great French military engineer, Sebastian Vauban. With its *place d'armes*, elaborate fortifications, protected harbor, and gridiron street system, Louisburg could have been one of the many cities planned or remodeled by Vauban in Europe. Although Louisburg served primarily as a garrison town, it was planned for a population of 4,000 persons and developed as an important commercial port as well. Yet for all its seemingly impregnable fortifications, Louisburg fell to the English twice, in 1745 and again in 1758. Some years after its final capture, the English demolished the fortifications, and the town virtually ceased to exist.

Montreal and the Linear Plan

Quebec and Louisburg must have seemed familiar to new colonists or travellers from Europe, the first growing like a replica of some medieval city, the second springing into existence as a Renaissance community. Quebec's great rival, Montreal, developed in quite a different pattern. A plan of Montreal in 1759 reveals the narrow, linear pattern that had been adopted for the town during its growth from its original small and compact form (Fig. 26). As at the lower town of Quebec, the restricted level area along the St. Lawrence River confined the community's growth in depth. But it is equally obvious that the plan reflects some overall direction of town development. Similar topo-

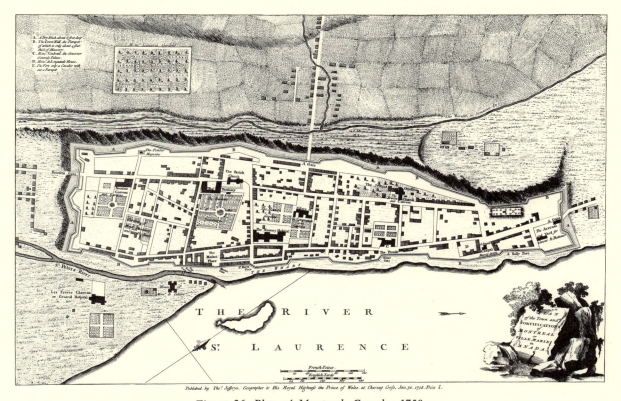

Published by Thos. Jefferys, Geographer to His Royal Highness the Prince of Wales, at Charing Cross, Jan.30.1758. Price 1.

Figure 26. Plan of Montreal, Canada: 1758

graphic features were also present in the case of Mobile, New Orleans, and St. Louis, whose plans closely resemble that of Montreal. It is likely that the planners of those later cities consciously imitated the Montreal plan.

Montreal's original plan, however, may have been derived from Champlain's first venture at town planning at Île Sainte Croix. That plan (Fig. 27), recently discovered in manuscript, apparently dates from the first year of settlement in 1642 when a group of missionaries, soldiers, nuns, and settlers arrived at Montreal Island.

The group that took up residence in 1642 had ventured to Canada as the pioneers of a movement supported from France by both money and prayers designed to bring the·Indians into the fold of Christianity. On the narrow point of land formed by the St. Lawrence River and the stream called the St. Pierre the first buildings were erected around a little square. The hospital, a small fort, and a number of residences made up the settlement during the bitter early years when Indian raids, the severe winters, and spring floods made life hazardous for these first settlers. By 1665 the population had reached 500, and within a few years expansion of the town became necessary.

The growth of Montreal coincided with changes in the colonial status of New France. The Sulpician order received the seigneurial rights for the Island of Montreal, and in 1672 Dollier de Casson, the Superior of the Sulpicians, supervised surveys for new streets and building sites. St. Paul Street, which on the map of 1759 can be seen connecting the market place and the Parade along the river, already existed as a curving lane serving the few houses that had been built

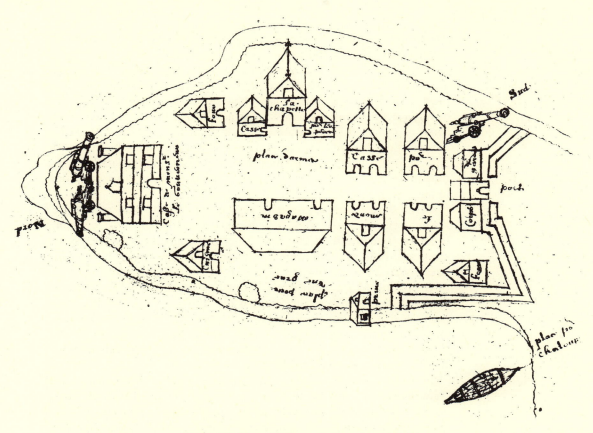

Figure 27. Plan of Montreal, Canada: ca. 1644

beyond the confines of the original settlement. This was now surveyed and building lines established.

Parallel with St. Paul Street and away from the river, Nôtre Dame Street was laid out 30 feet broad and in a straight line above and below the site set aside for the parish church of Notre Dame. The right-of-way for this street lay across cultivated fields, and for a year or so some of the proprietors ignored the surveyor's monuments. In 1673 these settlers received notices that the right-of-way must be observed and, further, that in accordance with the terms of the land grants they must enclose their lots and erect houses on them to prevent forfeiture of their lands.

Other streets were laid out at right angles to St. Paul and Notre Dame. Some of these were completely new, although most of them followed generally the location of lanes and trails affording access to scattered dwellings that were in existence at the time. These cross streets were quite narrow, 18 or 24 feet being the dimensions of most of them. In 1678 a third street parallel to the river, St. James, was surveyed, the same year that marked the completion of the church of Notre Dame. Within the framework of the newly established linear grid pattern the town began to grow. By 1680 the population was about 1,400, and in 1750, toward the end of the French regime, more than 8,000 persons lived in Montreal.

In 1721 a disastrous fire swept the town, destroying many of its frame buildings. This led to a series of regulations for the use of stone as the chief building material and also providing for new street lines, since, in the words of the regulations, "they are not large enough nor straight enough; that while this cannot be done without individuals suffering, yet at the present moment, seeing that there are only ruins in the streets, it would be easy for individuals, before rebuilding, to conform with the alignment which shall be drawn up by the Engineer. . . ."[3]

And so the first replanning of the city began, a process that continues to the present day as old plans and buildings are modified to meet the changing conditions of a new era. The modern metropolis of Montreal sprawls for miles beyond the boundaries of the old town, yet much of the 17th-century character remains. As in the lower town of Quebec, this older section of Montreal preserves the results of an earlier age of town planning, a previous heritage almost unique on a continent where all too frequently the residue of the past has been destroyed with awful finality.

French Towns in the American Interior

With Quebec and Montreal established along the St. Lawrence, French traders, explorers, and missionaries pushed on into the great central lake basins and river valleys of America. Champlain, Nicolet, Jolliet, Marquette, La Salle—these were but a few of the hardy Frenchmen who established a great empire in North America. It was a different kind of domain from that which the English were carving from the forests along the Atlantic coast. Based on a string of frontier forts and missions, with here and there a settlement large enough to be called a town, New France depended heavily on water transportation as the only reasonably speedy and effective means of communication and trade. The waterfront, or a military installation controlling

[3] As quoted by William H. Atherton, *Montreal*, Montreal, 1914, I, 347.

water transportation, was the important feature of most of these French colonial settlements.

The plan of Detroit, founded in 1701 by Antoine de la Mothe Cadillac, expressed its function as a fortress town dominating the Detroit River connection between Lakes Erie and St. Clair. The earliest printed map of Detroit in 1764 (Fig. 28) suggests nothing so much as one of the *bastide* towns of southern France in Cadillac's native Gascony. The fortifications enclosed a space about 600 by 400 feet. Streets were extremely narrow. The widest, Rue Sainte Anne, measured less than 30 feet, and the others were between 10 and 20 feet wide.

Outside the little town lay the farm plots of the settlers. The map shows the major field lines in the vicinity of Detroit, with the typical French pattern of long, narrow farms running back from the water's edge. This pattern was even more pronounced in the Canadian settlements along the St. Lawrence and, later, on the lower Mississippi in the neighborhood of New Orleans. In the case of New Orleans this pattern of rural land holdings helped to shape the expansion of that city as it grew beyond its original bounds. At Detroit, however, the French system of field division had little influence. After the town passed to the British and still later into American hands a fire completely destroyed the settlement. Congress authorized its replanning and gave jurisdiction over ten thousand acres of land in the vicinity to the Governor and Judges of Michigan Territory. Their plan completely wiped out the last traces of the French town and its surrounding farm lands.

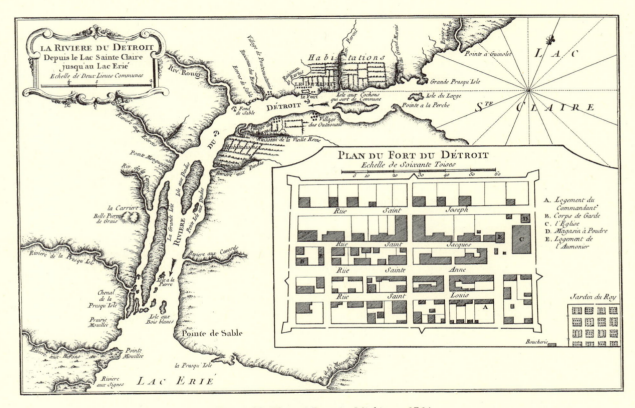

Figure 28. Plan of Detroit, Michigan: 1764

There were many other fortress communities erected by the French. Some, like Fort Duquesne, at the present Pittsburgh, were intended to stop the westward march of the English colonies. Others were established in an effort to consolidate French control over the vast interior valleys of the Great Lakes and the Mississippi River. While most of these settlements began as military garrison communities, they often included groups of missionaries and usually attracted traders and farmers.

By the end of the 17th century, French settlements began to appear along the Mississippi River and its major tributaries. Around Fort Pimitoui or Fort St. Louis, built at Peoria in the winter of 1691-92 a little settlement of traders and farmers developed. More important were the neighboring communities which were founded along the fertile alluvial plain on the east bank of the Mississippi stretching southward from the mouth of the Illinois River. The most northerly was Cahokia, which grew up around a mission founded in 1699. To the south were Prairie du Rocher and Kaskaskia, the latter being the site of a mission originally established by Marquette, moved once to Peoria, and finally relocated about 1703 on its third site near the southern end of the American Bottom. Here Captain Philip Pittman, who arrived in the area late in 1765 to survey the new territory taken by the English from France, found "by far the most considerable settlement in the country of the Illinois, as well from its number of inhabitants, as from its advantageous situation. . . . The principal buildings are, the church and Jesuits house, which has a small chapel adjoining to it; these, as well as some other houses in the village are built of stone, and, considering this part of the world, make a very good appearance. . . . Sixty-five families reside in this village, besides merchants, other casual people, and slaves."[4]

Pittman's plan of Kaskaskia reveals an irregular grid of narrow streets dividing the town into blocks of various sizes (Fig. 29). Between the church and the river appears some kind of open space which may have served as a market and mustering ground. Kaskaskia and the other primitive French settlements in this area, like the Spanish *pueblos*, were agricultural villages on the European pattern. The drawing shows the location of the common fields where farmers received allotments of land separated by two furrows. These strips stretched backward from the river and were from 100 to 500 feet wide and occasionally as long as one mile. A common fence bordered the fields, and each farmer was required to maintain his section of the fence. In addition to these cultivated fields, other common land provided for cattle grazing and timber.

Across the Mississippi from Kaskaskia lay Ste. Genevieve, founded in 1732. Later, in 1784, this town was relocated on higher ground and was planned on a much more regular pattern. By this time the west bank of the Mississippi was under Spanish rule, and the regularity of Ste. Genevieve's streets and its imposing central square may well have resulted from the application of the Laws of the Indies. In population and in architecture, however, the town was essentially French, a character which the modern little city has somehow managed to retain.

[4] Philip Pittman, *The Present State of the European Settlements on the Missisippi* (London, 1770), Frank H. Hodder, ed., Cleveland, 1906, pp. 84-85.

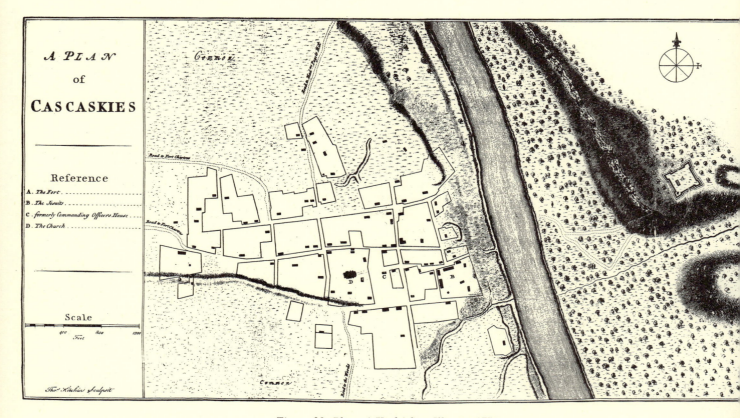

Figure 29. Plan of Kaskaskia, Illinois: 1770

St. Louis, the latest of the mid-Mississippi towns established under French sponsorship, became the largest and most important of all. Following their practice of granting exclusive trading privileges to a private company, French authorities in New Orleans conferred a monopoly of trade in the upper Missouri valley on the firm of Maxent, Laclede and Company in 1763. Pierre Laclede spent that fall and early winter in reaching the area and exploring for the most suitable site. The one chosen proved an excellent selection, a moderately sloping location without deeply incised stream valleys to interfere with the street plan and occupying the first high ground on the Mississippi below the mouths of the Missouri and Illinois rivers.

Auguste Chouteau, little more than a lad but designated by Laclede as his agent, tells of the founding of the town:

"Navigation being open in the early part of February, he fitted out a boat . . . and he gave the charge of it to Chouteau, and said to him: 'You will proceed and land at the place where we marked the trees; you will commence to have the place cleared, and build a large shed to contain the provisions and the tools, and some small cabins to lodge the men. . . .' In the early part of April, Laclede arrived among us. He occupied himself with his settlement, fixed the place where he wished to build his house, laid a plan of the village which he wished to found . . . and ordered me to follow the plan exactly, because he could not remain there any longer with us."[5]

[5] From Col. Auguste Chouteau's Narrative of the Settlement of St. Louis as quoted in Ina Faye Woestemeyer, *The Westward Movement*, New York, 1939, pp. 201-202.

An early plan of St. Louis drawn by Chouteau shows a close resemblance to that of Montreal (Fig. 30). Here is the same linear pattern, the rectangular street system, and the *place d'armes* opening to the river. Virtually this same design had been employed earlier at Mobile and New Orleans, and Laclede's knowledge of those cities may have influenced him at St. Louis. The streets were quite narrow: those running parallel to the river were 38 feet wide, while the short cross streets were only 32 feet in width. Common fields and common pasture and woodlands were provided nearby, and this land on at least one occasion provided the site for a second and smaller settlement, Carondelet, south of St. Louis.

Laclede may have envisaged his settlement as only a trading post, but the population of his infant town quickly grew as many French settlers on the east bank of the Mississippi moved to St. Louis to avoid English domination. What they did not know is that the French had secretly transferred the entire Louisiana Territory to Spain and that shortly a handful of Spanish officials would arrive to assume the reins of government. Under Spanish rule the city languished, and it was not until the opening of the trans-Mississippi west to American exploration and settlement that St. Louis outgrew the dimensions of its original plan. Then it grew rapidly and steadily, extending its gridiron plan up and down the river and to the west, absorbing in the process all of the old agricultural land and commons which had once surrounded the town. Today Lafayette Park, in the southern part of the city, is all that has remained open of these farm and pasture lands.

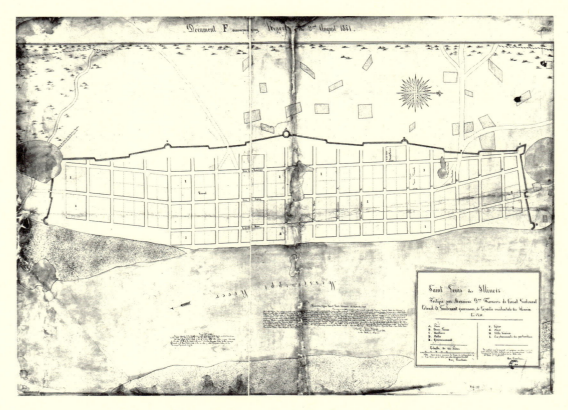

Figure 30. Plan of St. Louis, Missouri: 1780

Although the original intention of the founder apparently was to leave open a 300-foot-wide strip along the river, this land was in great demand, and it was made available for building sites. When Henry Brackenridge visited St. Louis in 1811 he was deeply impressed by the great commercial future of the city, but he was dismayed at its appearance along the river:

"It is to be lamented that no space has been left between the town and the river; for the sake of the pleasure of the promenade as well as for business and health, there should have been no encroachment on the margin of the noble stream. The principal place of business ought to have been on the bank. From the opposite side, nothing is visible of the busy bustle of a populous town; it appears closed up. The site of St. Louis is not unlike that of Cincinnati. How different would have been its appearance, if built in the same elegant manner! its bosom opened to the breezes of the river, the stream gladdened by the enlivening scene of business and pleasure, compact rows of elegant and tasteful dwellings, looking with pride on the broad wave that passes."[6]

Two hundred years after its founding, however, St. Louis was to remedy this defect that Brackenridge had noted. On a forty-block site cleared for the purpose the Jefferson Memorial Park has now taken form along the great river, which had previously swept by almost unseen near the heart of the city. A great steel arch, higher than the Washington Monument, symbolizes the gateway to the west which

[6] Henry M. Brackenridge, *Views of Louisiana Together with a Journal of a Voyage up the Missouri River, in 1811*, Pittsburgh, 1814, pp. 120-21.

was opened by the Louisiana Purchase. Regrettably in the process virtually all traces of the original French plan of St. Louis have been obliterated.

Bienville and the Planning of Mobile and New Orleans

One of the most prominent of the early settlers of Montreal was Charles le Moyne, whose seigneury of Longueuil across the river from the city was once almost as important and influential as that of Montreal itself. Eleven of his sons brilliantly served the cause of New France. Two of them were responsible for important cities: Pierre, Sieur d'Iberville; and Jean Baptisti, Sieur de Bienville. It was Iberville who, in 1698, sailed from Brest in command of an expedition under orders to discover the mouth of the Mississippi and secure the lower end of the great valley for France.

Early the following year Iberville and his brother reached the mouth of the Mississippi and explored the lower reaches of the river. Then, sailing eastward to Biloxi Bay, Iberville constructed a fort near its entrance as a temporary post. After further explorations he sailed for France, but in 1701 he returned with a new party, this time to establish a settlement on Mobile Bay. Early in 1702 Fort Louis was located on the Mobile River, and a rectangular gridiron village plan was marked out. Bienville, who had assisted his brother throughout these years, was installed as governor of the French settlement, and on the death of Iberville in 1706 became the leading figure in the Gulf possessions of France.

The original settlement survived only eight years. After a flood in 1710 inundated the site, Bienville determined to re-establish the town on another location, this time at the mouth of the Mobile River and on a more favorable spot. The design for this second Mobile was similar to the first, although more elaborate and more carefully laid out. A plan of the city drawn in 1711 included this detailed description of the city:

"There is in the fort only the governor's house, the *magasin* where are the king's effects, and a guardhouse. The officers, soldiers, and residents have their abode outside the fort, as is indicated, being placed in such manner that the streets are six toises [36 feet] wide and all parallel. The blocks are fifty toises [300 feet] square except those opposite the fort, which are sixty toises [360 feet] wide and fifty deep, and those nearest the river, which are fifty wide and sixty deep.

"The houses are constructed of cedar and pine upon a foundation of wooden stakes. . . .

"They give to all who wish to settle in this place land 12 1/2 toises [75 feet] wide, facing a street, by 25 [150 feet] deep."[7]

The letters on the map and the accompanying key show the allotments of land made at that time (Fig. 31). The most prominent settlers were given sites nearest the fort and bordering the tree-lined parade. One feature is of interest: the streets and blocks shown by dotted lines projected inland from those first laid out for the settlers moved from the old site. Evidently Bienville was confident that his new city would grow and that additional land would be needed.

[7] Peter J. Hamilton, *Colonial Mobile*, Boston, rev. edn., 1910, p. 87.

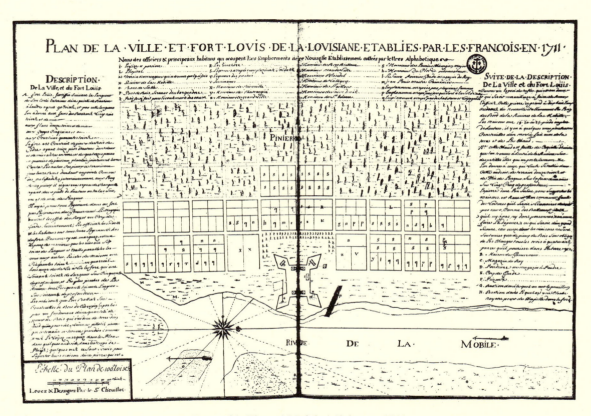

Figure 31. Plan of Mobile, Alabama: 1711

Note, too, the proportions of the city, ten blocks long by five blocks deep, and the parade ground or *place d'armes* opening to the river bank and centrally located.

Under the Treaty of Paris in 1763 Mobile passed to the English. Maps of that period indicate that with the passage of time some of the regularity of Bienville's original plan had disappeared. When the capital of the French territory was shifted from Mobile many years earlier the city lost some of its initial importance, and encroachments were made on the original straight streets and carefully surveyed city blocks. Yet the framework of the original plan can still be traced in the streets of the modern city.

Of all the French settlements in the United States, however, it is New Orleans where the most substantial portions of our French city planning legacy remain for inspection today. New Orleans, too, was a product of the energy of Bienville, who applied there what he had learned in laying out the two Mobiles. Bienville had always favored a city on the Mississippi. His interest was renewed by the promotional activities of one John Law, who had received a charter from the French government for his Western Company, one of the early examples in America of a speculative real estate promotion. Law's enterprise received wide publicity in France as he advanced extravagant claims for Louisiana's fertility, ease of settlement, and potential wealth.

As early as 1718 Bienville sent a few emigrants from Canada to clear the site and to erect temporary buildings, but it was not until 1722 that actual planning and town building began. It was in this year that Charlevoix visited the site accompanied by Adrien de Pauger, the engineer Bienville directed to survey and lay out the city.

Charlevoix had no doubt expected to find the city already in being, since before he left France for Canada he had read in *Le Mercure de France* and other newspapers the exaggerations of Law, who described the great city on the banks of the Mississippi as something only slightly less imposing than Paris itself. Charlevoix refers to these false impressions in his descriptions of the actual conditions at New Orleans as he saw them: "If the eight hundred fine houses and the five parishes, which our Mercury bestowed upon it two years ago, are at present reduced to a hundred barracks, placed in no very good order; to a large ware-house built of timber; to two or three houses which would be no ornament to a village in France; to one half of a sorry ware-house, formerly set apart for divine service, and was scarce appropriated for that purpose, when it was removed to a tent: what pleasure, on the other hand, must it give to see this . . . become the capital of a large and rich colony."[8]

An accurate plan of the town in 1764, four decades after its founding, shows that the city even then had not fulfilled the expectations of its promoters. The details of the plan, however, show clearly (Fig. 32). The focal point of the city is the *place d'armes*, the modern Jackson Square. As at Mobile, this appears at the water's edge. But this open ·square was plainly intended as more than a parade ground. On the inland side, facing the square and the river beyond, stood the principal church. To give this building further architectural

8 Charlevoix, *Journal*, ii, 257-58.

Figure 32. Plan of New Orleans, Louisiana: 1764

prominence the planners introduced an extra street dividing the central range of blocks terminating at the square. This strong axial treatment doubtless reflected the intentions of Bienville to create a capital city of beauty as well as utility. Stretching each way from the central square along the river ran the quay, broadening at either end where the river curved away from the town site.

As the capital city, New Orleans became the favored spot for French settlers and after them Spanish colonists, and it enjoyed a mild prosperity. Above and below the city on both sides of the Mississippi plantations were developed, laid out on the typical French pattern with relatively narrow river frontages and stretching back from the river for great distances. Yet even by 1797 we are told that not all of the land within the original city boundaries enclosed by its fortifications had been built on. Francis Baily's account of the city at that time is of considerable interest for his description of the *place d'armes*, the buildings around it, and the appearance of the city from the river bank:

"The church is a plain brick building of the Ionic order. . . . Not far from the square in which this church stands is the government-house, a plain edifice, in which the governor of the province resides: it stands facing the water at the corner of a street; it is built (as many houses in this place are) with open galleries facing the street, and is surrounded at the back by a garden. At an equal distance from the church, on the opposite side, and immediately facing the water, is a magazine of stores. . . . At the eastern corner of the city are the barracks. . . . Immediately adjoining the barracks is the convent, which is another very plain edifice, and holds about thirty or forty nuns. . . . The levee . . . here was a handsome raised gravel walk, planted with orangetrees; and in the summer-time served for a mall, and in an evening was always a fashionable resort for the beaux and belles of the place."[9]

Baily's impressions were thus not entirely favorable. The "plain edifices" he encountered doubtless seemed to him unimpressive, and it is true that they would have been regarded with amazement in Georgian London. Many of the city's buildings had been constructed or remodeled during the period of Spanish control from 1763 to 1801, and much of the elaborate cast iron grillwork which embellishes the façades of the buildings in the old part of the city dates from that period or later.

The French returned to govern for a brief period, but with the Louisiana Purchase in 1803 New Orleans came under the jurisdiction of the United States. It is from this time, with the opening of the Mississippi to river shipping from the heartland of the nation, that the city began to prosper and to expand its boundaries beyond its original limits. As occurred in many European walled cities, when the old perimeter fortifications were pulled down broad boulevards replaced them: the Canal Street, North Rampart Street, and Esplanade Avenue of the present day. A beautifully detailed plan of the city in 1815 clearly shows these and other changes in the urban pattern (Fig. 33).

[9] Francis Baily, *Journal of a Tour in Unsettled Parts of North America in 1796 and 1797*, London, 1856, pp. 300-302.

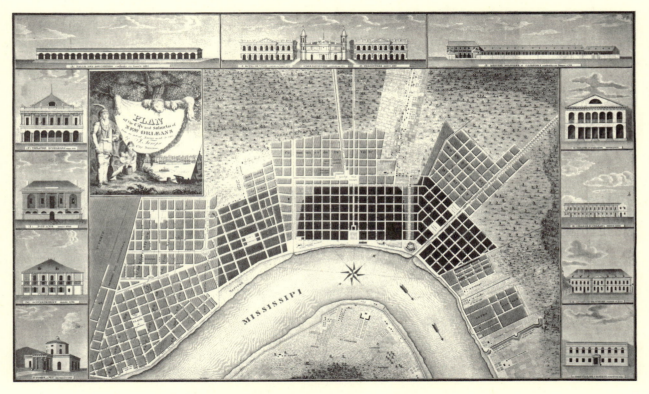

Figure 33. Plan of New Orleans, Louisiana: 1817

Above and below the old town new suburbs or "faubourgs" appeared. The curving river bank suggested a new orientation for the grid plan of these city extensions, a change in street directions that could have been disastrous except for the skill with which connections were designed.

Good planning and the influence of topography combined in another way to fashion a street pattern of beauty and interest as well as one that functions well even with modern traffic. As the long, narrow plantations adjoining the expanding community were subdivided, each was laid out in a little gridiron strip. But because the land back from the river was the least desirable owing to its location and its swampy character, the first subdivision of land occurred along the river. Each grid developed independently and rather slowly. Developers recognized the importance of short cross streets and arranged for connections across property lines.

New Orleans adopted one feature of its original plan, which was repeated at intervals as its boundaries expanded. This was the open square, often combined as a space opening off or terminating one of the numerous boulevards. In this respect, although the city was under American rule, it remained European in its use of the urban square as a major element of planning and growth.

In New Orleans, as in Quebec and Montreal, the French colonial plan survives, a valuable remnant that should be guarded and preserved with careful efforts and sensitive treatment. Fortunately, relics of the past are not without value as tourist attractions, aside from their historic worth. The modern city has already taken some steps to preserve the unique flavor of the *vieux carré* by regulations governing architectural changes and through the encouragement of restoration projects. Much has already been lost through neglect and barbaric commercialization of some of the finest parts of old New Orleans. Today's visitor must restrict his vision to escape the visual intrusions of neon signs, the ubiquitous automobile, and the dominating billboard. Yet in the little oasis of Jackson Square and in some of the surrounding streets one may recapture the atmosphere of French and Spanish New Orleans and imagine himself in Bienville's modest capital of the great province of Louisiana.

Not until the 16th century was drawing to a close did English interest in North America extend beyond occasional voyages of exploration, periodic raids on Spanish ports, and the use of the fishing banks off the mouth of the St. Lawrence. It was in 1585 that Sir Walter Raleigh dispatched seven ships carrying 108 persons in the ill-fated effort to establish a colony on Roanoke Island off the Carolina coast. We know very little about the shape of the settlement laid out by the governor, Ralph Lane, but contemporary drawings of English colonial forts of the period and fragmentary archaeological evidence indicate that the little community was a stockade-enclosed square, with pointed bastions along the sides of the square and an octagonal tower at one corner. This first English colonial effort in the New World ended in total failure and the mysterious disappearance of the tiny colony.

Jamestown, St. Mary's, and the
First Tidewater Towns

Some twenty years later the settlement that was to open a new era in the colonization of North America was finally established. At Jamestown, England finally succeeded in gaining a toehold on the new continent and began 170 years of colonization and town building.

The Virginia colony came into being as a result of the formation of a joint-stock enterprise under Royal charter. We shall be concerned here with the activities of one of the two major divisions of the Company, that underwritten mainly by London merchants and investors. The London Company received settlement rights .between the 34th and 41st parallels and in December 1606 dispatched three ships carrying one hundred settlers on the long voyage to Virginia.

In April of the following year the expedition landed at Cape Henry, near present-day Norfolk. Then a two-week search began for a suitable site for the first town. Finally, the site named Jamestown was selected some thirty miles inland on the James River where a narrow isthmus connected the mainland to a near-island.

In choosing this location the colonists followed instructions given them on their departure pointing out that a site well inland on a navigable river would have the trading advantages of a coastal situation but would be far easier to protect against attack. But unfortunately, through ignorance or carelessness, they disregarded the warning against "a low or moist place because it will prove unhealthful," and settled on an island surrounded by swamps and brackish water.

The instructions also included these general directions on the order of construction: "It were necessary that all your carpenters and other such like workmen . . . do first build your storehouse and those other rooms of publick and necessary use before any house be set up for any private persons, yet let them all work together first for the company and then for private men."

As to the layout of the town itself, the instructions were brief but admirably clear: "And seeing order is at the same price with confusion it shall be adviseably done to set your houses even and by a line, that your streets may have a good breadth, and be carried square about your market place. . . ."[1]

On May 14 work began on the fort. As one contemporary described it, "Now falleth every man to worke, the Councell contrive the Fort, the rest cut downe trees to make place to pitch their Tents; some provide clapboard to relade the ships, some make gardens, some nets, &c. The Salvages often visited us kindly. The Precidents [President's] overweening jealousie would admit no exercise at armes, or fortificatin but the boughs of trees cast together in the forme of a halfe moone."[2] Within a month the little fortified settlement had taken shape. Its form was a triangle, enclosed by a palisade of poles set in the ground vertically. The side parallel to the river was 420 feet long, the other sides being 300 feet each, and thus enclosing about one acre. At the corners "bulwarkes," each shaped "like a halfe moone and foure or five pieces of artillerie mounted in them," were erected. Inside were the church, storehouse, and the dwellings of the settlers.

No plan of the "town" has survived, and the original site has itself been destroyed by the river's eroding force. From the fragmentary early descriptions of the primitive community a modern replica has been constructed not far from its true location. A modern map drawn

---

[1] "Instructions . . . for the intended voyage to Virginia . . . ," September 10, 1606, the text of which appears in Alexander Brown, *The Genesis of the United States*, Boston, 1890, I, 84.

[2] William Simmonds, *The Proceedings of the English Colonies in Virginia*, in Lyon Gardiner Tyler, *Narratives of Early Virginia 1606-1625*, New York, 1907, p. 123.

in antique style records with reasonable accuracy the general character of Jamestown during its earliest years (Fig. 34). The meanest hamlet in rural England possessed more comforts than this crude community set in a clearing on the fringe of a vast continent.

The history of Jamestown and the other early settlements of Virginia is one of famine, disease, misfortune, and disappointments. By the beginning of fall half of the original settlers were dead. Reinforcements arrived from time to time, but in the winter of 1609-10 the population that had increased to 500 dwindled to 60 as a result of disease, Indian attacks, and starvation. In May 1610 Sir Thomas Gates arrived with supplies but, finding the town almost ruined, resolved to take off the survivors and abandon the colony. At the last minute Lord Delaware arrived with 150 new colonists, and Gates's ship put back to Jamestown for a new attempt.

The racking hardships were by no means over, but from that year the survival of Jamestown no longer seemed in doubt. A few additional settlements sprang up, one of which, Hampton, is the oldest of the surviving English colonial towns. Captain John Smith has left us an account of the founding of another of these communities, Henrico, farther up the James, laid out by Deputy Governor Thomas Dale in 1611:

". . . within ten or twelve daies . . . [Dale] . . . had invironed it with a pale, and in honour of our noble Prince Henry, called it Henrico. The next worke he did, was building at each corner of the Towne a high commanding Watch-house, a Church, and Store-houses. . . .

"This towne . . . hath three streets of well framed houses, a hand-

Figure 34. Plan of Jamestown, Virginia: 1607

some Church, and the foundation of a better laid (to bee built of Bricke)...."[3]

The only surviving graphic record of Henrico is of little help in reconstructing the original plan (Fig. 35). In its general representation of the coast and the James River the map is highly inaccurate. Doubtless the cartographer never set eyes on Virginia, and the representation of Henrico is a mere convention. The map is of interest, although for our purposes not helpful, in that it shows Jamestown, indicated by the name "Jackqueville."

At Jamestown, Henrico, Hampton, and their sister towns the colonists encountered continual difficulties in preventing the buildings and fortifications from falling into ruins. The early records contain repeated accounts of new governors arriving to find the towns in a state of decay and their efforts to promote rebuilding. Flimsy construction of unseasoned timber, excessive moisture in the low-lying town sites, inattention to regular maintenance, and destruction by frequent fires all contributed to the hardships of sustaining the physical basis for town life.

Geographic and economic factors contributed to the difficulties of maintaining towns. The Virginia coast, penetrated at frequent intervals by wide, slow-flowing, deep rivers, navigable for many miles inland, offered so many potential sites for settlement that no single spot stood out as clearly superior where a major city would develop. The

[3] Captain John Smith, *Generall Historie of Virginia, New England and the Summer Isles* (London, 1624), in Tyler, *ibid.*, pp. 304-305.

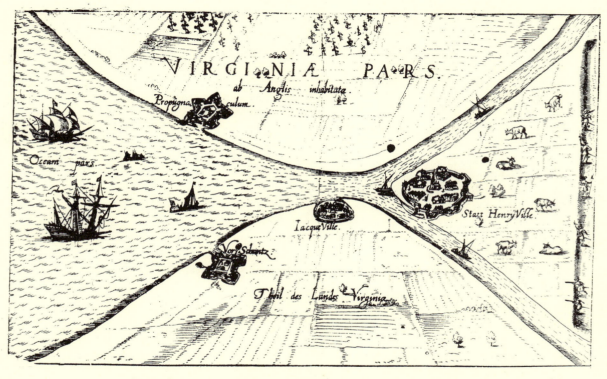

Figure 35. Map of the Coast of Virginia and the James River: 1611

second influence causing a dispersed pattern of settlement and impeding town development was the early adoption of tobacco as the dominant product of the colony. The most economical and efficient method of production was in large-scale farming operations. As tobacco plantations developed and cheap labor was introduced with the beginning of slavery, individual plantations became small communities with warehouses, shops, slave quarters, and the plantation residence. Because of the proximity to tidewater channels, docks and port facilities on each plantation furnished direct links with the markets in the mother country.

As the Reverend Hugh Jones, one of the earliest historians of Virginia, observed in 1724: "Thus neither the interest nor inclinations of the Virginians induce them to cohabit in towns; so that they are not forward in contributing their assistance towards the making of particular places, every plantation affording the owner the provision of a little market; wherefore they most commonly build upon some convenient spot or neck of land in their own plantation. . . ."[4] Under these circumstances town life was not likely to flourish in Virginia or, where almost identical conditions prevailed, in Maryland.

The London Company and the Crown had, however, visualized colonial life as centering on towns. Moreover, the warehouse and shipping facilities at the individual plantations, dispersed throughout the colony, added to the difficulties and expense of collection of customs duties and the control of trade. There was apparently a feeling,

[4] Hugh Jones, *Present State of Virginia* (London, 1724), Chapel Hill, 1956, pp. 73-74.

too, that the affairs of the colony would be furthered if one town in each district clearly became the center of trade, administration, and cultural activities. As early as 1623 rules required all cargoes to be shipped through Jamestown. These regulations were naturally resisted by the planters, as were later directives authorizing the use of a limited number of other ports. The first century of the colony saw a continued struggle between the planters, who favored shipment from individual plantations, and the Crown, which desired town and port development through which all commerce would be channelled.

Efforts to extend and enlarge Jamestown were made in 1623, when Surveyor General William Claiborne laid out the "New Towne" adjacent to the triangular fort. In 1636 house lots were made available at nominal rentals to anyone who would build in the town. In 1641 additional lots were granted. Finally, in 1662, the legislature passed an "Act for building a towne," which directed that each of the seventeen counties should erect one house in Jamestown. A minimum size and brick construction were specified, and grants of 10,000 pounds of tobacco were authorized for each county and each person building a house which met these standards. A tax of thirty pounds of tobacco a person was levied to raise the subsidy funds necessary. Counties were authorized to impress building workmen at specified wages to ensure a supply of construction labor.

But this elaborate legislation failed to achieve its goals; one account indicates that only four or five houses were completed under the Act of 1662. Some growth had occurred earlier on the land surveyed under Claiborne's directions into a little gridiron pattern stretching southward from the fort, but in 1675 the population probably did not exceed 100 freemen. Jamestown was scarcely more than a village, although it remained the seat of government. During Bacon's rebellion in 1676 most of the town was burned to the ground, a blow from which the town never fully recovered.

Meanwhile, across Chesapeake Bay in the Maryland colony, new attempts at town founding were made. In many respects the development of towns in Virginia and Maryland followed parallel courses. In both colonies the first settlers brought with them instructions on choosing a site for and laying out the first town. Legislation aimed at promoting town development followed within a few years of initial colonization. In both colonies topography, tobacco economy, and the resistance of planters largely nullified these urbanizing efforts. And in both colonies the original capitals were finally moved to new, planned towns of considerable interest and character.

The Jamestown of Maryland was St. Mary's. Here, on a point of land between the mouth of the Potomac and Chesapeake Bay, the first group of colonists sent out by Lord Baltimore settled in 1634. Baltimore's instructions directed "all the Planters to build their houses in as decent and uniforme a manner as their abilities and the place will afford, and neere adjoying one to an other, and for that purpose to cause streetes to be marked out where they intend to place the towne and to oblige every man to buyld one by an other according to that rule. . . ."[5]

[5] "Instructions . . . directed by the Right Honorable Cecilius Lord Baltimore . . . ," November 13, 1633, in Clayton Colman Hall, *Narratives of Early Maryland, 1633-1684*, New York, 1910, pp. 20-22.

The instructions also specified that a plat of the town should be sent to Baltimore at the earliest opportunity. This has not survived, and the exact layout of St. Mary's remains unknown. From contemporary descriptions we do know that, while St. Mary's did not suffer all the difficulties encountered at Jamestown, its growth was slow. As late as 1678 Charles Calvert could only report sadly that the town had "not above thirty houses, and those at considerable distance from each other, and the buildings . . . very mean and little, and generally after the manner of the meanest farm-houses in England."[6]

The New Town Acts of Virginia and Maryland

The Virginia Act of 1662 for the rebuilding of Jamestown also specified four other sites where towns were to be built in subsequent years. Through its tobacco tax provisions it further provided a means of financing town building and established a procedure for town development. The act became the precedent for a whole series of legislative enactments in Virginia and Maryland. Passed at the request or direction of the Crown, these laws designated sites for towns, established the method of land acquisition and land valuation, provided for their layout, and made provision for disposition of town lots. These towns were to be ports of entry through which all shipments were to pass; naturally this legislation was resisted by the planters and by their London agents. In Maryland a Governor's proclamation

[6] As quoted by Justin Winsor, *Narrative and Critical History of America*, Boston, 1884, III, 558.

of 1668 and Acts of 1683, 1684, 1686, and 1706 and in Virginia the Acts of 1680, 1691, and 1706 were each in turn repealed by the legislatures or voided by the Crown under pressure exerted by the planters and traders. Despite this erratic record of legislative vacillation, many towns were laid out. Although most of the original plats are no longer extant, a few have survived and provide interesting evidence of the state of colonial town planning.

The Virginia laws designated twenty sites for new towns, each to be built on fifty acres of land. The Act of 1680 established a flat price of 10,000 pounds of tobacco for each site, with half-acre lots available for 100 pounds of tobacco to any person agreeing to build a house and warehouse. The 1691 Act provided for purchase of the required sites by the justices of the county at a reasonable price and authorized a method of acquiring land by eminent domain should the owner be unwilling to sell. In 1706 the number of town sites was reduced to fifteen, and the law added liberal provisions for town government, including freedom from certain taxes for the residents.

Maryland legislation was even more ambitious. No less than fifty-seven sites of 100 acres each were designated in the Act of 1683, forty-four more than had been provided for in the Governor's proclamation of 1668. The Maryland legislation was also more specific in describing the land to be set aside for public use. The commissioners appointed to oversee the establishment of the towns in each county were directed to have the site "marcked staked out and devided into Convenient streets, Laines & allies, with Open Space places to be left On which may be Erected Church or Chappell, & Marckett house, or other publick buildings, & the remaining part of the said One hundred acres of Land as neare as may be into One hundred equall Lotts. . . ."[7]

A simple grid system was evidently regarded as the logical plan for these new towns in Virginia. At Yorktown there was a main street running parallel to the shore of the York River crossed by eight shorter streets leading back from the river (Fig. 36). Tappahannock, which became the county seat of Rappahannock and later of Essex County, had a more regular plan (Fig. 37). One entire block of four lots was set aside for public use. Three different street widths were used, with the widest streets flanking the public square and dividing the town in half being 82 1/2 feet wide. Three other streets were 66 feet wide, with the two narrower "lanes" being 49 1/2 feet in width. All lots were platted with the same dimensions, 165 by 132 feet, to equal exactly half an acre as prescribed by the statute.

Marlborough on the Potomac in Stafford County no longer exists, although it enjoyed a brief period of prosperity. The plan is a curious one, probably originating from the surveyor's uncertainty over which shore line to follow as the main axis for the town. Evidently he decided to use both, with the result that the blocks and lots are parallelograms, without a right angle to be seen (Fig. 38).

[7] An Act for Advancement of Trade, 1683, William H. Browne, ed., *Archives of Maryland*, Proceedings and Acts of the General Assembly of Maryland (October 1678–November 1683), Baltimore, 1889, p. 612.

Figure 36. Plan of Yorktown, Virginia: 1691

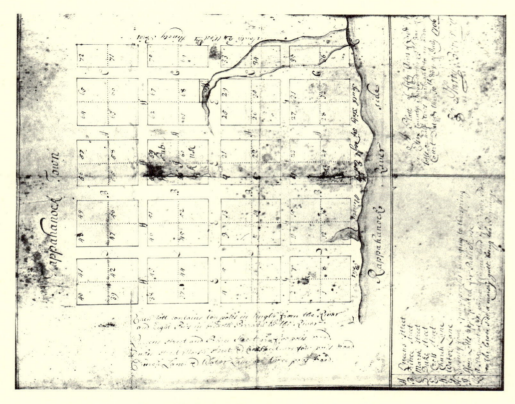

Figure 37. Plan of Tappahanock, Virginia: 1706

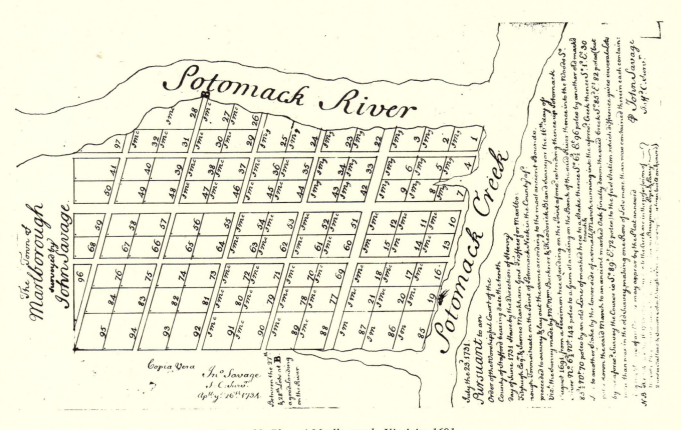

Figure 38. Plan of Marlborough, Virginia: 1691

Equally simple and elementary plan forms were also employed in the Maryland towns of this period. Vienna Town, Oxford (referred to as Williamstadt in the Act of 1694), and Wye are all primitive little gridiron settlements. At Vienna Town the surveyor was apparently at a loss as to where to locate the various public sites specified in the act. His solution was to lump them all together in a large rectangular tract and label them on his drawing as "Public Lands of Vienna Towne" (Fig. 39).

Ten years after the Virginia Act of 1680 had been suspended, the General Assembly passed a new and somewhat revised law. The Act for Ports differed from its predecessor chiefly in its provisions for land acquisition. Instead of establishing a fixed price for all town sites, the law authorized the justices of each county to purchase the required land at a reasonable price. If the owner was unwilling to sell, the justices could then empanel twelve freeholders to fix a fair price for the land. Half-acre lots could then be granted outright to persons agreeing to build a house 20 feet square within four months.

Further building was carried out under this second new town law, but again the act was repealed—this time by the Assembly itself on the grounds that the Crown had not specifically signified its approval of the measure. Subsequently, in 1699, the Assembly approved an enactment confirming land titles in these towns, indicating that construction had taken place on the sites despite the action to rescind the original legislation.

Finally, and again following royal instructions to the new governor, the Assembly in 1706 passed a third general town act. This law met

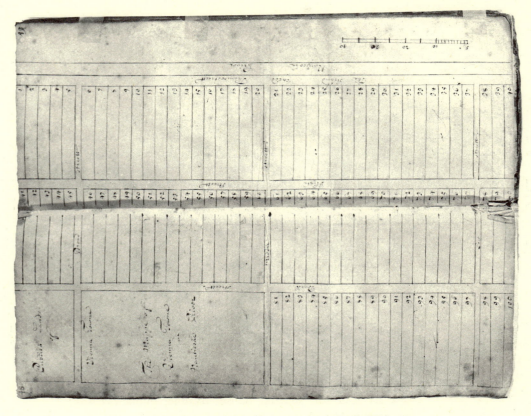

Figure 39. Plan of Vienna Town, Maryland: 1706

a fate similar to the earlier legislation, and the Crown suspended its provisions in 1709. This marked an end to the general town acts of Virginia and Maryland and the attempts at wholesale urbanization.

The planning of individual towns under public sponsorship, however, continued in both colonies. In Maryland no fewer than twenty-three such towns were established under special acts of the legislature during the period from 1728 to 1751. The same procedure was followed in Virginia. Alexandria, Virginia, is one example, dating from 1748, when the General Assembly authorized a town for the new county of Fairfax. The following year the county surveyor, John West, Jr., and his assistant, a young man named George Washington, laid out the usual grid system of streets and eighty-four half-acre lots (Fig. 40). Washington's drawing of the town plans reveals no innovations in urban design, and most of the 18th-century new towns in Maryland and Virginia were laid out in similar fashion following the tradition established during the abortive period of wholesale town development of the previous era.

One exception was Charlestown, Maryland, in Cecil County, founded by legislative action in 1742 as the county seat (Fig. 41). Here a common of 300 acres surrounded the town proper. In the center, marked "M," is the market place and the two lots for the "lord proprietors," designated "A" and "B." The two other large squares were set aside for "meeting houses or other public occasions," while the site marked "L" was reserved for a courthouse or other public building. The plan clearly demonstrates an attempt to provide a some-

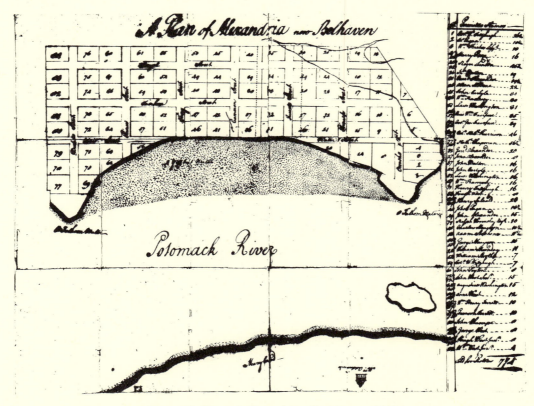

Figure 40. Plan of Alexandria, Virginia: ca. 1749

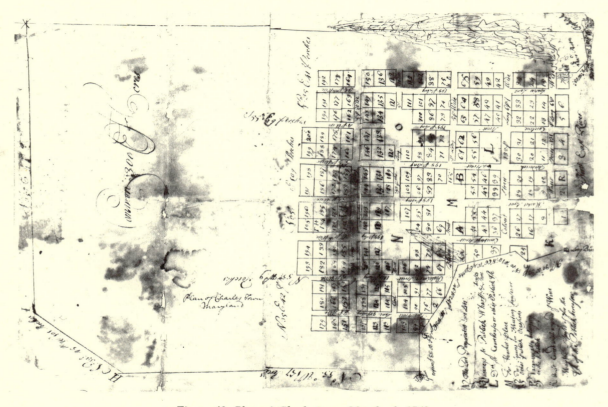

Figure 41. Plan of Charlestown, Maryland: 1742

what more elaborate setting for urban life than was common during this period.

Equally interesting was the town plan proposed in the 1730's by William Byrd II for a group of Swiss settlers whom he hoped to attract to his land, which he called Eden in Halifax County. The only surviving drawing shows three proposed villages along the river and an insert plan which reveals the details of the town layout (Fig. 42). With its nine city blocks, the central one being left open as a green or common, the plan closely resembles that of New Haven, Connecticut, of a century earlier. Whether Byrd knew of the earlier example or himself devised this design is not known. Unfortunately this scheme was never to be realized. The publication of the proposal in Switzerland had attracted some attention, and in 1738 a group of Swiss sailed for Virginia. They arrived during a violent storm, their vessel was wrecked, and most of the would-be colonists bound for the land of Eden were drowned.

Dating also from the early years of the 18th century are the remarkable isolated courthouse-square compounds of Virginia. These may be regarded as an expression of and a concession to the essentially rural character of the early commonwealth. Seats of local government, the basic unit of which was the county, were clearly needed. If towns stubbornly refused to spring up as county seats, then the only solution was to provide county buildings in a rural setting as centrally located within the county as possible. Some of these later became the centers of towns, as in the case of Gloucester. Others, like King Wil-

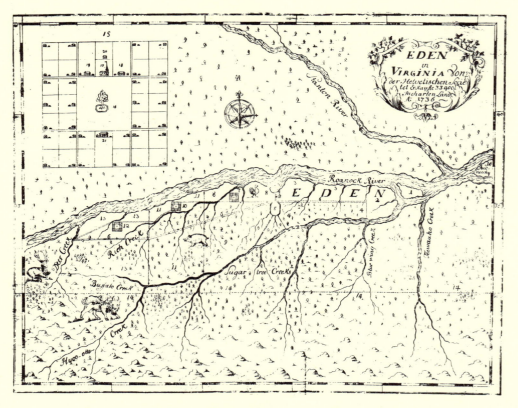

Figure 42. Map of Eden in Virginia with a Plan of one of the Proposed Towns: 1737

liam Court House, stand by themselves as solitary symbols of government.

Typically the compounds are surrounded by a brick wall. Inside can be found the courthouse, a jail, a caretaker's residence, and a row of lawyers' offices. Nearby usually stood a tavern and inn. These little administrative and legal communities came to life only when the court was in session or other sporadic governmental activities occurred. The architectural merit of many of the individual buildings is outstanding, and they deserve to be preserved as splendid examples of early group design of particular effectiveness.

Francis Nicholson's Tidewater Capitals

However interesting these ventures in town development may be, one can scarcely contend that, with the exception of Charlestown and Eden, the surviving plats indicate any great skill in or attention to the planning of towns. Furthermore, all evidence points to the conclusion that planning in three dimensions, except for the Virginia courthouse-square communities, was scarcely considered. But it is just this lack of noteworthy features in these provincial villages that makes the achievements in planning the capital cities of the Virginia and Maryland colonies the more remarkable.

The planning of Annapolis and Williamsburg stem from a similar concept or philosophy of civic design and from the activities of a single individual, although they differed markedly in the details of their layout. In the absence of proof to the contrary, Francis Nicholson must be credited with both plans on the basis of circumstantial evidence which, if not overwhelming, is at least highly persuasive.

Nicholson was a remarkable person whose American career included service as lieutenant governor or governor of no less than five of the colonies. The circumstances of his parentage and education are uncertain, only his birth year of 1655 being known. He served as page in the Yorkshire household of Lord St. John, whose natural son he may have been. Lord St. John, later the Marquis of Winchester and then Duke of Bolton, probably purchased Nicholson an ensign's commission in 1678 and over the years continued to aid the young officer in winning promotions and securing appointments.

Francis Nicholson saw a few months' service in Flanders, and then, in 1680, received a commission as lieutenant with the Second Tangier Regiment in Morocco. Two years later he undertook the first of a series of courier journeys between North Africa and England via Cadiz, Seville, Toledo, Madrid, Paris, and Dover. In 1686, following two years of garrison duty in England, he was appointed captain of an infantry company in the King's Dominion of New England to serve under its new royal governor, Sir Edmund Andros. At the age of thirty-one Nicholson left for America to embark on a new career as colonial administrator.

He proved an energetic and tireless servant of the Crown, and in July 1688 he received a promotion to lieutenant governor of the newly expanded Dominion of New England, with his headquarters in New York. His administration coincided with the Protestant Revolution in England, which provoked unrest in the colonies. In New York this included an eventual rebellion by the militia, and Nicholson, deprived of effective power to govern, surrendered Fort James and sailed for England in June of 1689. Although he had left his post without specific authorization and might have expected a reprimand or worse, Nicholson instead found himself appointed Lieutenant Governor of Virginia. In the absence of Lord Howard of Effingham, the governor, Nicholson became the chief executive of this important southern colony under the new sovereigns, William and Mary.

Nicholson's administration lasted from June 1690 until September 1692, but in this short period he achieved a great deal. He reorganized the militia and inspected and strengthened frontier outposts. He secured the passage, in 1691, of the second general town planning act, which directed anew the establishment of more than a dozen new towns or the re-establishment of those laid out under the Act of 1680. He also assisted Commissary James Blair in founding the College of William and Mary, himself subscribing £ 300 toward its development. He also managed to achieve a substantial measure of popular support. Certainly he hoped and had some reason to expect designation as governor, but this post was filled by Sir Edmund Andros, his former superior in New England, and Nicholson left for England in a furious temper.

His visit lasted several months, and during this time he developed close relations in London with authorities of the Anglican church through their mutual interest in the College of William and Mary. Lord Nottingham, the leader of the church party, and Nicholson's consistent patron, the Duke of Bolton, secured for him the governorship of Maryland. In that colony conflict between Catholic and Protestant elements threatened its further growth and development. Nicholson, with his excellent record as a civil governor in Virginia and his strong Anglican leanings, seemed the ideal appointment to establish Protestant domination of Maryland and to secure unquestioned loyalty there to William and Mary, the successors to the Catholic king, James II.

We know little otherwise of Nicholson's activities in London. It seems highly probable, however, that his interest in the new college would have led him to the office of Royal Surveyor, where all colonial buildings of importance were designed. At that time the office was directed by Christopher Wren. Almost certainly the old building of the College of William and Mary was designed in this office, although Wren's personal role in this remains unknown. It is at least possible that Nicholson and Wren may have discussed building problems in the colonies and that their conversations may have included the design and location of towns. Certainly Nicholson's ideas about town planning appear to have been stimulated at this time, and his subsequent involvement in this activity resulted in a drastic change in the practice of colonial urban design as heretofore typified by the Virginia and Maryland port towns laid out under the series of acts previously described.

When Nicholson arrived in Maryland he thus had already some experience with town planning, he had seen at first hand the residential expansion of London in a series of planned open spaces surrounded by terrace houses of uniform design, and he may have absorbed some of the ideas of the great Wren, whose plan for rebuilding London in 1666 had marked such a departure from previous English thought in this field. This knowledge and experience was not to be wasted.

In Nicholson's first year of office he obtained legislation to found two new communities. One was Oxford, previously settled in a rather casual manner but now regularized and constituted as a town. The other was Anne Arundel, strategically located at the mouth of the Severn River on Chesapeake Bay and virtually in the center of the colony. A later act, vigorously opposed by the Catholics and the residents of St. Mary's, designated Anne Arundel Town as the capital city, and in the year following, 1695, the name was changed to Annapolis, honoring Princess Anne, soon to become queen.

Direct evidence is lacking, but there is every reason to believe that Governor Nicholson himself assumed responsibility for the design of the town. We do know that one Richard Beard acted as surveyor and that he carried out his duties under difficulties not usually encountered in city planning. When the officials called on Beard for his finished plat of the town he reported "that for want of some Large Paper to draw the same on, it is not yet done. . . ." But it seems unlikely that Beard would have had the imagination to produce the plan which was finally adopted. Nicholson, in his first position as full colonial governor, with his European, New York, and Virginia background, and with apparent ambitions to make his mark in Maryland, doubtless furnished the inspiration.

The Annapolis plan was a novelty for North America (Fig. 43). With its two great circles, the imposing "Bloomsbury Square," and the several radiating diagonal streets, the layout introduced a new concept

Figure 43. Plan of Annapolis, Maryland: 1718

of civic design to colonial America. All the original drawings perished in the statehouse fire of 1704, but the Stoddert plat of 1718 faithfully reproduces the first layout, adding only the twenty lettered lots to the east of the town which were provided in 1718 as accommodations for tradesmen. This addition followed a law of 1695 which provided "that when any baker, brewer, tailor, dyer, or any such tradesmen, that, by their practice of their trade, may any ways annoy, or disquiet the neighbors or inhabitants of the town, it shall and may be lawful for the commissioners and trustees . . . to allot and appoint such tradesmen such part or parcel of land, out of the present town pasture, as . . . shall seem meet and convenient for the exercise of such trade, a sufficient distance from the said town as may not be annoyance thereto. . . ."[8]

The immediate sources on which Nicholson drew remain unknown. The general inspiration must have been the achievements of French Baroque designers, first applied in garden layout, as at Versailles, then to town extension and remodelling schemes on the continent, and later adapted by Christopher Wren and John Evelyn for the rebuilding of London after the great fire.

Following accepted planning practice of this style, Nicholson set aside the highest and most commanding sites for the statehouse and church. The "Public Circle" within which the statehouse now stands is slightly over 500 feet in diameter, while the "Church Circle" meas-

[8] An Act for Keeping Good Rules and Orders in the Port of Annapolis, as quoted in Elihu S. Riley, *The Ancient City: A History of Annapolis*, Annapolis, 1887, pp. 63-64.

ures approximately 300 feet across. The other great open space, Bloomsbury Square, is some 350 feet on each side. It may be sheer coincidence, but the proportions of these three open spaces are such that the square fits neatly inside the larger circle, while the smaller circle can be contained in the square, although with some room to spare. The other open area is the market square, 100 feet on each side. There were other public reservations as well: a school site, public landings, and common lands beyond the town proper.

One curious detail appears in the diagonal streets. Those leading into the statehouse circle have a pinwheel alignment; not one is directly on axis with the center of the circle. It is hard to believe that this was anything but deliberate, but the motives are unclear. It may well have been a case of Nicholson's lack of comprehension of one of the aims of Baroque design—that is, to create as many terminal vistas as possible by ending diagonal streets at some great public building or monument. The many lots bisected by the diagonal streets and the resulting awkward shapes of building sites testify also to the unfamiliarity of the planner with some of the problems inherent in this type of layout.

The derivation of Bloomsbury Square is suggested by its name. In London Bloomsbury was but one of many regularly planned residential developments grouped around an open space which had become the accepted pattern of urban expansion on lands owned by the great families adjoining the older portions of the city. Unfortunately, this portion of the Annapolis plans was never developed, and the interesting combination of the English square and the French *rond-points* was thus never to be experienced.

Something of the urbane character of Annapolis as it slowly developed during the century to follow may still be perceived by today's visitor. A mid-19th-century view also helps to reveal the main elements of the community a century ago (Fig. 44). It was fortunate that the center of commerce and industry soon shifted to Baltimore, for many of the older buildings of Annapolis doubtless thus escaped the destruction that surely would have accompanied an era of mercantile expansion.

Nicholson's plan for Annapolis was certainly not completely successful, but he was soon to have a second opportunity to create a capital city. In 1698 he found himself again in Virginia, this time with the full authority of the governor's office. He cared for Jamestown as little as he had for St. Mary's, and the burning of the Virginia statehouse in his first year of office furnished the excuse he needed to shift the capital site to a new location and away from the scene of so many disasters and hardships.

The favored site was a place called Middle Plantation, second only to Jamestown in population, and located on higher ground midway between the James and York rivers. There was much to recommend this location. From the site smaller streams led in two directions to the nearby rivers. It was certainly more healthful than Jamestown; almost any site would have been. For a brief period following Bacon's rebellion and his destruction of Jamestown the General Assembly had

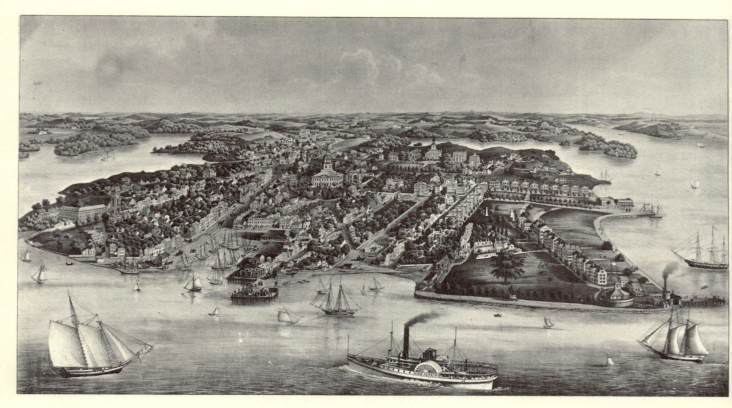

Figure 44. View of Annapolis, Maryland: ca. 1860

met at Middle Plantation. Here, too, was the infant College of William and Mary, the buildings of which might be used as temporary quarters for the legislature.

All accounts indicate that Nicholson exerted his influence to bring about this move, and he soon became deeply involved in the plans for the city. The legislation of 1699 which established the new town, and which doubtless Nicholson helped to draft, was beyond a doubt the most detailed town planning law yet adopted in the English colonies. It specified the exact amount of land to be set aside for the town proper, the capital building site, the public landing areas on the two rivers, and the roads leading from the town proper to these outlying river port areas. In great detail the law also spelled out the form and principal dimensions of the capital building, including the pitch of the roof, the size of windows, and many elevational specifications.

The principal street, Duke of Gloucester Street, was named in the act. All houses built on this street were to be set back six feet and to "front alike." For other streets the directors of the town were authorized to adopt rules and orders governing dwelling size and setbacks. The town was to be divided into half-acre lots to be sold after public notice. Each purchaser was required to construct a dwelling within two years. Minimum sizes were specified, with the larger houses required along the Duke of Gloucester Street. All lots on the main street had to be enclosed with "a wall, pails, or post and rails," within six months after the dwelling was completed.

Indeed, there was little omitted from this unique statute that the legislature could have provided to guarantee a capital building and a town which would, in the words of the act, result in a "convenient sitting . . . at a healthy, proper and commodious place, suitable for the reception of a considerable number and concourse of people, that of necessity must resort to the place where the general assemblies will be convened, and where the council and supreme court of justice for his majesty's colony and dominion will be held and kept."[9]

The evidence is fragmentary but strongly suggestive that two plans for Williamsburg were prepared and that, for reasons unknown, the first was rejected. Robert Beverley, a Jamestown landowner and foe of Nicholson, alluded to this first plan in his history of the colony written in 1705. Nicholson, he said "flatter'd himself with the fond Imagination, of being the Founder of a new City. He mark'd out the Streets in many Places, so as that they might represent the Figure of a W, in Memory of his late Majesty King William. . . ."[10]

And Hugh Jones, writing a few years later, mentions that Nicholson planned the city "in the Form of a Cypher, made of W. and M." for William and Mary. Then, in his description of Williamsburg as actually built, Jones refers to the Duke of Gloucester Street as "a noble

[9] For the text of the law of 1705 which confirmed the Act of 1699 see William Hening, *Statutes at Large . . . of Virginia*, New York, 1823, III, 419-32, An Act Continuing the Act directing the building of the Capitol and the City of Williamsburg.

[10] Robert Beverley, *The History and Present State of Virginia* (London, 1705), Chapel Hill, 1947, p. 105.

Street mathematically straight (for the first Design of the Town's Form is changed to a much better)."[11]

No copies of this first plan are known to exist, and the manner in which Nicholson planned to incorporate the initials of the Sovereigns in his city can only be conjectured. It may well be that the two diagonal streets diverging from the end of the Duke of Gloucester Street and bordering the college grounds are the remnants of one of the letters.

Whatever may have been the merits of Nicholson's first plan, it is just as well that he abandoned it. For the revised plan which guided the development of the town was, along with the plan of Savannah, the most successful essay in community layout in colonial America. Unfortunately, contemporary plans no longer exist; the earliest is the so-called Frenchman's Map of 1782 which shows the elements of the design (Fig. 45).

The principal axis of the composition is the Duke of Gloucester Street, 99 feet wide and three-quarters of a mile long, laid out to run along the divide between the two rivers. The College of William and Mary stands at the western end of this street, where two roads diverge at equal angles. The Capitol terminates the street at its other end, rising from the center of a square, 475 feet on each side, set aside by the legislature for this purpose.

Midway along the Duke of Gloucester Street appears the Market Square, on or near which are sites for the courthouse, magazine, and Bruton Parish Church. Close to this point a secondary axis opens at

[11] Hugh Jones, *op.cit.*, pp. 66, 68.

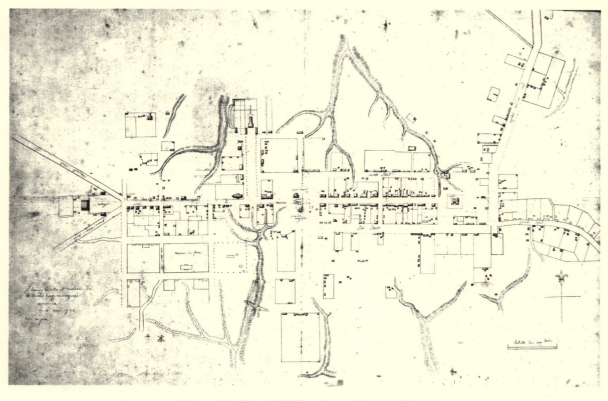

Figure 45. Plan of Williamsburg, Virginia: 1782

right angles to the north. This is the Palace Green, somewhat over 200 feet wide and approximately 1,000 feet long. Furnishing the terminal vista for this tree-lined expanse is the governor's palace. Beyond the palace, although concealed from the ordinary viewer, the secondary axis continues for some distance as the formal gardens to the rear of the executive mansion. The view to the south down Palace Green is unchecked, since the site on the Duke of Gloucester Street facing the governor's palace remains open.

Note how Nicholson provided additional building sites of special prominence by changing the spacing of the streets paralleling the Duke of Gloucester Street east and west of Palace Green. Opposite the termination points of these streets, houses could be erected from which long views could be enjoyed and which in turn closed the views from the other ends of these minor axes.

This elegant, neatly conceived plan represents a vast improvement over that of Annapolis, although both derive from the same school of civic design. At Williamsburg, however, the mere eccentricities that mar the plan of the Maryland capital disappear; nearly every feature is deftly placed. Here is a disciplined exercise in axial planning—formal, yet never pompous. Part of the success of the Williamsburg plan is surely due to its scale. Designed for a population of about 2,000, the little city must always have had an air of domesticity that balanced its miniature grand plan. And part of its appeal certainly stems from its three-dimensional quality—the architectural planning of at least some of the principal buildings at the same time that its ground plan was conceived.

For slightly more than three-quarters of a century Williamsburg served as the capital of Virginia. Then, in 1779, the recently constituted independent Commonwealth of Virginia resolved to move the seat of government to Richmond. From that time Williamsburg began to decline, its plan and buildings being rescued from further encroachments and destruction through the generosity of John D. Rockefeller, Jr., in 1927. The elaborate and painstaking restoration of the old colonial capital that has resulted provides us today with an unusual opportunity to observe one of the noteworthy accomplishments of our town planning tradition. Even in an age where mechanization has taken command, the merit of this plan for a town in a simpler era can still be appreciated, and it is not without lessons for modern planners.

V · Pilgrims and Puritans: New Towns in a New England

The first English efforts to settle New England occurred in the same year that Jamestown was founded. The leaders of the Plymouth Company, Sir John Popham and Sir Ferdinando Gorges, organized an expedition that set out from Plymouth in May 1607 and arrived off the coast of Maine two months later. At the mouth of the Kennebeck River they built a fort and made plans for a permanent town. But Fort St. George was abandoned the following year, after a severe winter and the death of several of the colony's leaders. Like Roanoke, Fort St. George soon lay in ruins. Not until 1620 was a permanent settlement established.

Village and Town: the New England Land Pattern

It was on the bleak shore of Plymouth Bay in Massachusetts that the Pilgrims, a self-exiled group of English who had broken with the established church, succeeded in building New England's first town. They selected a partially cleared and sloping site for their village, on which work was hurriedly begun. A description of this settlement a few years later by a visitor from New Amsterdam provides us with a clear picture of this primitive little village:

"New Plymouth lies on the slope of a hill stretching east towards the sea-coast, with a broad street about a cannon shot of 800 feet long, leading down the hill; with a . . . [street] . . . crossing in the middle. . . . The houses are constructed of hewn planks, with gardens also enclosed behind and at the sides with hewn planks, so that their houses and court-yards are arranged in very good order, with a stockade against a sudden attack; and at the ends of the streets there are three wooden gates. In the center, on the cross street, stands the governor's house, before which is a square stockade upon which four patereros are mounted, so as to enfilade the streets. Upon the hill they have a large square house, with a flat roof, made of thick sawn plank, stayed with oak beams, upon the top of which they have six cannon. . . . The lower part they use for their church. . . ."[1]

Within three years after the settlement of Plymouth a small fishing colony was established to the north on Cape Ann, in what is now Gloucester. The leaders of this little outpost succeeded in obtaining a patent for settlement of a much larger area in 1628. Sixty colonists were soon on their way to Naumkeag, the present Salem, to which the Cape Ann settlers had moved. In the following year a new charter was obtained directly from the Crown. This established the Massachusetts Bay Company, with both territorial and governmental powers.

Like the Plymouth colony, that of Massachusetts Bay stemmed from religious discontent. Its leaders were Puritans whose lot under Charles I had become increasingly uncomfortable. The drastic step of emigration seemed the safest course after the king dissolved Parliament in

[1] Letter written by Issack de Rasieres, in J. Franklin Jameson, ed., *Narratives of New Netherland 1609-1664*, New York, 1909, pp. 111-12.

1629 to begin his ten years of dictatorial rule. By 1630 the exodus was under way. Eleven ships left for Massachusetts in the spring of that year, and others came during the summer months.

Settlement in a single place being out of the question with so many persons to accommodate, several favorable locations were selected for towns, with surrounding farm fields, along the shores of Massachusetts Bay and on the principal rivers which flowed into it. Virtually all of these communities and those that followed as the colony grew were laid out on a common pattern. Unlike the later settlement pattern in farming areas beyond the Appalachians, the agricultural community in New England centered on the village. Farmers lived in the village in a compact community and daily went to their fields stretching outwards from the cluster of buildings. The complete rural-urban settlement was called a town, a word which encompassed not only a nucleated urban-type settlement but the entire community of village lots and farm fields as well.

The site for the home lots normally was selected near the center of the town. Usually these were grouped around an open space, on or fronting which the meetinghouse was erected. Large fields suitable for cultivation were then roughly surveyed. These were divided into many strips, usually rather long and narrow. The strips were then numbered, and the settlers drew lots to determine which strips would be assigned to them. Each settler ordinarily had several strips, the number depending on his share in the allotment. The purpose of this system was to ensure that each person obtained land no better and no worse than his neighbors.

While the strips themselves were not fenced, it was the usual practice to enclose the entire field by a wooden paling. Each farmer then became responsible for the maintenance of his proportionate share of fencing. These great fields were referred to as the common fields, but, except in the earliest years of some of the townships, common ownership was not the usual rule. On the other hand, in a number of the settlements the proprietors meeting as a group determined what crops would be grown, when they would be harvested, and what land should be left fallow. Common cultivation was thus carried out, although apparently crops harvested from each strip belonged to the person to whom the strip had been allotted. After the harvest and before the spring sowing the fields were also used in common, with cattle turned loose to graze on the stubble.

 These "common fields" or "proprietor's commons" were thus not open to subsequent settlers unless these newcomers were formally granted commoners' rights. The remaining lands, however, were open to all inhabitants of the town. These were the common pasture lands and common woodlands. Cattle and sheep were entrusted to the supervision of cowherds and shepherds. These herdsmen were paid a salary by the owners of the animals under their care. Like the pasture lands, the wooded areas of the town were also held in common ownership. Subject to town regulations, residents could fell timber and quarry stone for individual use, but the title to the land itself remained with the community.

Thus the land system of the typical early New England town combined ownership in severalty and ownership in common. Even where home lots and strips in the common fields were in individual ownership, by custom and by town regulations the welfare of the community as a whole predominated over individual desires or advantage. For communities only one crop removed from starvation and engaged in subduing a harsh wilderness, no other system would have met their requirements so well.

This pattern of land distribution, however, arose only in part because of the special environment of the frontier. In fact, a pattern essentially similar, although not so regular in its boundaries, prevailed in England at that time. The practice of narrow strip cultivation grew out of feudal systems of land tenure. Common pasture and woodland, too, marked many areas in England. Indeed, throughout most of Europe, the land was occupied by tightly grouped agricultural villages surrounded by strip fields interspersed with irregular pasture and forest plots.

The close similarity of the New England town and the Spanish colonial *pueblo* is obvious. Both English and Spanish colonial land systems had their origins in European land tenure patterns. There were, of course, differences between older European systems and that used throughout New England. Generally the holdings of land were greater in extent in New England. Field lines were also more regular, a feature to be expected where land was being divided at one time rather than gradually over the centuries.

Wethersfield, Connecticut, settled in 1640, is an example of the New England land and field system. A reconstructed map of land holdings show the home lots on streets leading to a central green

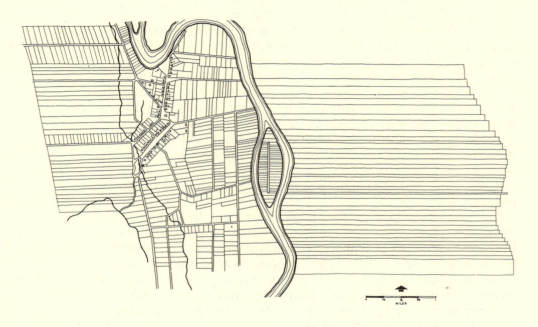

Figure 46. Plan of Wethersfield, Connecticut: 1640

(Fig. 46). Strip fields surround the town. Those to the east of the Connecticut River are approximately three miles long, but such extreme length was not typical of most of the early New England communities. Beyond this subdivided area lay the common pasture and woodlands.

Increased population forced adjustments in the settlement system. One solution seemed obvious: to parcel out the hitherto undivided common lands to newcomers. All of the towns used this method to accommodate additional residents, although these later settlers were not always granted the rights of commoners. Original proprietors benefitted from this process, since in subsequent divisions of land they were frequently given additional allotments. In a number of towns, as the supply of common land became scarce, a final division was made, at which time all the proprietors or their heirs received proportionate shares of the remaining undivided land.

The second method of providing for an increased population was the "hiving off" of groups of settlers from the old town and the establishment of a new town on newly granted land nearer the frontier. An early example is the founding of Sudbury through a grant made in 1637 by the Massachusetts General Court, a portion of which read as follows:

"Whereas a great part of the chief inhabitants of Watertown have petitioned this court, that in regard to their straightness of accommodation, and want of meadow, they might have leave to remove and settle a plantation upon a river which runs to Concord . . . it is hereby ordered that they . . . shall take view of the places upon said river and shall set out a place for them by marks and bounds sufficient for 50 to 60 families. . . . And it is ordered further, that if the said inhabitants . . . shall not have removed their dwelling to their said new plantation, before one year after the plantation be set out that then the interest of all such persons, not so removed . . . shall be void and cease."[2]

In the same manner the three early Connecticut River towns of Wethersfield, Hartford, and Windsor were established by groups moving from the Massachusetts Bay settlements. In turn, these three river towns subsequently sent out new groups into the vicinity; this led to the founding of ten additional towns. Until 1675, when King Phillip's war marked the beginning of a period of organized Indian resistance to further expansion, group settlement of new plantations and towns continued steadily.

The pattern of settlement changed in the 18th century. Where before grants were made mainly to organized groups desiring land for their own use, now an element of land speculation appeared. Large tracts of land, sizeable enough for several of the standard six-mile-square townships of previous years, were granted to a group of proprietors. These persons often had no intention of settling the land but in turn laid out one or two townships, offered lots free to those who would settle, and then made their profit from the sale of farms in the remaining townships.

[2] As quoted in D. H. Hurd, *History of Middlesex County, Massachusetts*, Philadelphia, 1890, II, 377.

Coincident with this development and to some extent because of it, there developed a trend toward larger home lots and away from the compact village design of the earlier years. In part this was simply a reflection of the deficiencies of the multi-field strip system of agricultural land allotment. As certain individuals began to consolidate their land holdings into contiguous and larger parcels, maintaining their residence in the village became a hardship. Then, too, the decreased danger of Indian attacks made the compact settlement pattern less necessary as a defense measure. Home lots of ten and twenty acres and even larger became common, where earlier custom had dictated lots of one, two, or perhaps six acres.

In summarizing this brief and barely adequate discussion of the New England system of land distribution, the importance of the group or community basis of settlement should be re-emphasized. It was the public welfare that was paramount, and public control over land distribution and land use was regarded as essential. In these small communities a rough but workable democracy prevailed. Whatever changes were made were subject to group discussion and approval. Dissension there must have been, but one has the impression that rarely since that time have important decisions been made about community planning in America with such harmony. The other feature of note is that the settlement of New England was an experiment in genuine regional planning. Both urban and rural land development were subject to conscious forethought and community controls. Only the Spanish *pueblo* rivaled the New England town in this respect.

The other element in the New England land planning system was the village. The simple plan of New England's first village, Plymouth, has already been described. While many of the later village plans were rather more elaborate, it was a characteristic of the New England communities that the elements used in their planning were limited in number and elementary in nature. New England never possessed counterparts of Annapolis or Williamsburg. Such formal planning in the Baroque tradition would not have been in keeping with the spartan, almost stern, outlook on life adhered to by the Puritan founders. But if the New England villages lacked the long, axial vistas of a Williamsburg, they achieved an intimate charm of their own which many of them have retained to the present day.

What were the distinguishing features of the New England villages? First of all, they were planned to accommodate a limited population. Once the home lots were taken up, with perhaps some modest expansion possible through platting undivided land, the expectation was that a new settlement would be formed elsewhere to accommodate newcomers. In actual practice, many of the villages did continue to increase in size as farm lots were divided into home lots, but in the early years, at least, community size remained within limited bounds.

Many, though not all, New England villages centered around some form of central open space—the village green or common. The motives behind this element of the plan appear mixed. The green often served as a site for the meetinghouse and later for other public buildings as well. It was also used as a mustering place and training ground for adult males serving as the local militia or village guard. While apparently some of the larger greens provided space for cattle grazing, this was not often a normal function. The green did, however, offer itself as a space into which cattle from the common pastures could be herded in case of a threatened Indian attack. Doubtless also the early village planners must have consciously attempted to create open spaces for purposes of community amenity and as an advantageous setting for dwellings.

Care was used in the siting of buildings. In some cases dwellings were required to set back from the street line some prescribed distance. Even where such requirements were lacking, builders seemed to observe good taste in locating buildings with repect to the street line and adjacent structures. The church or meetinghouse in this theocratic society naturally assumed great importance. A location on the green itself or facing it was favored.

Another feature of the New England village community was the sharp break between village and countryside. Although the 18th-century villages, with their much larger home lots, blurred this distinction between town and country, the earlier villages exhibited a compact group of houses and home lots quite apart from the surrounding farm lands. Modern suburban growth has obliterated this crisp distinction in the larger New England communities, but it can still be observed in the hill villages of New Hampshire and Vermont.

The oldest of the Massachusetts Bay villages was Salem. Here the informality that characterized many of the village plans is evident (Fig. 47). The main street, now the present Essex Street, ran along high ground forming the spine of the settlement. At irregular intervals

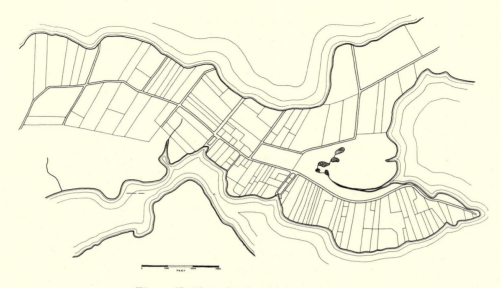

Figure 47. Plan of Salem, Massachusetts: 1670

short streets led to the water's edge. A large plot near the center was retained as town property, the western half of which now forms the majestic Salem Common.

Among the earliest towns of the period, along with Salem, Charlestown, and Boston, were Watertown and Medford on the Charles and Mystic rivers, and Newtown, later renamed Cambridge, on the tidal estuary of the Charles. Here, in the spring of 1631, a small community was begun. With the arrival of a new group of colonists the following year a village plan was adopted, streets were laid out, and house lots chosen. The newly formed town government decreed that "houses shall range even and stand just six feet in their own ground from the street," perhaps the earliest example of a front yard regulation in the English colonies.

The Cambridge plan differed from that of Salem, being more compact, regular, and less elongated (Fig. 48). The average home lot measured about 100 by 80 feet. Most of the streets were 30 feet wide. The market square in the northwestern part of the village was approximately 150 by 200 feet. Midway along the principal northwest-southeast street stood the meetinghouse on a plot slightly larger than those allotted for houses. The entire village with its little gridiron streets occupied a site hardly more than 1,000 feet square.

Cambridge was the prototype of one kind of New England village pattern—the compact, "squared," community in which the home lots were usually small in comparison with farm fields and where several streets led outward from a central green or square. Salem repre-

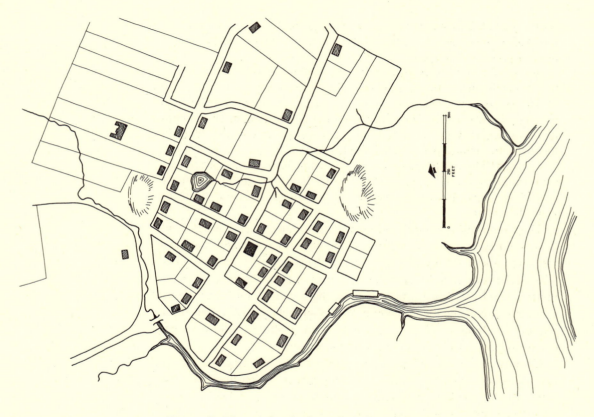

Figure 48. Plan of Cambridge, Massachusetts: 1637

sents another community form—the linear pattern, where a single street forms the spine of the settlement.

Although most of the New England villages fall into one of these two general plan forms, the variations within each category are almost endless. We can also distinguish within each type two sub-groups: those where the layout is more or less regular or geometric; and those where the plan is informal, irregular, or "organic." The problem of classification is made more difficult because some villages combine the geometric plan in some parts with an informal layout in others.

The most regular of the compact settlements was New Haven, settled in 1638 (Fig. 49). According to tradition, John Brockett was the planner of the town, which took the form of a square divided into nine blocks, the central block forming the common. Each of these great blocks measured 16 rods, or 825 feet, on a side. In later years these blocks were further subdivided by new streets, and the central green was split into two portions, one of which contained the churches and public buildings while the remaining section was left in open park.

As in other New England communities the village of New Haven formed one part of a rural-urban community unit. Farm field stretched out beyond the boundary streets and were supplemented by the common pasture and woodlands of the town. The New Haven records are apparently the earliest to describe allotments of farm lands so arranged that those owning home lots in each sector of the village could reach their fields easily. For a distance of one mile from the village bounds the land was divided into "quarters." The fields or out-lots

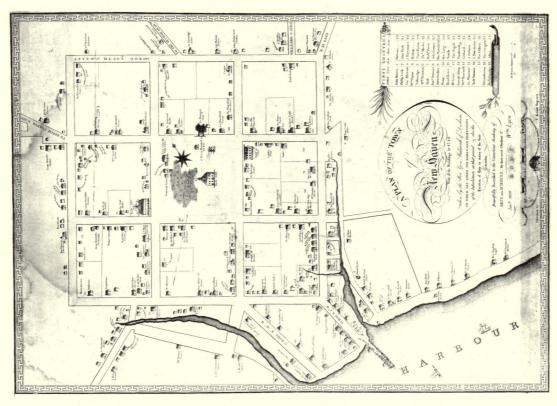

Figure 49. Plan of New Haven, Connecticut: 1748

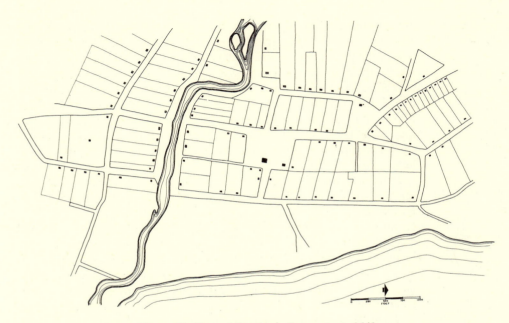

Figure 50. Plan of Hartford, Connecticut: 1640

granted in each quarter were assigned to those living in the village block contiguous to the inner line of these great farm divisions.

Although the plan of New Haven was perhaps the most striking among the early New England geometric compact villages, there were others that deserve mention. Hartford, planned in 1640, also exhibited a gridiron plan with a central square or green measuring a generous 500 by 650 feet (Fig. 50). The splayed lines of the square and of the short street entering in from the river side may have been designed to emphasize the importance of the central green and to enhance the vista into it.

Following the Pequot War in 1639, Roger Ludlow established the new settlement of Fairfield on Long Island Sound east of the New Haven colony. Ludlow laid out the first lots in that year, and in 1640 he completed the remainder of the village plan (Fig. 51). This shows a simple pattern of four square blocks with a village green and meetinghouse and school sites cut from the central corners of two of the blocks. While some of the village lots were as large as eight acres, most of them were about three and a half acres in size. The central green contained approximately ten acres, measuring roughly 850 by 500 feet. While the placement of the green in the village plan appears less skillfully handled than at New Haven or Hartford, the plan is an interesting one that is effective in its simplicity and compact grouping of home lots and civic open space.

Many other regular, compact villages were created throughout the colonial period of New England. Stratford and Litchfield, Connecticut; Pittsfield, Massachusetts; Hanover, New Hampshire; and New-

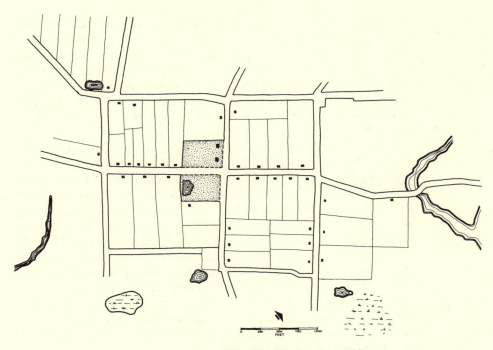

Figure 51. Plan of Fairfield, Connecticut: 1640

port, Rhode Island, are among the better documented ones. In one sense these village plans present no special problem in analysis: all of these regular layouts obviously resulted from advance planning and some degree of continued control, at least over the lines of streets and dedicated open spaces. Much more difficult to determine is the extent to which a preconceived plan or plans governed the development of those compact villages where the pattern is irregular or non-geometric.

Exeter, New Hampshire, is one example. It was founded in 1638 by John Wheelwright at the fall line of the Exeter River. A plan of 1802 shows the street pattern, the houses, and other buildings, probably little changed in most essentials from how the town must have looked a century before (Fig. 52). The town was and is a fascinating place, with one main street winding along the riverfront and the other leading inland to what is now the Phillips Exeter Academy. The widened space at the intersection of these two streets, where the map shows the courthouse, appears to be intentional, perhaps laid out as a market place near the wharves. Spring Street and Cross Street, two of the few straight streets that can be found on the map, appear to have been laid out with at least routine care. But these may well have been later additions; the New England town records are full of documents of such street changes and openings.

The plan of one of New England's most delightful late colonial villages—that of Woodstock, Vermont, which was settled in 1768—differs in form but raises the same questions. A 19th-century drawing shows the details of its original plan, although including many later

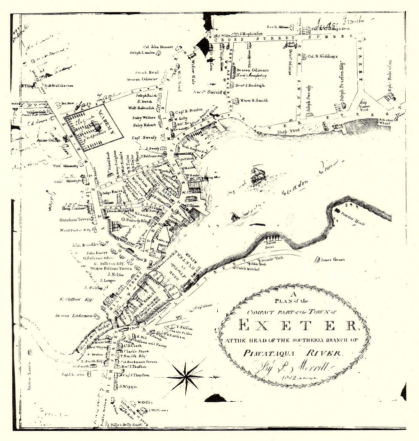

Figure 52. Plan of Exeter,
New Hampshire: 1802

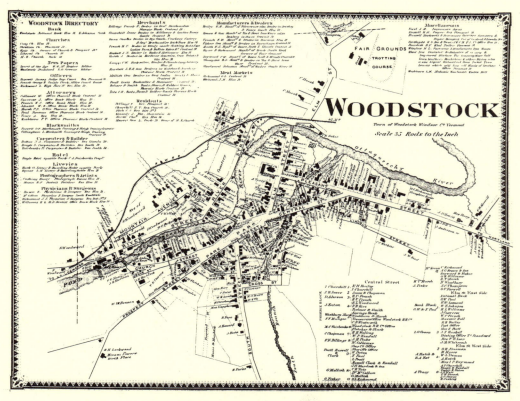

Figure 53. Plan of Woodstock, Vermont: 1869

additions (Fig. 53). Streets converging at acute angles at both ends of the town's center merge to form an irregular elongated space. In Woodstock the center of this space was developed as a sharppointed oval green on which houses and public buildings fronted, shaded in summer by lofty trees planted in the green along the streets. A local tradition has it that the shape and dimensions of the green duplicate the plan of the main deck of a ship once commanded by one of the town fathers.

Did this irregular pattern of the Woodstocks and the Exeters of New England come about through overall village planning? The answer here must be tentatively and cautiously in the negative. But if there was no comprehensive plan at Woodstock, for example, the visual satisfaction one discovers there is no mere accident. What the plan shows is the product of a century of fitting dozens of individual building projects into a harmonious pattern that makes less sense in two dimensions than it does in three. True, we can see in the plan something of the dignity of the central green, the commanding position of the church sites at the intersection of Prospect and Church Streets, and the quite different but equally effective treatment of the church placement at the terminus of Pleasant Street. But the plan alone cannot convey the pervading qualities of fitness, serenity, and congruity one encounters on the spot. This, too, is surely no mere accident, but such an architectural atmosphere was not necessarily the result of plans, regulations, and administrative controls. It came about because of a limited architectural vocabulary, limitations of major building materials to timber, brick, and stone, and a feeling of responsibility to both immediate neighbors and the greater community to build wisely and well. Our own era contrasts sharply in outlook and output. It would not be unfair to suggest that if Woodstock were to be planned today the two church sites mentioned would be occupied by gasoline stations, and the central green would no doubt be set aside as a metered parking lot.

Other villages of the compact type combine both formal or rectangular planning with informal and irregular elements. Both Lebanon, New Hampshire, and Fair Haven, Vermont, center on large rectangular greens of near-perfect regularity. Other portions of these villages, however, depart from this rectilinear design of what was probably the first part of each settlement. At Ipswich, Massachusetts, on the other hand, the original irregular green or central common reflects the broken topography, steep slopes, and rock outcrops of its surface (Fig. 54). In contrast, the later south common is rather formal in design. One side opens to the river through a cemetery, the other is lined with houses. At the western end the common narrows, partially closing the outward view in that direction. At the eastern end, square on axis, stands the imposing Congregational Church. Either one of these open spaces might be envied by any community; the two combined give Ipswich a rare architectural treasure and also provides a capsule history of New England town planning.

Those villages planned on a linear pattern, while not without interest, generally lack the variety and character of the compact form. The simple pattern of Springfield, Massachusetts, settled in the mid-1630's, furnishes one example (Fig. 55). Home lots ranged backward

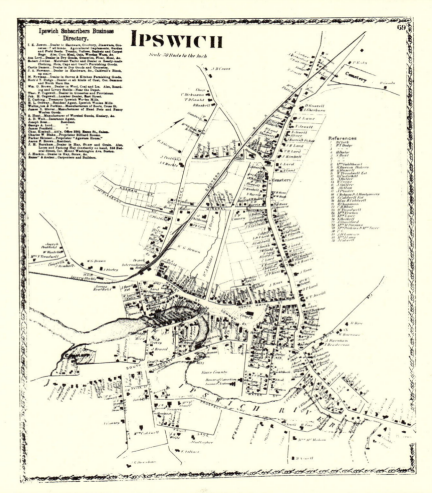

*Figure 54. Plan of Ipswich,
Massachusetts: 1872*

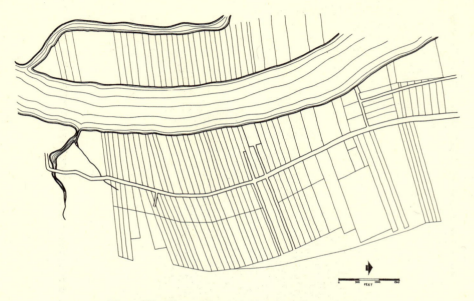

Figure 55. Plan of Springfield, Massachusetts: 1640

from either side of a road running parallel to the Connecticut River. Farm fields lay beyond and on the other side of the river. The usual common pasture and woodlands completed the familiar village and town complex.

Providence, Rhode Island, planned in 1638 on a site selected by Roger Williams, followed a similar pattern (Fig. 56). Here, however, the home lots were surveyed only on one side of "Towne Street," the north-south road that formed the spine of the village and which was laid out to follow the shore line. Long, narrow lots varied from 100 to 135 feet wide, 1,600 to 3,000 feet long, and 3 1/2 to 8 1/2 acres in area. These fronted on the road, where houses were built on level land, and extended up the steep slope to the farm fields allotted beyond the village proper.

The Providence plan resembles that of the French colonial settlements of the St. Lawrence and Mississippi valleys. Here, as there, settlers desired water frontage. To make that possible and still maintain a relatively close grouping of dwellings, very long and narrow house and garden lots were used. This early plan strongly influenced subsequent development. East-west streets, following or paralleling the old field lines, were later added to connect Towne Street (now South Main) and Hope Street, the original eastern boundary of the village. It is of interest to note that this College Hill section of Providence, three and a half centuries after its original design, is once again the scene of a major planning program as local authorities, organizations, and individuals are attempting to conserve and restore the many fine houses erected here in the heyday of the city's commercial

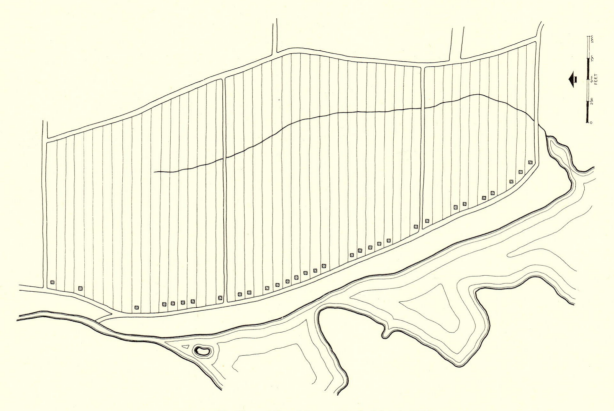

Figure 56. Plan of Providence, Rhode Island: 1638

prosperity and to rebuild those areas that have crumbled into decay during years of civic neglect.

Deerfield, Massachusetts, planned in 1670, and nearby Greenfield, dating from 1753, furnish other excellent examples of the linear type village. In both villages an additional element was introduced—small greens located on one side of the central street to provide a focus of sorts to the elongated community. At Greenfield, as in Springfield, later development at right angles to the original axis has obscured the linear character of the original plan. Deerfield, however, preserves its original form almost intact—a miraculous survival in the automotive era of a simple settlement form once widely employed. The village proper exists as one of those precious architectural and civic treasures now happily protected from incongruous "improvements" by its enlightened residents, who recognize that they hold their property in trust from history.

Boston

In the fall of 1630 Governor John Winthrop determined to move the seat of government from Charlestown to a new site. Across the Charles River to the south lay a hilly peninsula barely connected to the mainland by a low, marshy, narrow neck of land that could be easily defended. Good level farm land was lacking, but the harbor facilities seemed excellent. By the middle of the century a thriving city had developed. An observer, obviously impressed by what he had seen, described the city in these words:

"The chiefe Edifice of this City-like Towne is crowded on the Sea-bankes, and wharfed out with great industry and cost, the buildings beautifull and large, some fairly set forth with Brick, Tile, Stone and Slate, and orderly placed with comly streets, whose continuall inlargement presages some sumptuous City. The wonder of this modern Age, [is] that a few yeares should bring forth such great matters by so meane a handfull, and they so far from being inriched by the spoiles of other Nations. . . ."[3]

The lack of contemporary street plans prevents absolute certainty about the disposition of the "beautiful and large" buildings in their "comly streets," but the general arrangement of the land pattern in the 1640's has been reconstructed by a modern scholar and provides an accurate record of the city at that time (Fig. 57). The Boston of three centuries ago and only a decade after its founding already had become a sizeable village and seemed destined indeed to develop into a "sumptuous city."

Although Boston's plan could hardly be classified as regular, it was no more confusing than that of, say, Salem or Ipswich. Men not cows, as legend would have it, created the Boston street system, and by the standards of the 17th century it was reasonably well suited to the early community. The exact location of the rocky banks, the marshes, the low and muddy sinks of the virgin site were never recorded. The odds are, however, that these minor topographic variations shaped the early street pattern that has so persistently remained to plague the modern driver.

The longest street ran from the neck of land north-eastward to the

[3] Edward Johnson, *Wonder Working Providence* (London, 1654), as quoted in Nathaniel B. Shurtleff, *A Topographical and Historical Description of Boston*, Boston, 1871, p. 41.

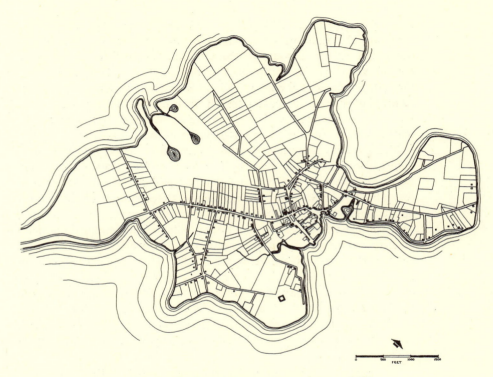

Figure 57. Plan of Boston, Massachusetts: 1640

cove where the town dock was located. Here Dock Square provided space for the handling of merchandise and the loading of cargo. A hundred yards or so south of Dock Square, Great Street (now State Street) led from the harbor to the main highway. This intersection formed the center of the village. Great Street here widened to 113 feet to provide space in its center for an open market. Fronting the market was the meetinghouse. In 1657 the town house was built on the market square, and the governor's house was located nearby.

Many of the prominent features appearing on the first published map of Boston in 1722 were well under way fifty years earlier. John Bonner's map provides our first detailed glimpse of the city's progress (Fig. 58). No great change in the street system of the 1640's appears. The density of buildings is somewhat greater, although gardens still exist to the rear of the houses. The vaguely defined common lay between the closely built-up section and the western shore. Greater changes have taken place along the border. Wharves now extend into the water, the most notable being the Long Wharf, which was begun in 1710. Bonner's map also shows the "Old Wharfe" connecting the two sides of the harbor. Started in 1673, this was intended to provide harbor defenses. Although finally completed, it soon fell into disuse, and outbound vessels used the stone from which it was constructed as ballast.

Shops and warehouses along one side of the Long Wharf furnished excellent shipping facilities and incidentally provided a dramatic entranceway directly into the center of the city. Other wharfs and docks can be seen on the Bonner map. These projects marked the

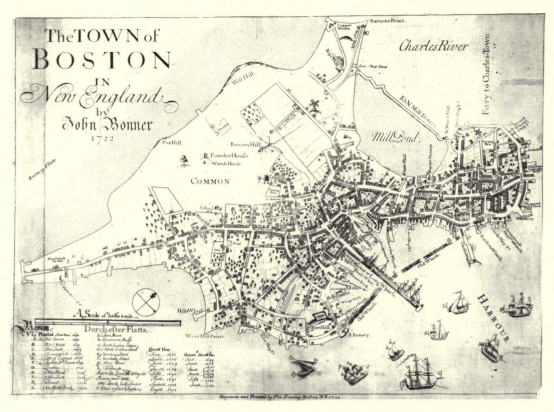

Figure 58. Plan of Boston, Massachusetts: 1722

beginning of Boston's reclamation of land originally under water. During the 18th century additional wharves were projected into the harbor. Often these were joined by cross wharves, and eventually the spaces between were filled and built on or occupied by buildings constructed on piles. Today every point on the waterfront extends well beyond the original shoreline. The scramble for urban land that was to mark the last century as an era of speculation was early anticipated in the colonial capital of New England.

At the time Bonner drew his map of the city, Boston's population stood about 12,000, the largest of the English colonial settlements. At the time of the Revolution the city had grown to 16,000, but by then Philadelphia and New York had outstripped Boston. This modest growth made possible the city's expansion on the peninsula and resulted in a compact community of restricted dimensions. A plan of Boston in 1800 shows few changes east of the Common (Fig. 59). But from the Mill Pond, which had been dammed in the mid-17th century, to the Common many new streets had been built. Cambridge Street led to the first bridge across the Charles River; this had been completed in 1786 as a private toll bridge and at once stimulated development on both sides of the river in the vicinity of its approaches. The grid pattern adopted here on the northern slope of Beacon Hill indicates a fairly early attempt to break away from the rambling alignment of the city's streets elsewhere.

The plan of 1800 shows two of Charles Bulfinch's many contributions to Boston. The State House appears north of the Common on the slope of Beacon Hill. Completed in 1798, this improvement led

Figure 59. Plan of Boston, Massachusetts: 1800

to the residential development of the Beacon Hill slopes to the west. Here the Mount Vernon proprietors used a grid pattern to develop the former pasture lands in the vicinity. The early years of the last century witnessed the construction on this site of some of America's most dignified town houses. The development included also some of the unaccountably few American residential squares on the London models. Louisburg Square, built from a plan prepared in 1826 but not substantially completed until about 1840, remains intact as a monument of urbanity and a model of what dignified city dwelling could be.

An earlier Bulfinch residential development also appears on the map. This is Franklin Place, midway between Fort Hill and the Common. Here in 1793 Bulfinch laid out a great crescent of sixteen brick row houses facing a straight line of eight houses in four units. Between lay a half oval, tree-planted green 300 feet long. The project proved a financial failure; if it had been successful Boston might well have become an American Bath, transformed like that English city into a town of elegant crescents, squares, and circuses.

The planning of Boston beyond this period cannot be followed in any detail. By 1850 the Common had become trim and cropped, in bold contrast to the untended pasture of colonial days. The Public Garden, approved by the voters in 1824 as an addition to the Common, provided Boston with additional open land at the city's core. Soon the city would be extended in a great grid pattern southwesterly from the Public Garden as the Back Bay was filled and laid out in streets to provide more land for the now rapidly growing city. The present Commonwealth Avenue, terminating at the Public Garden, formed the spine of this impressive project that still further altered the shoreline of the original colonial town.

The Heritage of New England Planning

So it was that the basis for town life was established in New England during the formative years. But the grace and charm of the New England village was long in the making. It should not be forgotten that the early years were harsh and that the first communities were frontier settlements. Some, like Windsor, Connecticut, in 1637, began as small fortress stockades, enclosing a square of dwellings little more than huts. In others, like Salem, the first residences were tiny dugouts scooped out of a bank or were bark-covered, sapling-framed shelters built in imitation of Indian dwellings. Even the surviving larger houses from the middle and late 17th century, with their unpainted plank or clapboard siding and their small windows, bear witness to the stern requirements of a pioneer existence. It was not for many years that the graceful architectural qualities we associate with the New England community began to take form.

During this period of development in building types and design, the village plans themselves doubtless underwent many changes. Agricultural lanes became residential streets as population increased, and planting fields became village house lots. Streets that may have been surveyed as straight lines developed irregularities as travellers took the easiest path around rock outcrops or low-lying wet spots in the right-of-way. Portions of the central green, where one existed, were occasionally sold for building lots or were allocated for public uses. Building encroachments on street lines apparently were fairly frequent and when tolerated resulted in minor shifts in street direction or width. Then, too, the sites of important buildings were sometimes changed; in Hartford, for example, the first meetinghouse site evidently was in one corner of the meetinghouse square some distance from the site used for its replacement a few years later.

There can be little doubt, however, that in addition to the irregularities that occurred, almost imperceptibly, in the original plans there were many "planned" irregularities from the beginning. Some of these seem deliberate—the sudden widening of a main street to form a narrow green or market space, as in Waterbury, Connecticut, or Greenfield, Massachusetts, are cases in point. Others may have been "planned" only in the sense that existing topographic features too strong to ignore were recognized and the otherwise regular pattern was adjusted accordingly. The neat precision of a New Haven with its nine equal, straight-sided blocks is something of a rarity among these early settlements.

It is just these frequent departures from regular geometry that add the charm of the unexpected and the variety in building site to the New England village today. That this resulted from deliberate attempts on the part of the early planners to create a community-wide aesthetic experience seems highly unlikely. This is not to deny that good taste and foresight in the advantageous siting of individual buildings was practiced. The location of the meetinghouse at Ipswich, Massachusetts, atop a lofty and rocky acropolis-like site or the site chosen at Topsfield, Massachusetts, fronting a spacious common are but two examples of such micro-planning.

Close study of these town plans leads inescapably to the conclusion that the very real visual distinction of the New England village stems less from the merits of their two-dimensional plans than from the combination of buildings and plant materials that developed by semi-accident many years after their layout. Perhaps this merely proves that simple plan forms often adapt best to changing circumstance. New England experience would seem to add its weight to this argument. So while the plans were simple but varied, it is the third dimension of the villages that is cherished. The scale, the materials, the architectural designs inherited from abroad but modified to meet the new environment—all of these things combined with the village layout to produce a total quality of community that has yet to be equalled in America except in isolated towns of outstanding character.

The New England pattern influenced the layout of towns in other parts of North America. William Penn's agricultural villages may well have been based on the design of New Haven. The frequently encountered system of in-lots and out-lots in the town plans of the Northwest Territory doubtless stemmed from the New England system of home lots and related farm fields. In northeastern Ohio within the Western Reserve dozens of little New England villages were recreated in regularized form by Connecticut settlers who duplicated on the new frontier the forms that had served so well on the old.

The planning heritage of New England, buried for the most part under the clutter of later accretions, remains less known, although hardly less important, than its architectural heritage. Modern planners concerned with central city renewal and suburban expansion alike could do worse than study the lessons of New England town and village design.

accepted the West India Company's terms and who, with later arrivals from Holland, began the building of a town called New Amsterdam. The orderly Dutch directors of the company sent with these settlers detailed written instructions on how the town should be laid out and delegated to company officials accompanying the expedition the power to put these plans into effect (Fig. 60).

Engineer Cryn Fredericksz, who accompanied the settlers, was first of all directed to survey a ditch 24 feet wide and 4 feet deep enclosing a rectangle extending back 1,600 feet from the water and 2,000 feet wide. Ten house and garden plots, each being 200 by 200 feet were to be laid out for the first farmers and were to be assigned by lot. Farm lands were to lie beyond the ditch. These parcels were long and narrow, 450 rods long and varying in width from 55 to 80 rods. A rectangular pattern of roads and ditches, the latter presumably for controlled drainage and irrigation on the Dutch pattern, was specified to serve the farm parcels. The remaining land on either side of the fort was to be used for vineyards.

The town proper was to be located within a five-pointed fortress. The distance from the perimeter to the central square was to be about 500 feet. A street 25 feet wide was to connect the two gates of the fort, and along this street twenty-five house lots, each 25 by 50 feet were to be laid out. In the center was to be a market square, 100 by 165 feet, at one end of which were to be located the school, hospital, and church. The instructions also mentioned additional streets, house lots, and sites for storehouses and shops.

This neat symmetrical pattern conceived in the security and com-

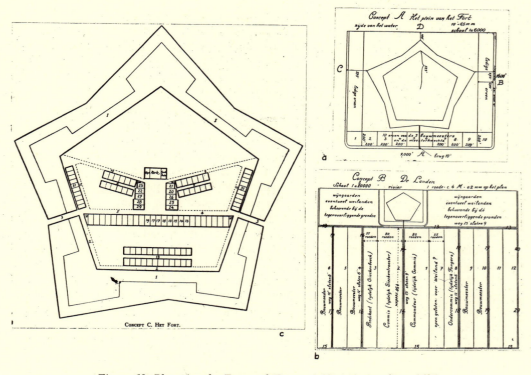

Figure 60. Plans for the Fort and Town of New Amsterdam: 1625

fort of the company's offices in Amsterdam proved unsuitable to the site on the tip of Manhattan and was beyond the resources of the colonists to carry out. It was soon abandoned, and the town developed with little in the way of an overall plan for its growth. New streets were laid out from time to time as they were needed, usually following the lanes that had become established naturally as men and animals followed the most convenient paths between houses, farms, and the fort. This method of growth resulted in streets of irregular alignment and width. As the population increased and land near the fort became more valuable, encroachments on the streets added to the lack of order.

Orderly town growth was also inhibited by the failure of many persons to whom land had been granted to build houses on their lots. Thus, in 1647, we find the director general and his council taking action to overcome this difficulty and to establish more conscious control over haphazard development. Their ordinance, one of many aimed at improving municipal affairs and eliminating the hazards of fires, read in part:

"As we have seen and remarked the disorderly manner . . . in building and erecting houses, in extending lots far beyond their boundaries, in placing pig pens and privies on the public roads and streets, in neglecting the cultivation of granted lots, the Director General Petrus Stuyvesant and Council have deemed it advisable to decide upon the appointment of three Surveyors . . . whom we hereby authorize and empower, to condemn all improper and disorderly buildings, fences, palisades, posts, rails, etc. . . . Likewise we warn all and everybody, who may heretofore have been granted lots, that they must erect on their lots good and convenient houses within 9 months . . . or in default thereof such unimproved lots shall fall back to the Patroon, or Landlord, to be given by him to such, as he pleases."[1]

Many of the streets in lower Manhattan originated in the early days of New Amsterdam. A detailed map of the city redrawn from the original of 1660 shows the extent of the infant community (Fig. 61). Leading northward from the fort, Broadway connected the settlement at the tip of the island with the farms and estates beyond. The map also shows the street running from the East River to Broadway and following the line of fortifications marking the northern limit of the city. This was and is Wall Street, originally built to serve the wall or palisade hurriedly erected in 1633 when an English attack threatened. In the little plot of grass before the fort at the foot of Broadway can be discerned the beginnings of Bowling Green.

A minute description of New Amsterdam just one year later furnishes us with other details of conditions in the city. We are told of the "gutte" or canal, "whereby at high water boats goe into the towne," and of the town hall on Pearl Street, which followed the bank of the East River. The four-pointed fort contained "the Church, the Governor's house, and houses for soldiers, ammunition, etc." The city already had developed as a center of trade, with products from New England and Virginia as well as furs from inland areas being bought,

[1] *The Records of New Amsterdam*, I, 4, as quoted in James Ford, *Slums and Housing*, Cambridge, 1936, I, 28.

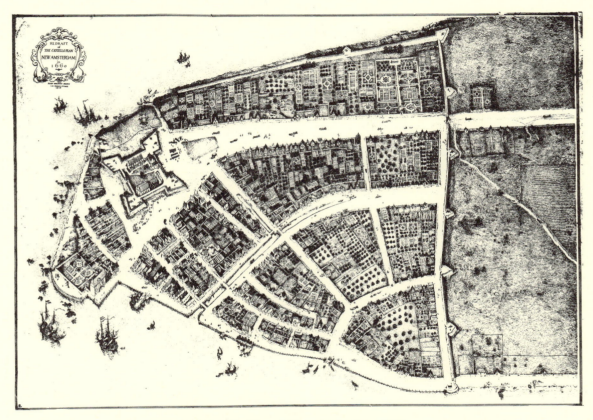

Figure 61. Plan of New Amsterdam: 1660

sold, and transported by "severall sorts of trades men and marchants and mariners."[2]

New Amsterdam was not the only Dutch settlement on Manhattan. Beyond the city lay a number of villages. Bowery Village was one, not far from the main town. Farther to the north along the Harlem River another little settlement developed. At Harlem each settler had a town plot about 90 feet square, a garden lot approximately one-third of an acre, and a twelve-acre farm. Harlem was planned with two parallel straight streets leading inland from the river, with the town plots located between them, the garden lands beyond the village to the southwest and bordered by the two main streets, and the farm parcels laid out at right angles to the streets and stretching away to the northwest and southeast across the streets from the houses.

Several other settlements sprang up along the Hudson River. Here were the great estates of the patroons, the feudal lords under the Dutch system of land distribution. At a ferry or perhaps a natural harbor along the river, little villages developed. Wiltwyck, renamed Kingston by the English, was typical of these river communities. The plan of the town as it appeared in 1695 shows a little gridiron street plan with a stockade and blockhouse for protection (Fig. 62). Stuyvesant constructed these fortifications in 1658 as added protection for a town which had been laid out five years before on the site of a Dutch trading post dating from 1615. A plan of Albany, also dating from 1695, shows a similar, although larger, urban pattern (Fig.

[2] *Description of the Towne of Mannadens* (1661), in J. Franklin Jameson, ed., *Narratives of New Netherland, 1609-1664*, New York, 1909, pp. 412-24.

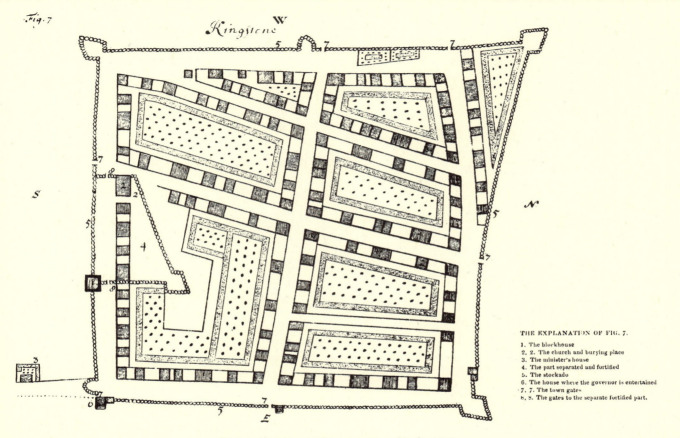

Fig. 7

Kingstone

THE EXPLANATION OF FIG. 7.

1. The blockhouse
2, 2. The church and burying place
3. The minister's house
4. The part separated and fortified
5. The stockado
6. The house where the governor is entertained
7. 7. The town gates
8. 8. The gates to the separate fortified part.

Figure 62. Plan of Kingston, New York: 1695

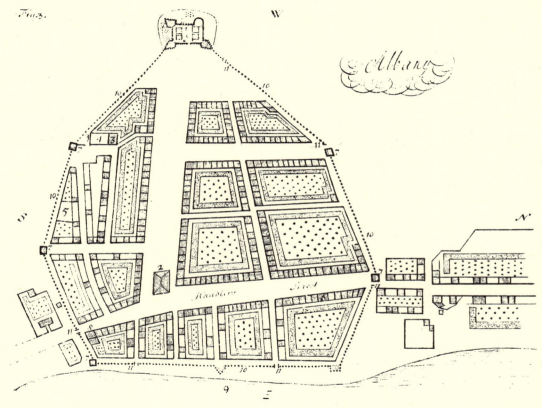

Figure 63. Plan of Albany, New York: 1695

63). Stuyvesant also established this town, originally called Beverwyck, in 1652, although there is some evidence that he merely extended and regularized the street system that had already taken shape as settlers gathered near the fort and began that ancient town.

Early New York Under English and American Rule

Dutch rule came to an end in 1664, except for the brief period from 1672 to 1674. Within a year New York, as it was renamed by the English, received its first charter. Municipal powers were renewed and extended in 1686 by the so-called Dongan Charter. This conferred municipal jurisdiction over the entire island of Manhattan, established public ownership of all land between high and low water marks, and, of even greater importance, granted the city ownership of all remaining lands on the island not yet allotted to individuals.

Manufacturing, trade, and shipping increased in importance. These expanded commercial activities attracted new residents and generated a need for additional land development. By 1700 new streets and building sites were being surveyed north of the old city wall or stockade. Expansion also occurred along the East River where major harbor facilities were located. This expansion, however, took place without the benefit of a systematic growth plan. Instead, street by street, lot by lot, relatively small parcels of land were surveyed and sold by the owners of farms adjoining the city in any way they pleased.

Perhaps the earliest large-scale subdividing was carried out by a group of tanners and shoemakers who, forced out of the more crowded parts of the growing city, purchased a tract of land north of Maiden Lane and along William and Nassau streets and had it surveyed into rectangular streets and lots in 1696. Such developments, however, remained rare, and elsewhere land sales continued to be made one or two lots at a time as demand arose.

Toward the middle of the 18th century increased need for developed land finally resulted in the subdivision of several large tracts for building purposes. Lands lying along the Hudson belonging to Trinity Church were platted in a rectangular pattern by the city surveyor, Francis Maerschalck. He was also responsible for two other such projects. One lay to the west of Bowery Lane and was surveyed in 1763. The other was located to the east of the Bowery on property originally belonging to James DeLancey. Both of these subdivisions were rectangular, but the DeLancey plan included a large open square, possibly modeled on one of the great residential squares of Georgian London.

These three land development schemes, which helped to establish the rectangular street system in New York, can be seen on the Ratzer Map of New York in 1767 (Fig. 64). This map shows the approximate condition of New York immediately before and during the war for independence. With the occupation of the city by British troops, the normal commercial and land development activities in the city were suspended, the trend of population growth was reversed, and in 1776 and again in 1778 fires swept the city and destroyed many of its buildings.

By 1789, when New York became the temporary capital of the new nation, trade once more began to flourish, and by the beginning of the 19th century New York had become the economic capital of the

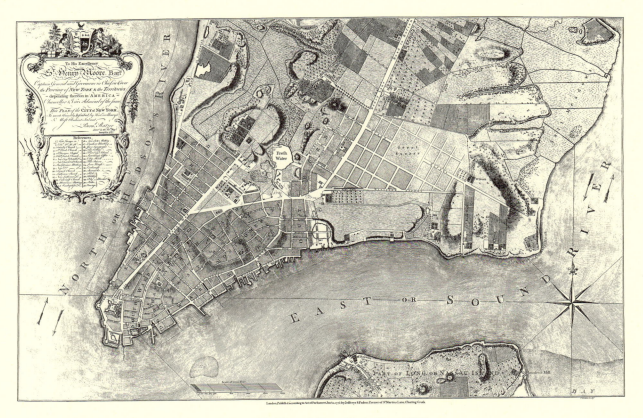

Figure 64. Plan of New York City: 1767

country. This position of dominance resulted in new population growth and the extension of the city. A map of the city in 1797 reveals some of the changes that had taken place (Fig. 65).

The great square of the DeLancey subdivision no longer existed. This and other land owned by loyalists had come into public ownership. The square, New York's first planned open space, was subdivided and sold to obtain badly needed revenues. A new open space, Hudson Square, does appear, although it, too, was ultimately to vanish. For revenue purposes the city also directed its surveyor, Casimir Goerck, to survey the public lands north of the city that had come into municipal ownership at the time of the Dongan Charter. Goerck first laid out these lands in 1785 in large rectangular parcels. Later, in 1797, he platted several north-south streets each 100 feet wide with cross streets running east and west each 60 feet in width. This action began a series of events that culminated in a street plan for most of the Island of Manhattan.

In 1804 the mayor and aldermen of New York decided to survey all existing street and building lines in the city. Two years later they concluded that they should also seek more extensive powers to lay out new streets in the area covered by Goerck's survey and even beyond. In an effort to detach this important task from the frictions of local politics and the conflicting claims of property owners, the city requested the state legislature to appoint a commission for this undertaking. In 1807, Simeon DeWitt, Gouverneur Morris, and John Rutherford began this work, not to be completed until 1811 when their plan and an accompanying report was made public.

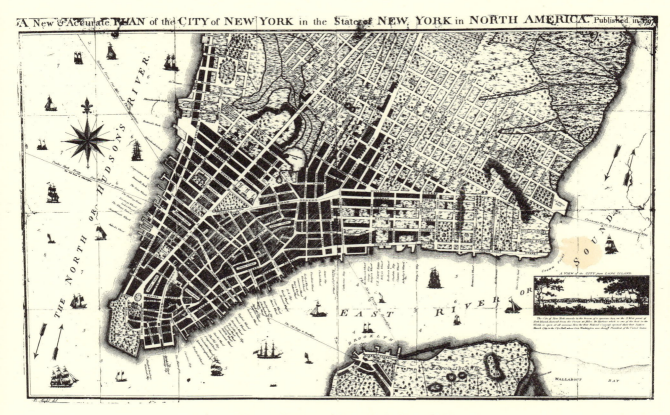

Figure 65. Plan of New York City: 1797

The appointment of the commissioners started a flurry of land speculation. Owners hurried to plat their property into blocks and streets. Surveyors employed by the commissioners were greeted with general hostility. According to one account, they were often driven off property they were attempting to survey, in one case being pelted with artichokes and cabbages by an irate woman who had made a living for twenty years by selling vegetables and who did not intend to have her property divided by strangers.

The commissioners found it impossible to adjust their plan to the irregular property boundaries and the random streets that already existed in the vast territory under their jurisdiction. Perhaps this is one reason their report had such a curiously defensive tone. In the end they employed a mechanical and rigid grid, the reasons for which their report expressed in these words:

"That one of the first objects which claimed their attention, was the form and manner in which the business should be conducted; that is to say, whether they should confine themselves to rectilinear and rectangular streets, or whether they should adopt some of those supposed improvements, by circles, ovals, and stars, which certainly embellish a plan, whatever may be their effects as to convenience and utility. In considering that subject, they could not but bear in mind that a city is to be composed principally of the habitations of men, and that strait sided and right angled houses are the most cheap to build, and the most convenient to live in. The effect of these plain and simple reflections was decisive."[3]

[3] "Commissioners' Remarks," in William Bridges, *Map of the City of New York and Island of Manhattan*, New York, 1811, p. 24.

Giving effect to this decision proved simple (Fig. 66). A dozen north-south avenues, each 100 feet wide, were laid out. Crossing these at right angles every 200 feet were no less than 155 streets, 60 feet in width, connecting the two rivers. The similarity to the earlier Goerck plan for the old common lands of central Manhattan is obvious. Not only are the street widths and intervals identical, but the location of the streets between 23rd and 93rd Streets and 5th and 6th Avenues coincided exactly with the Goerck survey of 1796.

In one respect the commissioners were farsighted. They established a plan for an area far in excess of what anyone believed would be needed even in the distant future. Their comments on this point are of interest:

"it may be a subject of merriment, that the commissioners have provided space for a greater population than is collected at any spot on this side of China. They have in this respect been governed by the shape of the ground. It is not improbable that considerable numbers may be collected at Haerlem before the high hills to the southward of it shall be built upon as a City; and it is improbable, that (for centuries to come) the grounds north of Haerlem Flat will be covered with houses. To have come short of the extent laid out, might therefore have defeated just expectation and to have gone further, might have furnished materials to the pernicious spirit of speculation."[4]

The reference to topography in this passage is the only indication that the commissioners took any notice whatsoever of the marked and often sharp changes in elevations on the island. Certainly the street

[4] *ibid.*, p. 30.

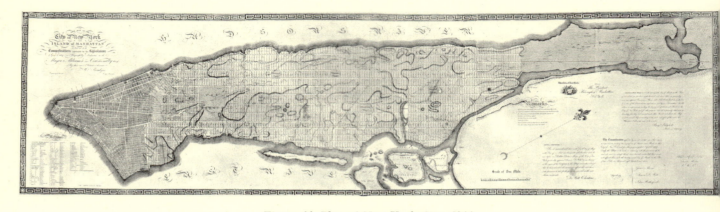

Figure 66. Plan of New York City: 1811

system they established is totally unrelated to the contours of the land. Along with the general mechanical dullness produced by their gridiron pattern, this is one of the outstanding defects of the commissioners' plan. Not only did they overlook major topographic features, but they ignored important existing roads. One or two of these, notably Broadway, did manage to survive the rigid grid as development took place, but the others gave way under the subsequent relentless expansion.

The commissioners were also directed to lay out open spaces for the future city. They set aside slightly less than 500 acres for various purposes, the largest site being the Parade bounded by 14th and 34th Streets and 3rd and 7th Avenues. They designated this to be used "for Military Exercise" and as a place to "assemble, in case of need, the force destined to defend the City." Several small parks occupying the space normally used for four blocks appear on the plan, a slightly larger site between 4th and 5th Avenues at 90th Street was designated as the location of a future reservoir, and they planned a site for a public market located between 7th and 10 Streets and extending back from the East River to 1st Avenue.

Although the amount of open space seems parsimonious by modern standards, they would have improved existing conditions substantially had they been followed. The commissioners anticipated possible criticism of the plan on the grounds of insufficient open land and advanced the following explanation:

"It may, to many, be matter of surprise, that so few vacant spaces have been left, and those so small, for the benefit of fresh air, and consequent preservation of health. Certainly, if the City of New York were destined to stand on the side of a small stream, such as the Seine or the Thames, a great number of ample spaces might be needful; but those large arms of the sea which embrace Manhattan Island, render its situation, in regard to health and pleasure, as well as to convenience of commerce, peculiarly felicitous; when, therefore, from the same causes, the price of land is so uncommonly great, it seemed proper to admit the principles of economy to greater influence than might, under circumstances of a different kind, have consisted with the dictates of prudence and the sense of duty."[5]

The unfortunate results of the prejudices and mistakes of the planners of 1811 are well known today. The lack of suitable sites for public buildings, the traffic congestion at the frequent intersections, the absence of enough north-south arteries, the overbuilding on narrow lots that inevitably resulted from the shallow blocks—these are but a few of the shortcomings. Even by the standards of the early 19th century the plan was inadequate. In their efforts to escape criticism on the grounds of economy and practicality the commissioners ignored well-known principles of civic design that would have brought variety in street vistas and have resulted in focal points for sites of important buildings and uses.

True enough, no one could have foreseen the rapid growth of the city and the changes in transportation that lessened the importance of the river-to-river cross streets while placing an increased load on the less numerous north-south avenues. But one cannot avoid the conclusion that the commissioners, in fixing upon their plan, were moti-

[5] *ibid.*, pp. 26.

vated mainly by narrow considerations of economic gain. Their surveyor, Randel, was later to defend the plan by steadfastly maintaining its utility for the "buying, selling and improving of real estate." As an aid to speculation the commissioners' plan was perhaps unequalled, but only on this ground can it justifiably be called a great achievement. The fact that it was this gridiron New York that served as a model for later cities was a disaster whose consequences have barely been mitigated by more recent city planners.

New Sweden on the Delaware

A few years after the Dutch began their colonization efforts at New Amsterdam and along the Hudson, another European power attempted to establish itself to the south in territory claimed by both the Dutch and the English. In 1638 a Swedish colony was planted on the shores of the Delaware River, beginning a brief and unsuccessful episode in colonization and town planning. The Swedish settlers were led by Peter Minuit, who had earlier bought Manhattan Island for the Dutch from the Indians. Minuit repeated this accomplishment after negotiations with the Indian tribe on the new site. He neatly posted the boundaries of the tract of land as "New Sweden," and constructed Fort Christina at the mouth of a creek within the boundaries of the modern city of Wilmington.

In the spring of 1639 and again in 1641 new arrivals at Fort Christina strengthened the little colony, and in 1642 the Swedes built two additional forts along the Delaware, New Gothenburg and New Elfsborg. Around these three forts little villages developed, although the total population probably never exceeded 200. In 1654 Queen

Christina of Sweden determined to expand the colony. This time a major expedition was equipped, and more than 350 colonists left Gothenburg for New Sweden. The Dutch garrison at Fort Casimir, located on the site of the present New Castle, was captured, and with the territory of New Sweden apparently secure, the first real town was planned.

Peter Lindstrom, a military engineer, laid out the tiny community near Fort Christina, calling it Christinahamm (Fig. 67). Lindstrom's town was a little gridiron with three main streets and one cross street located inland from the fort. This settlement enjoyed only a brief existence under Swedish rule. The year after its establishment the Dutch appeared with an army of 600 troops under Peter Stuyvesant and soon overwhelmed the colony. Most of the Swedish settlers remained on the Delaware under Dutch and then English jurisdiction, but Sweden's experiment in American colonization and town planning had come to an end.

William Penn and the Planning of Philadelphia

Between the Delaware settlements and New York stretched the flat coastal plains of New Jersey and eastern Pennsylvania. With the removal of the Dutch as a colonial power in North America, this territory lay open to English settlement. Here was to be planned the most important city of colonial America.

The city was Philadelphia, planned by William Penn as the capital of a great colony founded on the principle of religious toleration and freedom. Penn had become governor and proprietor of Pennsylvania

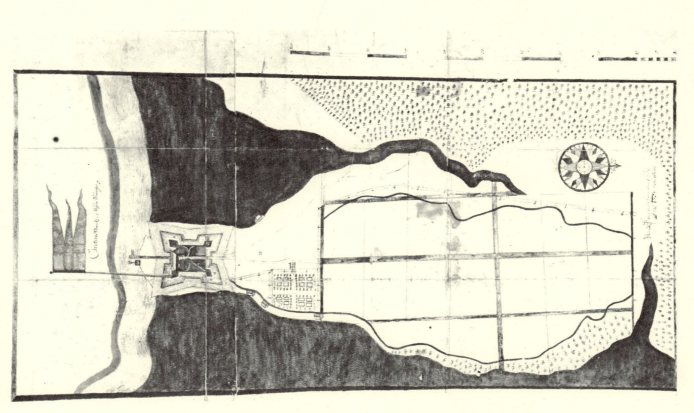

Figure 67. Plan of Fort Christina and Christinahamm, Delaware: 1654

in the spring of 1681 when Charles II put his signature to a charter and in return was freed from a sizeable debt he owed to the estate of Penn's father. Perhaps it was not entirely a business deal. Doubtless the king hoped to be rid of the troublesome Quakers and expected that many of them would migrate to America with Penn as their leader.

Within four months Penn produced his general scheme of colonization. In July he published the conditions of settlement, including a statement that "a large town or city" would be laid out and that every "purchaser and adventurer" would be given land in proportion to his investment in the enterprise. Every person buying 500 acres of land in the colony would be assigned a ten-acre parcel in the city. Penn then selected three commissioners to accompany the first group of settlers. To them he handed a long and detailed memorandum of instructions dealing with the establishment of his proposed city. These instructions, dated September 30, 1681, were specific, practical, and comprehensive. They dealt first with the selection of a suitable town site and the amount of land that would be required:

". . . let the rivers and creeks be sounded on my side of Delaware River, . . . and be sure to make your choice where it is most navigable, high, dry, and healthy; that is, where most ships may best ride, of deepest draught of water, if possible to load or unload at the bank or key side, without boating or lightering of it. It would do well if the river coming into that creek be navigable, at least for boats, up into the country, and that the situation be high, at least dry and sound, and not swampy, which is best known by digging up two or three earths, and seeing the bottom.

"Such a place being found out, for navigation, healthy situation, and good soil for provision, lay out ten thousand acres contiguous to it in the best manner you can, as the bounds and extent of the liberties of the said town."[6]

Penn, in trying to foresee every contingency, suggested what could be done if the best site for the town was already occupied by earlier settlers:

". . . you must use your utmost skill to persuade them to part with so much as will be necessary, that so necessary and good a design be not spoiled . . . urging my regard to them if they will not break this great and good contrivance, and in my name promise them what gratuity or privilege you think fit, as having a new grant at their old rent; nay, half their quit rent abated, yea, make them as free as purchasers, rather than disappoint my mind in this township. . . ."

Once the site was selected and made available, the commissioners were to proceed with the planning of the city. Penn was quite definite in specifying a regular street pattern and uniform spacing of buildings:

"Be sure to settle the figure of the town so as that the streets here-

[6] This and the following two quotations are from Penn's "Instructions . . . to . . . my Commissioners for the Settling of the . . . Colony . . . ," in Samuel Hazard, *Annals of Pennsylvania*, Philadelphia, 1850, pp. 527-30.

after may be uniform down to the water from the country bounds; let the place for the storehouse be on the middle of the key, which will yet serve for market and statehouses too. This may be ordered when I come, only let the houses built be in a line, or upon a line, asmuch as may be. . . .

"Let every house be placed, if the person pleases, in the middle of its plat, as to the breadth way of it, that so there may be ground on each side for gardens or orchards, or fields, that it may be a green country town, which will never be burnt, and always be wholesome."

These instructions, containing a statement of principles and practice for the planning of towns, were the work of a man to whom town design was no novelty. Penn had been closely involved in the establishment of two communities in the Jersey colonies. Burlington, founded in 1677, and Perth Amboy, settled at the same time as Philadelphia, resulted from these efforts. Neither plan exhibited anything out of the ordinary; Burlington had a single street with lots on both sides, while Perth Amboy had a simple grid of streets and a central market square. But Penn was thus able to draw on this earlier experience as he set out to shape a new urban pattern on a much greater scale.

The commissioners left for the new colony in the autumn of 1681. The next spring Penn appointed Captain Thomas Holme Surveyor General of Pennsylvania. Holme arrived at the site the commissioners had selected in June and began the work of planning the city. Penn himself was making ready for his first visit to the colony. The tedious preliminaries were at last complete; the stage was set for the planning of Philadelphia.

Between June and September 1682, Holme and the commissioners were busy with the design of the new city. The town they laid out, contrary to general belief, encompassed only a part of what is always referred to as the original plan. No plat of their work survives, and we can only infer that it encompassed the area between the Delaware River and a point roughly mid-way to the Schuylkill. A drawing for lots in this portion of the town was held on September 9, and a list of lot owners was certified by Holme and the commissioners, Whether or not the plan as then established provided for the public squares which appear on the first published map of the city cannot be determined.

Penn arrived in the colony in October of that year. Whatever other changes he may have made in the city's plan, his major contribution was to extend the bounds of the city westward to the Schuylkill River. The evidence of this is fragmentary but conclusive. Penn, in a published report of his activities appearing in 1685, wrote "Tho this Town seemed at first contrived for the Purchasers of the first hundred shares . . . I added that half of the Town, which lies on the Skulkill, that we might have Room for present and after Commers. . . ."[7] And Holme, in his description of the city which appeared two years earlier, observed, "The City is so ordered now, by the Governour's

7 William Penn, *A Further Account of the Province of Pennsylvania* (London, 1685), in Albert C. Myers, *Narratives of Early Pennsylvania, West New Jersey and Delaware, 1630-1707*, New York, 1912, pp. 261-73.

Care and Prudence, that it hath a Front to each River, one half at Delaware, the other at Skulkill. . . ."[8]

By the beginning of 1683, then, the basic plan had been prepared, lots surveyed and conveyed to their owners, a whole new portion of the town added, and the first buildings erected. In an effort to attract new settlers, a plan and description of the city was prepared by Holme and published in London later that year (Fig. 68). It was de-described by Holme in these words:

"The City of Philadelphia, now extends in Length, from River to River, two Miles, and in Breadth near a Mile. . . .

"The Model of the City appears by a small Draught now made, and may hereafter, when time permits, be augmented; and because there is not room to express the Purchasers Names in the Draught, I have therefore drawn Directions of Reference, by way of Numbers, whereby may be known each man's Lot and Place in the City. . . .

"The City, (as the Model shows) consists of a large Front-street to each River, and a High-street (near the middle) from Front (or River) to Front, of one hundred Foot broad, and a Broad-street in the middle of the City, from side to side, of the like breadth. In the Center of the City is a Square of ten Acres; at each Angle are to be Houses for Publick Affairs, as a Meeting-House, Assembly or State-House, Market-House, School-House, and several other Buildings for

[8] *A Short Advertisement upon the Situation and Extent of the City of Philadelphia and the Ensuing Plat-form thereof, by the Surveyor-General* (London, 1683), in Myers, *Narratives*, pp. 242-44.

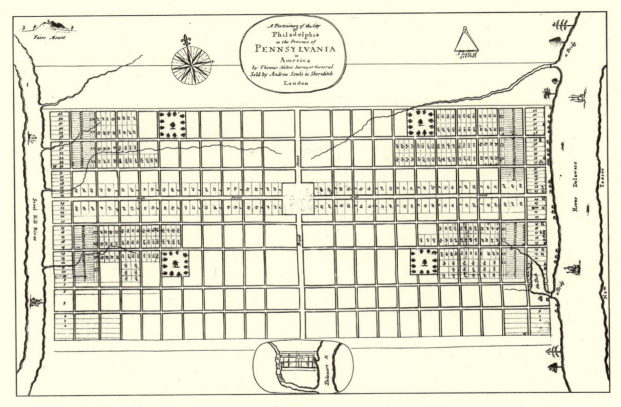

Figure 68. Plan of Philadelphia, Pennsylvania: 1683

Publick Concerns. There are also in each Quarter of the City a Square of eight Acres, to be for the like Uses, as the Moore-fields in London; and eight Streets (besides the High-street), that run from Front to Front, and twenty Streets, (besides the Broad-street) that run cross the City, from side to side; all these Streets are of Fifty Foot breadth."[9]

What were the origins of the plan of Philadelphia as laid out by Penn and Holme? What were the models from which its regular streets and neatly balanced open spaces were drawn? No fully satisfactory answers are possible, but there are remarkable similarities in the Philadelphia pattern to earlier city planning concepts and achievements.

Penn apparently had studied previous English colonization experience. Doubtless he knew of New Haven, with its nine squares and central open green. He certainly was aware of the earlier English colonial settlements in the Londonderry plantations of northern Ireland. He was familiar with Inigo Jones's great design for Covent Garden in London and with the nearby Lincoln's Inn Fields where he had studied law at Lincoln's Inn in 1665. It is highly likely that he had seen the several plans submitted to the king for the rebuilding of London after the great fire in 1666. One of these, by Richard Newcourt, closely resembled Penn's plan for Philadelphia, having a regular gridiron street system and five open squares similarly located. The scale of the plans for London coincided almost exactly with that of Philadelphia. Newcourt's scheme, for example, was for an area approxi-

[9] *ibid.*

mately one by one and a half miles, a tract nearly the size of Philadelphia's great grid.

Penn and Holme thus had a number of models from which to draw, but they did more than copy any existing or proposed city plan of the past. Philadelphia was much larger than previous colonial new towns, and in setting aside the four smaller squares "for the like Uses, as the Moore-fields in London," that city's recreational grounds, they established America's first designated public parks. By 17th-century standards the two principal streets each 100 feet wide and the other streets half that width were exceedingly generous. Thus in its scale, its open squares, and its consistent use of wide streets intersecting at right angles Philadelphia represented something of an innovation in colonial town design.

Lands were also surveyed outside the city for the farm tracts. These constituted the so-called "liberty lands," in extent some ten thousand acres. Each settler was entitled to a farm in this location as well as to one or more city lots within the bounds of Philadelphia. The liberty lands appear on the first map of Pennsylvania, drawn by Holme, probably in 1687. A later version of this map also provides a valuable source of information on the planning of rural settlements in the hinterland (Fig. 69). Penn's description of the layout of these agricultural villages, two of which may be seen near the right-hand border of the map, is of interest:

"Our Townships lie square; generally the Village in the Center; the Houses either opposit, or else opposit to the middle, betwixt two houses over the way, for near neighborhood. We have another Method,

Figure 69. Map of the Vicinity of Philadelphia, Pennsylvania: 1720

that tho the Village be in the Center, yet after a different manner: Five hundred Acres are allotted for the Village, which, among ten families, comes to fifty Acres each: this lies square, and on the outside of the square stand the Houses, with their fifty Acres running back, where ends meeting make the Center of the 500 Acres as they are to the whole. Before the Doors of the Houses lies the high way, and cross it, every man's 450 Acres of Land that makes up his Complement of 500, as that the Conveniency of Neighbourhood is made agreeable with that of the land."[10]

Penn was also concerned with the development of good lines of communication. In the published conditions of settlement he promised that the planning of a road system would receive early attention and that no encroachments on public rights-of-way would be permitted. These roads, 40 feet wide, were to be planned before the lands were divided for farming purposes, thus ensuring that the best routes could be freely selected and would not be blocked by property owners unwilling to allow the road to cross their lands. In the breadth of his outlook and in his attention to such details, Penn was unsurpassed as a colonial regional planner and administrator.

Construction of houses in Philadelphia began immediately after the allocation of city lots. By August of 1683 Penn could report that eighty houses had been completed, that farms were being cultivated, and that tradesmen and merchants were already busy. By the time he left for England a year later Philadelphia had 357 houses. Robert Turner, writing to Penn toward the end of the summer of 1685, told

[10] Penn, *A Further Account.*

the founder of Philadelphia that there were then 600 houses in the town, that two new meetinghouses were under construction, and that "Lots are much desir'd in the Town, great buying one of another."

The growth of Philadelphia continued at the same rapid rate for many years. Gabriel Thomas, a Welsh Quaker who had arrived with the first band of settlers, wrote this account of the city in 1698: ". . . the Industrious (nay Indefatigable) Inhabitants have built a Noble and Beautiful City . . . which contains above two thousand Houses, all Inhabited; and most of them Stately and of Brick, generally three Stories high, after the Mode in London, and as many as several Families in each. . . .

"Here is lately built a Noble Town-House or Guild-Hall, also a Handsom Market-House and a convenient Prison. . . ."[11]

But Thomas also records the beginning of a practice that was to create many later problems. He describes the cutting up of Holme's generous city blocks by additional streets, most of which were extremely narrow. Thus began a tradition of overcrowding that was to turn much of Penn's "green country town" into a city of tightly packed row houses and alley dwellings. Other changes occurred. Originally Front Street, along the Delaware, was to have no structures on the river side. This area quickly developed as the port, and warehouses and wharfs were built on the water's edge. Eventually a new street was constructed along the river parallel to Front Street which became

[11] Gabriel Thomas, *An Historical and Geographical Account of Pennsilvania and of West New-Jersey* (1698), in Myers, *Narratives*, pp. 317-31.

almost entirely commercial and industrial in character. Thus at an early date Philadelphians were denied easy access to the great river that had made the site so attractive.

More important alterations were made to the city plan as originally laid out by Holme and Penn and were recorded by Nicholas Scull on his detailed city map of 1762 (Fig. 70), Broad Street, the main north-south artery, was moved two blocks to the west of its first location, the street pattern along the Schuylkill River was rearranged somewhat, and the four park squares were encroached upon, one being used as a burying ground and another as a brickyard. These serious departures from the published plan of 1683 were made by Penn and Holme when it was discovered that the distance between the Delaware and the Schuylkill Rivers was greater than preliminary surveys indicated. Topography played a part also when it was discovered that the highest ground lay somewhat to the west of the first location assigned to the central square. Broad Street was therefore moved westward and additional north-south streets were added to the plan to occupy the additional space. These changes were to cause considerable confusion over land titles in subsequent years, but they did not alter the general pattern of the city plan.[12]

[12] My discussion of this modification to the first published plan in *The Making of Urban America*, Princeton, 1965, pp. 169-72 is incorrect. The details of how and why the plan was changed appear in a recent examination of the founding of Philadelphia which traces in great detail the system of land surveys and allotments in the city. See Hannah Benner Roach, "The Planting of Philadelphia, a Seventeenth-Century Real Estate Development," *Pennsylvania Magazine of History and Biography*, Vol. 92 (1968), pp. 3-47, 143-94.

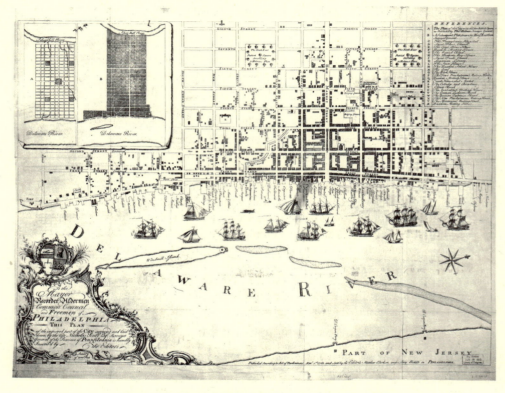

Figure 70. Plan of Philadelphia, Pennsylvania: 1762

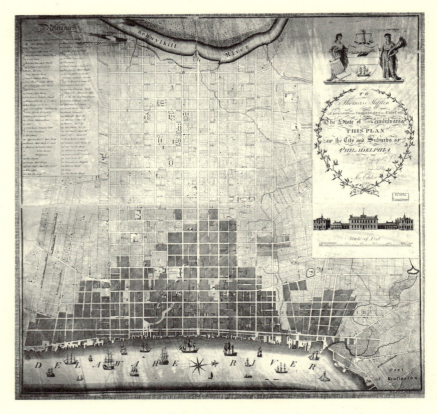

Figure 71. Plan of Philadelphia, Pennsylvania: 1794

The missing squares reappeared and exist today, although one has been modified in form, as valuable open spaces in an overcrowded city. A series of city ordinances passed in the early part of the 19th century officially named the squares, prohibited their use as burying grounds or as dumps, appropriated funds for their improvement, and, as a final reassertion of Quaker respectability, even provided for a fine of two dollars for any person smoking "a segar or segars, pipe or pipes, in any of the public squares."

Until the Revolutionary War Philadelphia continued to grow. By 1755 the population had reached 20,000. At the outbreak of the war Philadelphia was the largest city in any of the American colonies and was surpassed in England itself only by London. Most of the city's growth took place along the Delaware. A map of the city published in 1794 reveals that the built-up portion scarcely extended inland as far as the central square (Fig. 71). North and south of the original bounds of the city new streets had to be laid out to accommodate those who wished to locate on or near the river. Unfortunately, these city extensions did not incorporate a regular pattern of open spaces, and the map shows almost solid building in these newer sections of the city. By 1800 Philadelphia had become an imposing city with many fine town houses, elegant public buildings, and numerous churches. It was also a busy industrial and mercantile city, and the waterfront bustled with activity connected with the port. As the nation's capital city until 1800, Philadelphia was also the locus of political pomp and power. The infant University of Pennsylvania and several learned societies contributed to the intellectual life of the community. By the standards of any society, Philadelphia had become a great city, and its influence on the life of the country was far-reaching.

In particular, the Philadelphia city plan materially affected the subsequent course of town design in America. As the first large American city to be laid out on the gridiron pattern, Philadelphia has always been identified, usually unkindly, as the inspiration for the great era of rectangular town planning during the preceding century. This influence is undeniable, but it was not always unfortunate. Even where the results proved unhappy, part of the blame must be assessed against those who disregarded the good features of the gridiron or who extended an original settlement with mechanical regularity in disregard of topography.

The original city of Philadelphia was built on comparatively flat land, and a regular street system was not illogical. Street widths were more than ample for the traffic of the time and were almost extravagant by European standards. Moreover, the plan at least provided for even wider major streets, a feature often overlooked by subsequent gridiron planners. If the original provision of open spaces is judged inadequate by the standards of today, that is simply an indication that standards have changed, not that the original plan was deficient by the standards of its own time.

The Philadelphia of Penn and Holme, while large, was a city in which the human figure was never dwarfed by either the plan or the buildings. All parts of the city could be reached comfortably on foot, and even the chief buildings remained almost domestic in size. The first planners clearly intended a compact yet uncrowded settlement with a sharp distinction between the urban core and the surrounding rural region. The liberty lands to the north of the city functioned as a green belt that crisply defined the boundary between town and country.

Penn and Holme, as generous in their vision as they were, did not foresee today's sprawling metropolis that stretches into the countryside and blurs this distinction between what is urban and what is rural. Nor did they anticipate what might have been more obvious—the early development of the city north and south along the banks of the Delaware, outside the bounds of the original plan, instead of westward toward the Schuylkill. It was unfortunate that these later extensions did not incorporate the same sense of order in the street system or provide the same proportion of open space as did the planners of what is still the central portion of that great city.

For many of the towns that sprang up later during the westward march of urbanization, Philadelphia served as the model. The regular pattern of streets and one or more public squares were features that became widely imitated. Throughout Pennsylvania there are dozens of towns, large and small, that incorporate these elements in their plans. Reading, Allentown, Lancaster, York, and Pittsburgh were laid out with open squares or rectangles having four streets intersecting the middle of the square's sides. In Lancaster County alone at least six communities use the Philadelphia square as the central motif.

This pattern of grid and public square appears throughout the south and midwest and beyond, copied from Philadelphia or from another imitation. In at least two state capitals, Raleigh, planned in 1792, and Tallahassee, surveyed in 1824, the identical distribution of five open squares may be found, and a half-dozen or so smaller and less important cities also imitated this plan. As population spread beyond the first colonies, westward migrants must have had a strong psychological motivation to duplicate a familiar community element in the midst of unfamiliar surroundings.

The single open square in the center of the town became the typical expression of the Philadelphia plan as it was transplanted west. However inadequate the public square of the midwestern towns may be as a symbol of civic consciousness or a focus of architectural attention, it at least supplies a break in the almost intolerable rhythm of a relentless grid. If Philadelphia must share the blame for the ubiquitous gridiron, it should also be credited as the source of an occasional open square occupied by public buildings or used for park purposes.

Perhaps speculation on the influences of the Philadelphia plan is less important than understanding its place in the American tradition of city planning. Well before the great urban revolution of the 19th century there was a wealth of experience in the planning of towns and a realization that some degree of municipal control over land development was not incompatible with a democratic society. New Haven, Annapolis, Williamsburg, Charleston, and Savannah are all a part of that tradition. Not the least among them is the Philadelphia of William Penn.

By 1664 the English had gained control of the American eastern seaboard from Maine to Virginia. The Dutch, who earlier had absorbed the Swedish settlements along the Delaware, were themselves removed as a colonizing and town-founding power, and their towns gradually assumed the appearance of those established under English rule. Only Pennsylvania and the southern flank of Anglo-America remained for new colonial expansion. Both of these areas were to provide interesting and, in some cases, novel examples of city planning. William Penn's great city of Philadelphia has already been described, and it is to the Carolinas and Georgia that we now turn our attention.

Charleston and the Carolina Towns

Charles II established the Carolina Territory as a reward to eight court favorites in 1663. On these Lords Proprietors he conferred powers similar to those previously granted Lord Baltimore in Maryland. John Locke drafted the plan of government, an elaborate and essentially unworkable system by which the remnants of feudal rule were to be transplanted to the New World.

In 1669 the Proprietors resolved to attempt systematic colonization of their vast domain rather than a haphazard extension of settlement southward from Virginia. The following year a party entered the mouth of the Ashley and Cooper rivers and laid out a little town a short distance from the coast. This miserably unhealthy site soon proved unsatisfactory, and in 1672 Lord Anthony Ashley-Cooper instructed Sir John Yeamans, the governor, to lay out a new town on the peninsula between the two rivers. The original plan apparently was fairly ambitious, but the limited resources of the colony permitted only a portion of it to be carried out immediately. An early drawing of the town in 1704 shows a little gridiron design fronting on the Cooper River, with a line of fortifications surrounding it (Fig. 72).

Maurice Mathews, writing in 1680, described the community in these words: "The Town is run out into four large streets. The Court house which we are now building is to be erected in the middle of it, in a Square of two ackers of land upon which the four great streets of 60 foot wide doe center, and to the water side there is laid out 60 foot for a publick wharfe as also for other conveniences as a Church yard, Artillery ground, etc., and without there is care taken that the front lines be preserved whereby wee shall avoid the undecent and in-commodious irregularities which other Inglish Collonies are fallen unto for want of ane early care in laying out the Townes."[1]

By 1717 Charleston had grown to some 1,500 persons, and ex-pansion of the boundaries became essential. A plan of the town in 1739 shows how the so-called "Grand Modell" as originally con-ceived by the proprietors was then carried out (Fig. 73). The central square, only half of which was included in the first plan, was obvi-

---

[1] "A Contemporary View of Carolina in 1680," *South Carolina Historical Magazine*, Vol. 55 (1954), pp. 153-54.

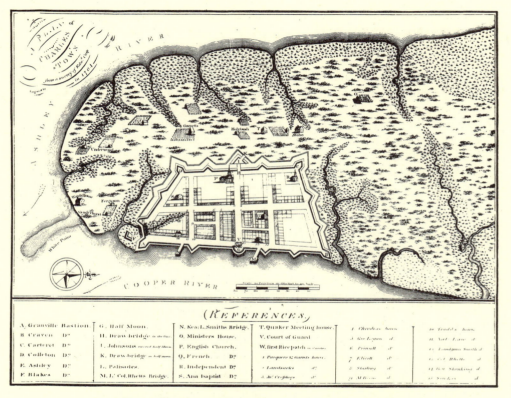

Figure 72. Plan of Charleston, South Carolina: 1704

ously intended as the focal point of the city. Yet, as the plan indicates, most of the intensively built-up portions of the town were near the waterfront facing the numerous docks and wharfs extending into the river.

The square, instead of being preserved as an open civic space, was soon to be occupied by buildings. As early as 1739 the market building stood on one corner. In 1761 a church was constructed in another corner, and in 1780 and 1788 the remaining two corners furnished the sites for an arsenal and the courthouse. The park and promenade along the Ashley River, which are such notable features of the present city, belong to a later era.

No other city of the southern colonies rivaled Charleston in size and prosperity. Unlike Virginia, where the indented coastline provided numerous opportunities for direct shipment to and from plantations, South Carolina offered limited sites for good ports, and Charleston's location was clearly the best for this purpose. The proprietors, moreover, in exercising their central control over the pattern of settlement, concentrated their resources at this spot. By the end of the colonial era the town was a handsome one with elegant town houses fronting the regular streets of the interior of the city and with a bustling warehouse and mercantile section stretching along its crowded dock area.

Urban development of North Carolina came later and more closely resembled the experience in Virginia, whose geographic features it also shared. Here, within the low-lying sand bars and islands stretching northwest and southeast from Cape Hatteras, was the same pattern of deep, wide river estuaries flowing into Albemarle Sound and

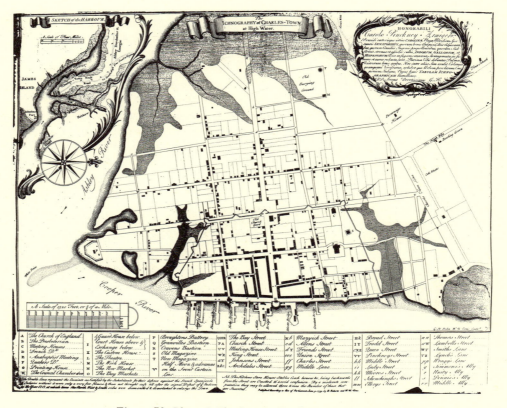

Figure 73. Plan of Charleston, South Carolina: 1739

Pamlico Sound which make up the northern coastline. The southern part of the coast offered less protected and fewer sites, but even here there were numerous locations for town development within the spits and bars which closely hug the mainland. It was along this coast that the earliest towns were founded, and it is not surprising that they were to be both more numerous and less imposing than in South Carolina.

The six port towns of significance were Brunswick and Wilmington on the Cape Fear River in the south; Beaufort, approximately midway along the coast; New Bern, on the Neuse River; Bath, on the River Tar; and Edenton, on the north bank of Albemarle Sound not far from the Virginia boundary. All date from the 18th century, all were officially designated as port towns for the purposes of customs and control of trade, and all of them were planned with rectangular street patterns orientated toward the waterfront. Wilmington, Edenton, and New Bern were the most important by the end of the colonial era and can be regarded as fairly typical of the others, although the exact layout varied from place to place.

Wilmington, the only one of the six to retain some importance as a seaport, began its existence as Newton in 1733. Its site was a few miles upstream from the older Brunswick which was then the official port of entry. Gabriel Johnston, who became governor in 1734, took a dislike to Brunswick and established his residence in Wilmington. Six years later the county seat and port officials were transferred to Wilmington temporarily, and later the General Assembly decided to meet here as well as at New Bern. The act of incorporation in 1739 included provisions for town regulations, and doubtless by this time it had assumed the form shown in the survey made by C. J. Sauthier in 1769 (Fig. 74).

Its plan could scarcely have been simpler. A single major street ran back from the waterfront. The other important street paralleled the river, and at the intersection of the two stood the courthouse. Two streets beyond could be found the jail, facing an open square on which was located the church. Two other streets led from the river street to form the balance of the city blocks.

New Bern owed its origins to the efforts of a Swiss nobleman, Baron Christopher de Graffenried, who founded the town in 1710 as a settlement for Swiss and Palatine refugees. Aided by John Lawson, Graffenried platted the town on a triangular site at the juncture of the Trent and Neuse rivers, surveying the main street so as to bisect the angle made by the two rivers. A second street crossed the first at right angles, running from one river to the other. The following year saw the Tuscarora Indian uprising and the complete destruction of the town, and it was not until 1723 that it was re-established on a new and more orthodox pattern. It remained a small and relatively unimportant settlement for some years; in 1741 a census revealed only twenty-one families residing there.

With the meeting of the Assembly in New Bern from 1745 to 1761 the town increased in importance, and in 1767 Governor William Tryon began construction of his imposing residence, regarded by many as the most beautiful building of colonial America. It was shortly thereafter that Sauthier prepared his drawing of the community, one of a series of North Carolina settlements recorded by this skillful

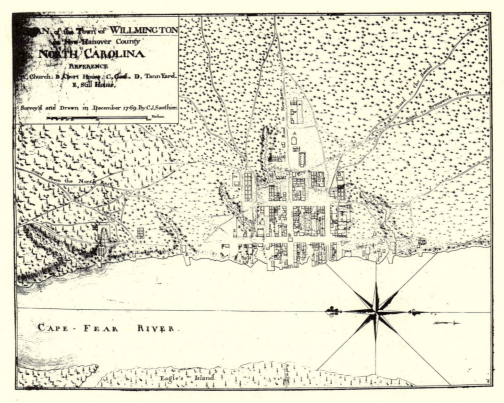

Figure 74. Plan of Wilmington, North Carolina: 1769

draftsman (Fig. 75). Again we see the use of the gridiron street system, broken only by one diagonal lane in the northern part of the settlement, which may mark the remaining portion of Graffenried's original plan. The courthouse, marked "C" on the drawing, occupies a commanding site at the intersection of two streets each leading from the waterfront. Near the courthouse is the jail identified by "D," and the church, shown by the letter "A." To the west of the church and fronting on the longest street in the city appears Tryon's "palace," with its second front opening out to the Trent River.

Edenton, the other important coastal settlement of the period, originated as did many of the Virginia and Maryland towns through an act of the General Assembly in 1712. The act directed commissioners to lay out the town and to designate sites for the public buildings and lands of the community. The treatment of the courthouse and jail site is of considerable interest. Shown by the letters "B" and "C" on Sauthier's drawing, these buildings occupy the center of a wide mall leading up from the waterfront (Fig. 76). The church is located some distance away, fronting on the wide main street that runs roughly north and south and divides the town into two parts. West of this street, along the strand, another mall appears to lead inland almost symmetrically with that of the courthouse mall. Still farther west another stretch of unbuilt land extends inward from the water. The purpose of these latter two plan elements is not clear. Perhaps they were intended to provide views to and from sites for important buildings that would have faced the Sound from the first or second street inland running parallel to the shore.

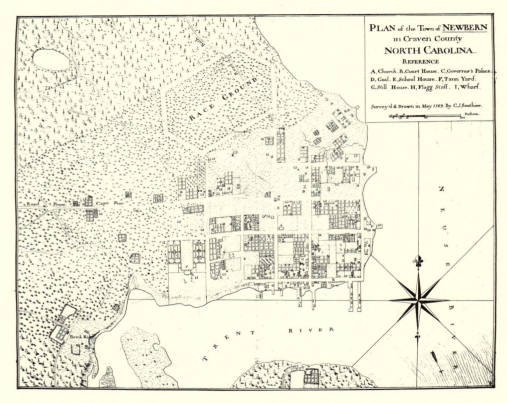

Figure 75. Plan of New Bern, North Carolina: 1769

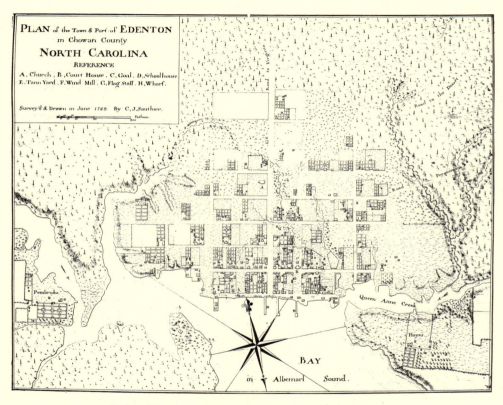

Figure 76. Plan of Edenton, North Carolina: 1769

While these and such other Carolina settlements of the piedmont region as Salisbury and Hillsborough are far from uninteresting, the plan forms and the land policies employed in the Georgia colony are considerably more novel. In the capital city of Savannah not only did the original plan possess distinctive qualities not found elsewhere, but both the form and spirit of its original pattern were followed for more than a century during the city's gradual expansion.

Sir Robert Mountgomery's Margravate of Azilia

The founding of the colony of Georgia and the planning of Savannah were preceded by an abortive settlement proposal under the Carolina Proprietors whose jurisdiction extended southward to Spanish Florida. In June 1717 they granted Sir Robert Mountgomery permission to create a separate province between the Savannah and Altamaha rivers, to be called the Margravate of Azilia. Settlement had to be undertaken within three years or the grant would become void.

Sir Robert lost no time in attempting to promote colonization. Within a few months he published a tract in which he set forth his scheme of settlement along with a plan of one of the districts or "county divisions" of the Margravate (Fig. 77). He rejected the concept of a series of isolated communities scattered throughout the territory. Instead he proposed nothing less than a fortified line surrounding the entire county, a square twenty miles on each side. As Mountgomery explained the proposal:

"The district is defended by sufficient numbers of men, who, dwelling in the fortified angles of the line will be employed in cultivating

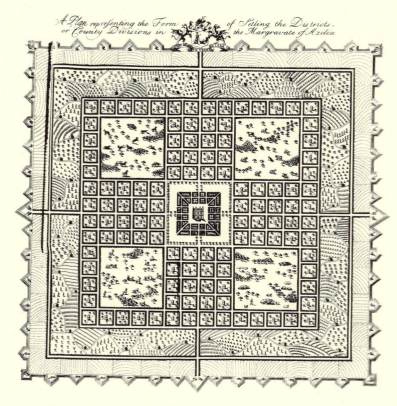

Figure 77. Plan for the Margravate of Azilia, Georgia: 1717

lands which are kept in hand for the particular advantage of the Margrave: these lands surround the district just within the lines, and everywhere contain in breadth one mile exactly.

"The men thus employed . . . shall have a right of laying claim to a certain fee-farm. . . . The lands set apart for their purpose are two miles in breadth, quite round the district. . . . The 116 squares, each of which has a house in the middle, are every one a mile on each side, or 640 acres in a square, bating only for the highways which divide them. These are the estates belonging to the gentry of the district. . . .

"The four great parks, or rather forests, are each four miles square, that is, 16 miles round each forest, in which are propagated herds of cattle of all sorts by themselves, not alone to serve the uses of the district they belong to, but to store such new ones as may from time to time be measured out on affluence of people."[2]

Then Mountgomery turned to the town proper which was to occupy the center of the county district. This, as he described it, was to be surrounded by a greenbelt of open land:

"The middle hollow square, which is full of streets crossing each other, is the city, and the bank which runs about it on the outside surrounded with trees, is a large void space, which will be useful for a thousand purposes, and among the rest, as being airy and affording a fine prospect of the town in drawing near it.

[2] Sir Robert Mountgomery, *A Discourse Concerning the Design'd Establishment of a New Colony to the South of Carolina in the Most Delightful Country of the Universe* (London, 1717), reprinted in George P. Humphrey, *American Colonial Tracts*, No. 1, Rochester, 1897.

"In the center of the city stands the Margrave's house, which is to be his constant residence, or the residence of the Governor, and contains all sorts of public edifices for dispatch of business; and this again is separated from the city by a space like that, which as above, divides the town from the country."

Mountgomery's attempts to raise funds for this ambitious and quite impractical venture failed, and his right to settlement in Georgia lapsed. But his novel town-country community proposal may well have influenced the pattern of settlement ultimately adopted a few years later. It is to this venture that we now turn.

James Oglethorpe and the Planning of Savannah

In 1729 the Lords Proprietors of Carolina surrendered their rights to the Crown. Three years later George II conveyed the southern portion of this territory to The Trustees for Establishing the Colony of Georgia in America, and thus began a novel colonial undertaking. The leading figure among the trustees was James Oglethorpe, and it was under his immediate supervision that the towns of the new colony were planned and built. Oglethorpe had served in the English army and later under Prince Eugene of Savoy. Returning to England to take over his family estate, he was elected to the House of Commons in 1722. He soon interested himself in prison reform, particularly the treatment of debtors. In 1728 he served as Chairman of a Commons committee investigating the conditions of the London jails. Out of this experience grew his idea of promoting a colony in the new world where those confined to English jails by their creditors could find a new life. Not only debtors would be sought for the venture, but other persons of modest means and little future who, for economic or religious reasons, felt the weight of oppression or discrimination.

The details of the proprietory grant by the king and the conditions of land settlement established by the trustees contained provisions aimed at preventing land speculation. No colonist could be granted more than 500 acres of land, and trustees were prohibited from owning any land while members of the corporation. Land grants to colonists transported and settled at the trustees' expense were set at 50 acres, and this land could not be sold. Succession in title was to be to the male heir only, to prevent breaking up of plots into holdings of uneconomic size.

The trustees were men of means and influence, and in a short time were successful in raising sufficient funds for the first expedition. One hundred and fourteen persons signified their willingness to meet the conditions for joining the colony. In November 1732 they sailed from Depford, accompanied by Oglethorpe, who characteristically had volunteered to lead the first group, paying his own expenses and acting as the trustees' representative.

After two months at sea the colonists arrived at Charleston and were welcomed by the governor and his council. Colonel William Bull was assigned to accompany Oglethorpe and assist him in locating and laying out a town site. Early in February Oglethorpe wrote to the trustees describing the beginnings of settlement at the spot he had selected on the Savannah River:

"The river here forms a half-moon, along the south side of which the banks are about forty foot high, and on the top flat. . . . The plain high ground extends into the country five or six miles, and along the river side about a mile. Ships that draw twelve foot of water can ride within ten yards of the bank. Upon the river-side in the centre of this plain I have laid out the town. . . . The whole people arrived here on the first of February. At night their tents were got up. Till the seventh we were taken up in unloading, and making a crane, which I then could not get finished, so took off the hands, and set some to the fortification, and began to fell the woods. I marked out the town and common; half of the former is already cleared, and the first house was begun yesterday in the afternoon."[3]

On March 16 three gentlemen from Charleston arrived in Savannah to observe what was taking place. Their impressions appeared in the *South-Carolina Gazette* the following week: "Mr. Oglethorpe is indefatigable. . . . There are four houses already up . . . and he hopes . . . to finish two houses a week. . . . He was pallisading the town round, including some part of the common. . . . In short, he has done a vast deal of work for the time, and I think his name justly deserves to be immortalized."[4]

When by July substantial progress had been made, Oglethorpe called the colonists together to reveal the plan of the town, the names of the streets and wards, and the assignment of town, garden, and

[3] Letter to the trustees, February 10, 1733, in *Reasons for Establishing the Colony of Georgia* (London, 1733), reprinted in Georgia Historical Society, *Collections*, Vol. I, Savannah, 1840.

[4] *South-Carolina Gazette*, No. 62, March 24, 1732 [1733].

farm lots to individuals. The *South-Carolina Gazette* reported the event: "On the 7th of July . . . the Inhabitants were assembled, on the Strand Prayers were read, by way of Thanksgiving. The people proceeded to the Square. The Wards and Tythings were named, each Tything consisting of ten Houses, and each Ward of four tythings. An House Lott was given to each Freeholder. All the people had a very plentiful Dinner."[5]

But the occasion was not entirely a happy one, since, as the account continues: "Some of the People having privately drank too freely of Rum are dead; and that Liquor which was always discountenanced here, is now absolutely prohibited."

While this division of land was carried out in July, it was not until December that the settlers received the deeds to their lands. A portion of one of them, interesting because it provides information about the peculiar method of land grants, reads as follows:

"Whereas . . . James Oglethorpe, hath set out and limited . . . a Town called Savannah, with Lotts for Houses, and left a Common round the Town for convenience of Air; And, adjoining to the Common, hath set out Garden Lotts of Five Acres each, and beyond such Garden Lotts hath set out Farms of Forty Four Acres and One Hundred and forty and one Pole each, and hath drawn a Plan of the Town, and Plot of the Garden Lots and Farms respectively, with proper Number, references, and Explanations for the more easy understanding thereof. . . .

[5] *South-Carolina Gazette*, No. 84, August 25, 1733.

"Now know Ye, that we . . . do Grant and Enfeoff unto John Goddard one House Lot . . . containing sixty feet in front and Ninety feet in depth, and one Garden Lot containing Five Acres . . . and one Farm . . . To have and to Hold the said Fifty Acres of Land."[6]

A map dating from 1735 shows the general regional pattern of land settlement as it then existed (Fig. 78). The town proper is the tiny rectangle near the river shown divided into six parts. To the north and east are the five-acre garden lots. Then come the farms of forty-four and a fraction acres. Finally, the large squares are the 500-acre estates granted to persons of means who would emigrate to the colony at their own expense.

The common does not show clearly on the map of 1735. But a redrawing of the early division of land around Savannah shows its outlines (Fig. 79). This map also reveals another unusual feature—the triangular shape of the five-acre garden lots, indicated by the dotted lines running diagonally through the squares which measure ten acres in area. In modern Savannah a few diagonal streets exist which developed from the original lanes or roads leading to the garden plots and following the old boundary lines. Here certainly is an example of a true regional plan—one quite as highly organized as Mountgomery's Azilia, but without some of the impractical features of that earlier scheme.

Most remarkable, however, was Oglethorpe's plan for the town lots, streets, and open spaces in Savannah itself (Fig. 80). As the

[6] As quoted in Charles C. Jones, *The History of Georgia*, Boston, 1833, I, 156-60.

Figure 78. Map of the County of Savannah, Georgia: 1735

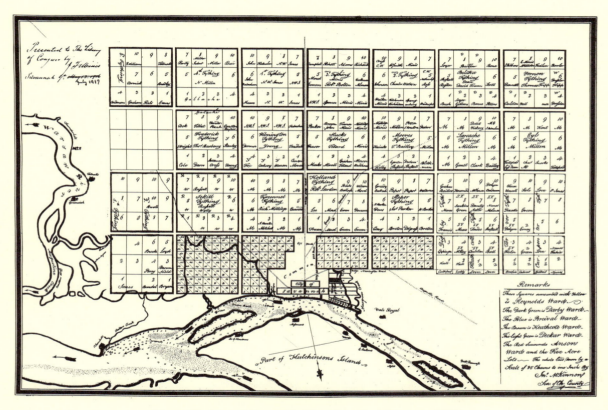

Figure 79. Map of Savannah, Georgia and vicinity: ca. 1800

basic unit he created a number of wards, each consisting of forty house lots, 60 by 90 feet. Four tithings of ten lots each constituted a further subdivision of the town. At the center of each ward Oglethorpe provided an open square 315 by 270 feet. Fronting the square on two sides were trustee lots, set aside for churches, stores, places of assembly, and similar uses. Main streets were 75 feet wide, with minor streets half that dimension. Lanes 22 1/2 feet wide provided access to the rear of all house lots.

On this admirable pattern Savannah gradually developed into a small town. In 1745 the *London Magazine* could report that it "has very near 350 houses . . . beside the public Buildings, which are, the store-house of the Trustees, an handsome Court-House, a Gaol, a Guard-House, and a public Wharf, projected out many feet into the River. The Streets are wide and commodious. . . . Many of the Houses are very large and handsome, built generally of Wood, but some Foundations are brick'd. . . ."[7] By the Revolution the population of Savannah exceeded 3,000 persons, and the city ranked as the twentieth largest town in the American colonies.

The Georgia trustees were anxious to develop other settlements, and they extended their charitable aid to a group of Protestant Salzburgers who had been driven from their home through religious persecutions. The first of this group arrived in Savannah in 1734. For them Oglethorpe selected a site for a town several miles north of Savannah. There, at Ebenezer, the Salzburgers cleared the land and laid out their community. The site proved unsatisfactory, and in 1736

[7] *London Magazine* (1745), p. 603.

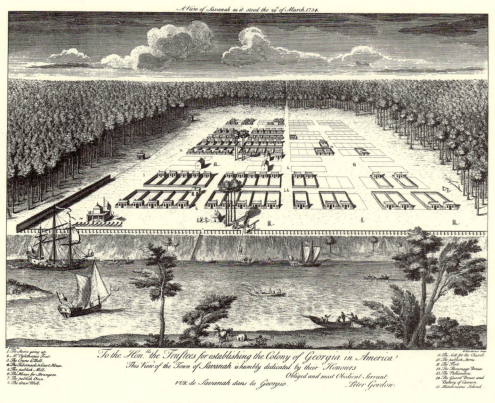

Figure 80. View of Savannah, Georgia: 1734

Oglethorpe granted them a new one a few miles to the east. Here New Ebenezer was planned, following the same pattern that had proved successful at Savannah (Fig. 81). The town common lay to the westward of the town lots, the five-acre garden lots were along the north and south boundaries, with the farm lots ("Plantationes") beyond.

The Georgia trustees also settled a group of Scots south of Savannah near St. Simons Island in 1735. Called New Inverness, or Darien, this tiny community had a single open square surrounded by four ranges of town lots set out like one of the wards in Savannah or Ebenezer. Darien appears in the lower left-hand corner of an undated map of St. Simons Island which shows another town—Frederica—planned in 1735 (Fig. 82). Much of the island was divided into farm lots on a pattern similar to but on a much larger scale than the town of Savannah. The inner boundary of the Frederica garden lots is a line describing one-half of a dodecagon. Between this line and the town proper appears a semi-circular open space approximately 1,000 feet wide, which apparently was the town common. The town itself appears on this map as the small symmetrical trapezoid above the fort at the bend in the river. More detailed plans of the town reveal that here Oglethorpe did not employ the Savannah model. Frederica, however, was designed as a garrison community to strengthen the defenses against the Spanish. This difference in function perhaps explains the difference in form.

There were other communities planned during this period. As Oglethorpe reported in 1737, Augusta was founded, and "there were several villages settled by gentlemen at their expense." The villages re-

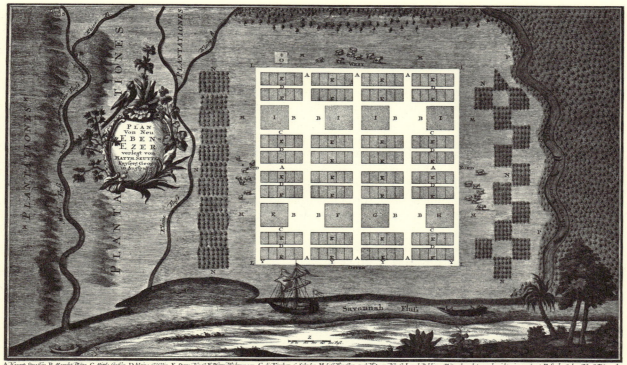

Figure 81. Plan of New Ebenezer, Georgia: 1747

Figure 82. Map of St. Simons Island, Georgia: ca. 1740

ferred to probably included such minor settlements as Josephs Town, Abercorn, Thunderbolt, Highgate, and Hampstead. Here the plots of land were wedge shaped, radiating outward from a central point where the houses probably were grouped in a small village cluster. A similar pattern had been earlier employed by William Penn in establishing the plan of farm villages near Philadelphia. An even earlier example was Gravesend on Long Island. Quite possibly the design of the Georgia villages was based on these earlier experiments. But the derivation of the Savannah plan, as employed also at Ebenezer and Darien, cannot be explained so easily. Oglethorpe combined both tradition and invention in his town planning venture in an effective manner which deserves further discussion.

It seems highly improbable that the layout of these towns resulted from some inspiration of the moment. Oglethorpe and his fellow trustees carefully planned all other aspects of their enterprise, and it seems unlikely they would have done otherwise with the layout of their first city. Perhaps they prepared at least preliminary plans before the first boatload of emigrants left England. Certainly they had available to them a considerable body of previous town building experience both in the colonies and in England from which to draw. In addition, Mountgomery's abortive plan for the very area the trustees proposed to settle must have been thoroughly reviewed.

The most obvious parallel in the New World was Penn's colony of Pennsylvania. The plan of Philadelphia had been widely circulated in England and would have been familiar to the Georgia trustees. The similarity of the agricultural villages in the two colonies is suggestive, but the plan of Philadelphia hardly seems to resemble that of Savannah except in the grid arrangement of streets. More likely is that Oglethorpe may have adopted the idea of Philadelphia's "liberty lands," and used this as his model for the Savannah garden and farm lots, of course making the divisions geometrically perfect instead of imitating the irregular boundaries used by Penn in allotting farm tracts to the purchasers of Philadelphia town lots.

Another possible influence were the towns planned in northern Ireland at the beginning of the 17th century by the London Companies on land seized by the Crown from the Irish lords. This was referred to in a tract published anonymously in 1732 and attributed to Oglethorpe as "a precedent of our own for planting Colonies, which perhaps, in Part, or in the Whole, may be worthy of our Imitation."[8] The chief cities of this experiment in urban and regional planning were Londonderry and Coleraine. Significantly, the central square of Coleraine is an almost exact duplicate in shape and in its pattern of access streets to that of the several open spaces at Savannah.

One contemporary account of the reasons for the numerous open squares of the Savannah plan appears in a tract published in 1744 by Francis Moore, who sailed with the band of colonists bound for the new town of Frederica in 1735. Moore first described the system of town, garden, and farm lots used at Savannah and then added this statement:

". . . every forty houses in town make a ward, to which four square

[8] *A New and Accurate Account of the Provinces of South Carolina*, London, 1732.

miles in the country belong; each ward has a constable, and under him four tithing men. Where the town lands end, the villages begin; four villages make a ward without, which depends upon one of the wards within the town. The use of this is, in case a war should happen, the villages without may have places in the town, to bring their cattle and families into for refuge, and to that purpose there is a square left in every ward, big enough for the outwards to encamp in."[9]

This is an ingenious explanation and one that cannot wholly be disregarded. Moore's account of the Georgia colony, however, came at a time when the trustees' land and governmental policies were under attack by critics in the colony and in England and was designed both as a vindication of the land policies and as a piece of promotional literature. His description of the Savannah squares as a place of refuge for settlers outside the town may well have been an attempt to allay the fears of potential colonists apprehensive about Indian raids.

The plan of Savannah has also been attributed to a design by Robert Castell in his volume, *Villas of the Ancients*. Oglethorpe's name appears as one of the patrons of this book, and it was Castell's plight, among others, when he was confined in debtors prison, that awakened Oglethorpe's interest and sympathy in prison reform. But Castell's volume contains no town plan; what does appear are drawings of classical villas surrounded by neat rectangular garden *parterres*. This grid pattern of solids and voids is similar to the Savannah plan,

[9] Francis Moore, *A Voyage to Georgia Begun in the Year 1735* (London, 1744), reprinted in Georgia Historical Society, *Collections*, Vol. I, Savannah, 1840.

but this scarcely establishes a valid claim for Castell as the source of inspiration for the Savannah plan.

Mountgomery's design doubtless had some influence. The scale is different, but the proportions of open space are almost identical if we compare all of Azilia with the much smaller area occupied by the Savannah town lots. It is not inconceivable that the Georgia trustees simply reduced the size of the Azilia plan in keeping with the more modest land grants contemplated for their own colony.

Both Mountgomery and the sponsors of the Georgia colony were well aware of the emerging pattern of land subdivision in Georgian London. During the preceding century a series of speculative building developments surrounding existing open spaces or newly created private residential squares had sprung into existence. It is worth recalling that Penn's surveyor described the four neighborhood squares in Philadelphia "to be for the like uses, as the Moore-fields in London." At that time Leicester Fields, Covent Garden, Lincoln's Inn Fields, Bloomsbury Square, and Soho Square had also been developed. By the time of the Georgia colony a number of new residential squares had been created: Red Lion Square (1684), St. James's Square (1684); Grosvenor Square (1695), Hanover Square (1712), and Cavendish Square (1720), among others. John Roque's great map of London, begun in 1737 and published in 1746 is the best graphic record of this new pattern taking shape in 18th-century London (Fig. 83).

Some of the Georgia trustees were active participants in developing these squares. Sir William Heathcote built what is now Chatham

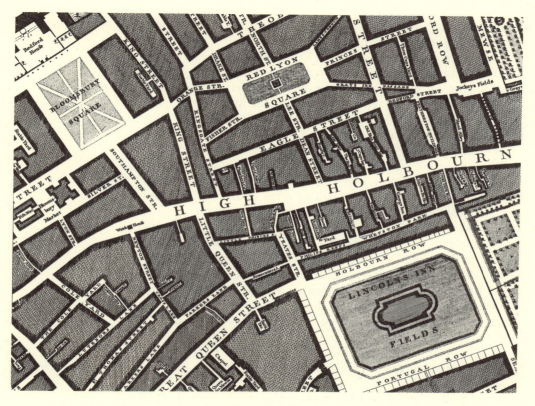

Figure 83. Plan of a Portion of London, England: 1746

House in St. James's Square in 1734. General Carpenter and several fellow officers were among the first residents of Hanover Square. The plan of Hanover Square, one of the last to be laid out before the colonization of Georgia, is, like the square of Coleraine, strikingly similar in form and size to those of Savannah. It is difficult not to conclude that the squares of Georgian London furnished the chief models after which the plans of Savannah and the other towns of the colony were fashioned.

Finally, in view of Oglethorpe's military background, the treatises dealing with castrametation or the art of military encampment must not be overlooked. These were standard works that may well have been consulted by Prince Eugene, under whom Oglethorpe once served. In one of them, written by an Englishman, Robert Barret, in 1598, appears a model encampment plan which closely resembles Savannah's layout.

Yet having duly noted all these possible sources in town planning tradition, one must grant that Oglethorpe, aided perhaps by a person or persons unknown to us, fashioned a new community pattern out of these older models. The Georgia settlements were real innovations in urban design. The basic module—ward, open square, sites for community facilities, and local streets—provided not only an unusually attractive, convenient, and intimate environment but also served as a practical device for governing urban expansion without formless sprawl. These little neighborhood units, scaled to human size, must also have promoted a social pattern desirable for a frontier settlement where cooperation and neighborly assistance were essential for survival.

For many years the six wards of early Savannah provided sufficient space for the newly stabilized population. Then, following the Revolution, Savannah began a steady expansion (Fig. 84). Each increment of growth faithfully retained the original concept of the Oglethorpe plan. Development took place by the orderly addition of one or more ward units when additional accommodations were needed. All but one of these squares remain today and give to modern Savannah a distinctive character enjoyed by no other American city. Not until the mid-19th century did this system of urban growth give way to the more usual pattern of gridiron extensions unrelieved by public open space.

The explanation is a simple one and not without lessons for modern planning in America. The common land which originally had separated the town proper from the garden lots passed to municipal control. Instead of permitting indiscriminate sales of this public resource, town officials released it for development purposes only after establishing the pattern of streets, building lots, open square, and public or semi-public sites as originally conceived by Oglethorpe. Like Stockholm, Amsterdam, and many other well-planned modern European cities, Savannah employed the only effective way of securing planned development. By 1856 the supply of common land was exhausted. Thereafter private decisions as to the form of urban growth prevailed, and the desire for individual profit ran counter to the social goals which had previously guided the city's expansion.

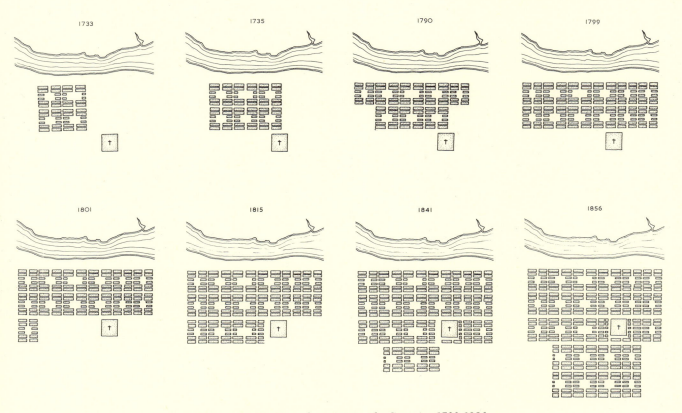

Figure 84. The Growth of Savannah, Georgia: 1733-1856

This history of a century and a quarter of controlled and planned urban growth is all the more remarkable because elsewhere on the continent municipal authorities and land developers alike ignored the spirit of the many fine plans established during the colonial period. At Philadelphia, to select only one example, town extensions took place without the care and attention that Penn had devoted to the initial layout. At one time even the four neighborhood squares disappeared, being used for brick yards and burying grounds.

Only Savannah escaped for a time the speculative mania for developing the maximum number of building lots on a given tract that characterized much of the 19th century in America. A view of the city looking toward the river slightly more than a century ago shows the superb character the town had attained (Fig. 85). When James Silk Buckingham visited Savannah in 1840 he was quick to note the unique qualities of the city that set it apart from all others: ". . . there are no less than eighteen large squares, with grass-plots and trees, in the very heart of the city, disposed at equal distances from each other in the greatest order; while every principal street is lined on each side with rows of trees, and some of the broader streets have also an avenue of trees running down their centre. . . ."[10]

One of the great misfortunes of American town planning was that the Savannah plan seemingly exercised no influence on the layout of towns outside Georgia. Even there, only Brunswick, planned in 1770, followed the novel and effective neighborhood pattern. The peripheral

[10] James Silk Buckingham, *The Slave States of America*, London, 1842, I, 118-19.

Figure 85. View of Savannah, Georgia: 1855

location of the city with respect to the westward movement of population undoubtedly accounts for the slight impact of Savannah's plan on subsequent urban projects elsewhere. Had Savannah been located, as were Philadelphia and New York, on the main routes leading to the interior, at least some of our midwestern cities might have achieved some of the charm and urbanity that still marks the Savannah of James Oglethorpe.

For the first century and a half following the English colonization of North America the Appalachian barrier and the menace of unfriendly Indians restricted the growth of settlement. Population increase, however, generated pressures for development of the lands beyond the mountains. Slowly, and with many interruptions because of wars and Indian raids, an irregular penetration of the mountain region began. Except on the friendlier eastern slopes, where isolated farmsteads might be maintained with less risk of Indian attack, the first settlements were in compact and tightly clustered communities designed for ease of defense. Only after these initial dangers seemed safely past did other and more spacious urban plans become common. Thus where there were people there were towns. Some were destined for oblivion, while others survived to become important cities.

The Town at the Forks of the Ohio

The defeat of the French, who had controlled the Mississippi and Ohio valleys, opened the path for settlement in western Pennsylvania. Easily the most important site existed at the confluence of the Monongahela and Allegheny rivers, where the French had constructed Fort Duquesne. In 1758 this fell to a British force and received the name of Fort Pitt. By 1760, according to one early account, there were 200 houses clustered around the fort grouped in a tiny grid of rectangular blocks fronting on the Monongahela.

John Penn, who had succeeded to the proprietorship of this land, greatly expanded the little settlement in 1784. He established a new base line parallel with the Allegheny River, surveying two streets, Penn and Liberty, in a roughly east-west direction (Fig. 86). The old grid settlement was then extended in both directions so as to fill most of the triangular area between the rivers. A courthouse square on the pattern of that at Philadelphia was set aside near the center of the newly enlarged town. Liberty Street was intended as the most important, with a width of 80 feet. Other streets were 60 and 40 feet wide, with a number of alleys 10 and 20 feet across.

Pittsburgh, as the city came to be called, rapidly developed as the place of departure for settlers bound for new homes in the valley of the Ohio. By far the easiest method of travel was by water, and dozens of flatboats, rafts, and keelboats started the journey down the river each week from the city. Braddock's Road from Baltimore and Washington and Forbes' Road, leading from Philadelphia, both terminated at Pittsburgh, and by the early years of the 19th century the town was a busy and prosperous community.

Additional expansion soon took place. A detailed plan of Pittsburgh and vicinity in 1815 reveals urban growth along the rivers beyond the confines of the Penn plan as well as completely new communities that had been laid out in the region to share the trade and manufacturing wealth of the area (Fig. 87). Of particular interest is the town of Allegheny, planned in a neat square of thirty-two blocks, with an open central green four blocks in size. A common surrounded the town on all sides, beyond which lay the garden or farm

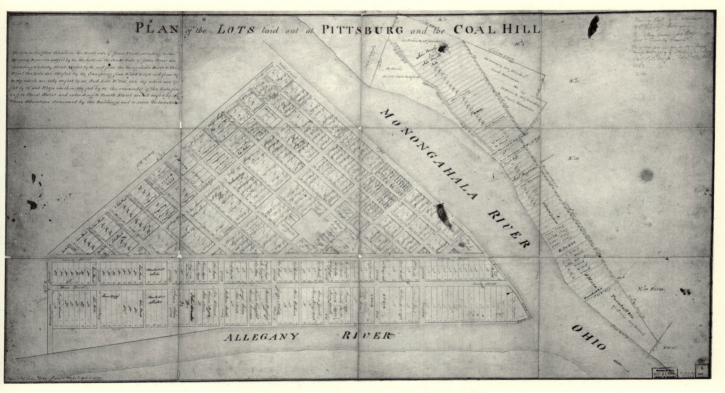

Figure 86. Plan of Pittsburgh, Pennsylvania: 1787

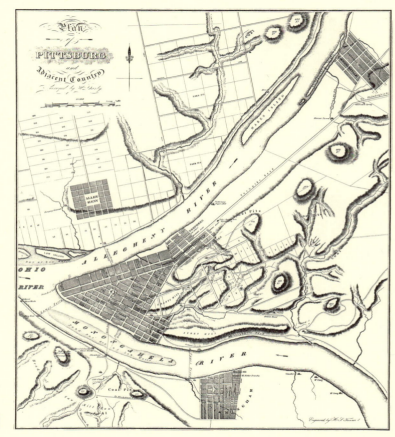

Figure 87. Plan of Pittsburgh, Pennsylvania: ca. 1815

lots of the community. Land sales here began in 1788, starting a rivalry between Allegheny and Pittsburgh that was not to end until the newer settlement became part of Pittsburgh many years later.

The Allegheny plan bears a marked resemblance to that of New Haven, and the common lands and farm lot division certainly has a New England touch. Whether David Redick, who surveyed the site in 1784 by order of the Supreme Executive Council of Pennsylvania, knew of the New Haven plan and consciously imitated it is uncertain. The plan is also of interest because it resulted from public rather than private initiative. Pennsylvania had reserved the area for land grants to reward veterans of the Revolutionary War, and the planning of the town was thus carried out as a governmental venture. This was not the only such public new town developed by that state. Not far down the Ohio from Pittsburgh stood another reserved site planned in 1791 by Pennsylvania as the city of Beaver with a central square occupying the space of four blocks and four additional one-block public open spaces, one at each corner of the town.

The later development of Pittsburgh lies beyond the scope of this work, but its growth was steady and at times rapid. With the construction of the National Road to the west Pittsburgh lost some of its importance as a stopover and outfitting station for pioneer emigrants, but coal and iron, canal and railroad provided a new basis for prosperity. In the era of mercantile and industrial expansion that followed, however, urban growth proceeded with little attention to sound planning and orderly development. The drabness of its endless gridiron extensions stamped on the rugged terrain of the site was matched by the conditions of the atmosphere produced by coal-powered industry. When James Silk Buckingham visited there for a few days in 1840 he was moved to describe Pittsburgh as "the most smoky and sooty town it has ever been my lot to behold. The houses are blackened with it, the streets are made filthy, and the garments and persons of all whom you meet are soiled and made dingy by its influence."[1]

The Towns in the Hills of Kentucky

Although the British government proclaimed the trans-Appalachian region closed to further settlement at the conclusion of the French and Indian War, this scarcely deterred the westward movement. Small bands of settlers as early as 1769 hacked their way through the heavily wooded ridge and valley region of western Carolina and eastern Tennessee to establish rude communities on the Wautauga River. Among these early arrivals was Daniel Boone, who had already explored much of the back country. From Wautauga, Boone resumed his early explorations of Kentucky, and his stories of fertile river valleys of the Kentucky, Cumberland, and the Licking rivers soon led to attempts at settlement.

Late in 1774, Judge Richard Henderson of North Carolina formed the Transylvania Company to purchase land from the Indians and sell it for white settlement. With Boone's help Henderson was able to purchase from the Cherokees a vast tract amounting to about half of the present state of Kentucky. Boone and an advance party set out

[1] James Silk Buckingham, *The Eastern and Western States of America*, London, 1842, II, 185.

through the Cumberland Gap for a site on the Kentucky River that he had previously noted. They erected a few temporary log huts, and when Henderson arrived a few weeks later a permanent settlement was established nearby on somewhat higher ground. This was first named Fort Boone, later changed to Boonesborough.

From a plan drawn by Henderson in 1775 a conjectural sketch has been prepared which shows twenty-six cabins arranged in a rectangle (Fig. 88). The cabin walls formed a stockade about 260 feet long and 180 feet wide. Two-story block houses with overhanging upper floors formed the corners of the fort. Not everyone in the settlement lived in the enclosure. There were a few isolated cabins on farmsteads located in forest clearings, and some settlers continued to live in the temporary settlement located in the hollow below. But here was the store, here families gathered for social or religious occasions or at times of Indian raids, here new settlers first arrived and found temporary housing, here was the land office of the Transylvania Company, and here was the "capital" of the newly proclaimed government of Transylvania. In short, this rough, log-enclosed quadrangle performed the historic functions for which towns throughout the world have been founded.

Despite Indian raids that began in 1776 and increased in frequency and violence, Boonesborough maintained its precarious existence. The famous siege in the fall of 1778 marked the peak of Indian hostility, but this too failed to dislodge the settlers from their tenuous foothold in Kentucky territory. Although Boonesborough was finally created a town by the Virginia legislature in 1779, the community that

Figure 88. View of Fort Boonesborough, Kentucky: 1778

survived the war could not endure in peace. Kentucky became a state in 1792 with Boonesborough as one of its chief towns. But by 1810 it had declined in size as more favorable sites elsewhere became available for settlement, and in a few years it disappeared altogether.

Lexington, first settled in 1779, was more fortunate. Here, too, the first town took the form of a stockade enclosure or "station" from which Indian attacks were successfully resisted. Even while the fighting continued the settlers petitioned the General Assembly of Virginia for a formal land grant, submitting with their application a plan of the town they proposed to develop. This was a traditional gridiron with three principal parallel streets 82 feet wide intersected by seven cross streets 50 feet in width. At the center of the town was a two-acre open square set aside for a courthouse.

Although Lexington lacked river transportation, it quickly became a prosperous settlement. The rich limestone soil of the surrounding bluegrass country and the infant Transylvania College made Lexington an agricultural trading center and the focus of higher learning for Kentucky. For a time it was the largest and most important town of the west, but after the turn of the century its rate of growth failed to keep pace with those cities more strategically situated for industrial and commercial development.

Lexington's fame and the settlement of other parts of the new state lured land speculators seeking quick fortunes in town lot promotions. Near the end of the 18th century a group of speculators, probably English, set about promoting land sales in two towns which existed only on paper (Fig. 89). Both Franklinville and Lystra, plans of

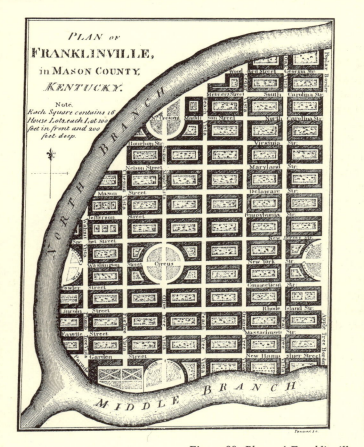

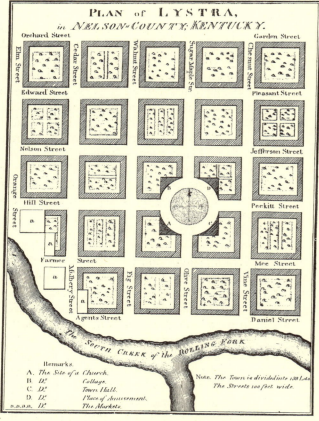

Figure 89. Plans of Franklinville and Lystra, Kentucky: 1796

which date from 1796, were described in glowing phrases and represented as having town halls, churches, colleges, theaters, and all other essentials and luxuries of great cities. Both were designed as elaborate communities with squares, circles, and other monumental architectural features. It is quite likely that not even a surveyor's stake graced the sites of these towns, and any purchasers of town lots who ventured to their locations quickly realized that they had been duped. The mania for land speculation in town lands that was soon to sweep the midwest thus had an early start in the hills of Kentucky.

Franklinville and Lystra were the forerunners for hundreds of similar speculative enterprises. The Land Ordinance of the Continental Congress in 1785 made available land in the public domain. Although early sales were few in number, some settlement did take place in the first seven ranges of townships in eastern Ohio. Soon more favorable purchase terms were extended, requiring a smaller initial payment and a longer period in which to pay the balance. As land thus became easier to acquire, speculation in both farms and town lots developed as a major activity on the frontier. Francis Baily, on his travels through the Ohio valley in 1796 and 1797, observed the operations of one such speculator:

"In order to found a colony at first, he holds out an encouragement to settlers by giving them a town lot and four acres of ground for nothing. . . . This he does only to the first twelve or twenty that may offer themselves. . . . In order to manage this concern to the best advantage, the land-owners will always take care and not sell all their land *contiguous to each other*, but only at *certain distances*, so that the whole face of it may be cultivated, and the intermediate uncultivated parts consequently rise in value. . . .

"The town he had laid out at right angles, nearly on Penn's plan, with a square in the middle, which he told me, with a degree of exulting pride, he intended for a court-house, or for some public building for the meeting of the legislature; for he has already fallen into that flattering idea which every founder of a new settlement entertains, that his town will at some future time be the seat of government."[2]

Another English observer, Joseph Briggs, emphasized the more fraudulent aspects of speculative town planning:

"A speculator makes out a plan of a city with its streets, squares, and avenues, quays and wharves, public buildings and monuments. The streets are lotted, the houses numbered, and the squares called after Franklin or Washington. The city itself has some fine name, perhaps Troy or Antioch. This is engraved and forthwith hung up in as many steamboats and hotels as the speculator's interest may command. All this time the city is a mere vision. Its very site is on the fork of some river in the far West, five hundred miles beyond civilization, probably under water or surrounded by dense forests and impassable swamps. Emigrants have been repeatedly defrauded out of their money by transactions so extremely gross as hardly to be credited."[3]

[2] Francis Baily, *Journal of a Tour in Unsettled Parts of North America in 1796 & 1797*, London, 1856, p. 215.

[3] As quoted by Walter Havighurst, *Wilderness for Sale*, New York, 1956, p. 106.

Newspapers usually enthusiastically supported local efforts at town promotion, often being owned by the speculator himself. But on occasion, when nearby communities threatened to attract attention or when local excesses became too pronounced, editorial condemnation resulted. A favored device was satire, although this of necessity had to be exceedingly broad to distinguish it from the exaggerated claims of the real town promoters. One paper, with mock seriousness, announced in the 1820's the planning of the city of "Ne Plus Ultra." This town was described as having streets one mile wide, blocks of one square mile, a vast forested mall, and two main streets, "one from the south pole to Symnes's hole in the north, and another from Pekin to Jerusalem."

The most elaborate plan of this area and period—one which eclipsed even the designs of Franklinville and Lystra—was that for the proposed town of Hygeia on the Kentucky side of the Ohio River opposite Cincinnati (Fig. 90). Here, in 1827, William Bullock, an English traveller and lecturer, purchased a tract of land for "a small town of retirement" which he "determined to have . . . laid out to the best possible advantage, with professional assistance. . . ."

On his return to England, Bullock engaged John Buomarotti Papworth, self-styled "Architect to the King of Wirtemburg," as town planner. Papworth's plan for Hygeia shows in considerable detail a proposed town incorporating most of the building types and plan forms developed in England during the preceding century. Detached villas, semi-detached houses, and terrace dwellings all appear. The four small and two larger residential squares were typical planning layouts of the Georgian and Regency builders. While these are skill-

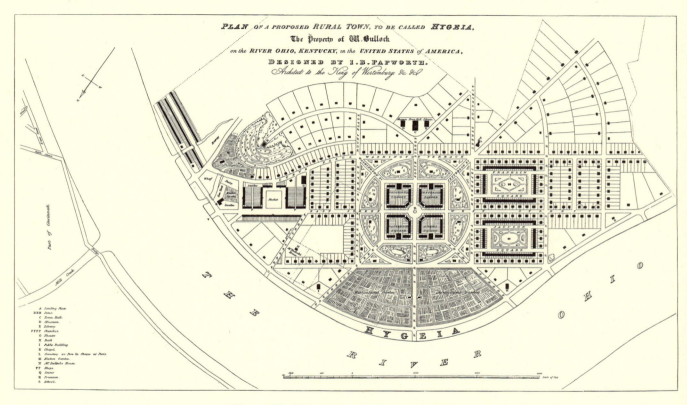

Figure 90. Plan of Hygeia, Kentucky: 1827

fully handled, the street pattern appears more as an abstract design than a functional system. The four diagonals lead from the outer corners of the small squares to nowhere, and, with no real focus of architectural interest at either end, these streets are largely meaningless. Nor is there any real civic center in the town. Museum, town hall, and library seem relatively isolated at one end of the long street leading upward from the river. The market place at the eastern edge of the town appears unrelated to other features of the plan. Of some interest, however, is the design for the cemetery, laid out in the romantic fashion of English landscape design. This anticipated by a year or so the famous rural cemetery of Mount Auburn in Cambridge, Massachusetts, which had a number of imitators and whose style was to be adopted after the middle of the 19th century in the planning of large public parks.

Although Mrs. Frances Trollope admired Bullock's "taste and art," the Hygeia speculation proved a failure. Perhaps the Baroque design seemed too advanced for the simple river settlers or even the more sophisticated Cincinnatians. In any event, Hygeia joined Lystra and Franklinville on the growing list of speculative paper towns that failed to live up to the inflated claims of their sponsors.

The Towns of the Great Falls of the Ohio

One of the Ohio Valley's great cities, Louisville, had its origins in the 18th century. It was in 1778 that George Rogers Clark reached the great rapids of the Ohio and settled some of his soldiers and their families on Corn Island. This first settlement took the form of a typical frontier station. Later, after Clark achieved his military victories over the British in Indiana and Illinois, the settlers moved to the south bank of the river and erected a similar stockaded village surrounded by farms and gardens. In April 1779, the inhabitants formally organized a town government, agreed on a town plan for the land east of the fort along the river, and, at the suggestion of Clark, adopted the name of Louisville in honor of the French king.

An early plan of the town attributed to Clark has survived (Fig. 91). This shows all the land between the present Main Street and the river as public property. In addition, another strip of public land extended along the entire length of the town on its southern boundary. One account states that Clark intended to repeat this open strip of common land after every third street as the town was extended to the south. Unfortunately, this unique pattern was not to be realized.

Louisville was forced to sell its common lands to satisfy a debt owed by John Connolly, the original owner of the site, to one John Campbell. Campbell exercised his influence with the Virginia legislature to secure the passage of a series of curious laws which in effect made the town liable for Connolly's obligations. For $3,300 the town disposed of its lands and lost an opportunity to retain a feature in its design which would have been as attractive and functional as it would have been unusual. That some attempt was made to salvage the linear common feature of the first plan is indicated on a map of 1836, which shows the remnants of the old common or a start of a new one located one tier of lots south of the first location (Fig. 92). This same drawing shows regular parallel strips of outlots of five, ten, and

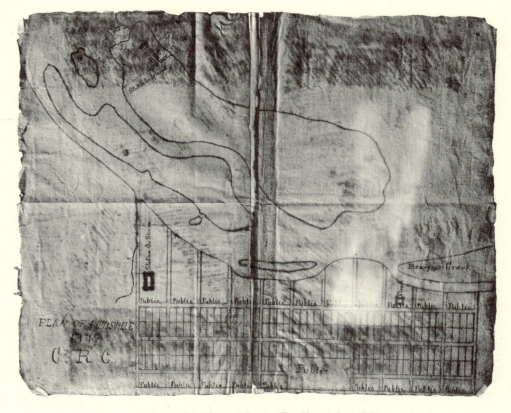

Figure 91. Plan of Louisville, Kentucky: 1779

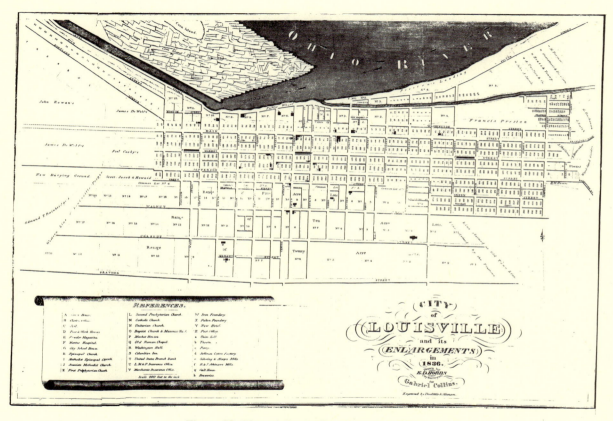

Figure 92. Plan of Louisville, Kentucky: 1836

twenty acres. Like the common, these agricultural field divisions have given way with the growth of the city far beyond the boundaries ever contemplated by Clark.

When Francis Baily visited Louisville in 1797 he noted that the city contained some 200 houses. He also described Clarksville, "a little village consisting of about twenty houses," on the opposite shore two miles down river. Soon other settlements sprang up in the vicinity, each with hopes of becoming the metropolis that would one day surely develop at such an important site. Portland, Shippingsport, and New Albany were all laid out with this possibility in view. The canal which was required to ensure reliable river transportation, was finally located to favor Louisville, and its rivals were soon outstripped in population and in commercial and industrial importance.

Across the river from Louisville lay Jeffersonville, another city of unusual design. This Indiana town, like its Kentucky sister community, was destined to witness the ultimate substitution for this novel layout of another of quite conventional quality. The circumstances of its founding and eventual redevelopment are of considerable interest. No less a personage than Thomas Jefferson was responsible for its first plan, at least in its general character. The peculiar form of the city resulted from a suggestion apparently first made by Jefferson to William Henry Harrison, the Governor of Indiana Territory, who, on August 6, 1802, wrote the following letter to the President:

"When I had the honour to see you in Philadelphia in the spring of the year 1800 you were pleased to recommend to me a plan for a Town. . . . As the laws of this Territory have given to the Governor the power to designate the seats of Justice for the Counties, and as the choice . . . was fixed upon a spot where there had been no town laid out, I had an opportunity at once of gratifying them—of paying respect to your recommendation and of conforming to my own inclination—The proprietor of the land having acceded to my proposals a Town has been laid out with each alternate square to remain vacant forever (excepting one Range of squares upon the River)—and I have taken the liberty to call it Jeffersonville. . . ."[4]

The distinctive feature of the plan, as Harrison pointed out, was the alternating pattern of open squares and subdivided blocks (Fig. 93). Jefferson had conceived this system of urban development as a measure to prevent yellow fever, a disease then plaguing American cities. Jefferson, in a letter to his friend the Comte de Volney, described his plan and its advantages:

"Take, for instance, the chequer board for a plan. Let the black squares only be building squares, and the white ones be left open, in turf and trees. Every square of houses will be surrounded by four open squares, and every house will front an open square. The atmosphere of such a town would be like that of the country, insusceptible of the miasmata which produce yellow fever."[5]

In one respect the plan of Jeffersonville departed from the ideas

[4] Letter from Harrison to Jefferson, August 6, 1802, U.S. Department of State, *The Territorial Papers of the United States*, Vol. VII, *The Territory of Indiana, 1800-1810*, Washington, 1939, pp. 66-67.

[5] Letter from Jefferson to C.F.C. de Volney, February 8, 1805, in A. A. Liscomb and A. L. Bergh, eds., *The Writings of Thomas Jefferson*, XI, 66-67.

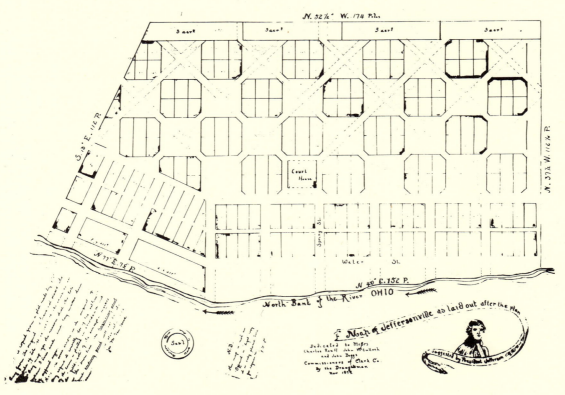

Figure 93. Plan of Jeffersonville, Indiana: 1802

of the President. Diagonal streets were introduced cutting through the open squares so that the gridiron street system ran at an angle of forty-five degrees to the checkerboard axis of the city blocks. Perhaps John Gwathmey, who laid out the town, wished to employ the most up-to-date features of civic design, presumably as then embodied in the radial plan for Washington. Even with the streets destroying much of the open space the plan of Jeffersonville was a remarkable achievement in town design. Whether the repeating open squares would have produced the results that Jefferson hoped cannot be known, since within fifteen years of the town's founding the proprietors obtained legislation allowing them to replat the town into a conventional grid pattern, perhaps the first example of urban redevelopment in America.

The motives for this action were doubtless economic. At a time when there had developed a lively trade in town lots in the vicinity and when Jeffersonville seemed a likely candidate as the chief metropolis of the Ohio falls, all those squares lying idle and unimproved doubtless became too much of a temptation to resist. Thus vanished a variation on the gridiron plan which rivalled that earlier adopted at Savannah in potential interest and effectiveness. The Jeffersonian system was to be used a few years later at Jackson, the new capital of Mississippi, but there· too the open spaces were eventually used for building sites, and few traces of this feature of the city's original plan have survived.

Marietta on the Muskingum

While the Land Ordinance of 1785 provided for sales of land in the public domain in townships of 36 square miles or sections of

640 acres, Congress was soon approached by groups wishing to purchase much larger tracts. Revenues obtained under the Land Ordinance system proved to be far less than expected, and these new proposals for wholesale acquisition seemed to offer opportunities for obtaining badly needed funds for the operation of governmental affairs.

Most of the would-be purchasers saw a chance for speculation in western lands with small risk and great potential gain. One of the first of such proposals, however, came from quite a different group. This was the Ohio Company of Associates, a band of army veterans chiefly from Massachusetts but including persons from Rhode Island and Connecticut. The Ohio Company organized in 1786 under the leadership of Colonel Rufus Putnam and sent the Reverend Manasseh Cutler as its agent to negotiate the terms of the proposed land purchase with Congress. By the fall of 1787 Cutler had secured congressional approval for the purchase of 1 1/2 million acres of land at $1.00 an acre, with a portion of the purchase price to be paid within three months and the remainder in installments.

In order to gain sanction for this departure from established land policy, Cutler was forced to enter privately into an agreement with Colonel William Duer, secretary of the Board of the Treasury. Duer pointed out to Cutler that Congress was badly in need of funds and would be more likely to approve a request for a much larger tract than needed by the Ohio Company. Cutler and Duer reached an agreement, the exact nature of which remains obscure, for the Ohio Company to petition for some 5 million acres. Duer and his associates, usually referred to as the Scioto Company, would then take over

3 1/2 million acres for their own purpose. It was this larger area that Congress agreed to sell.

The Scioto scheme was an out-and-out land speculation. The Ohio Company project, on the other hand, was a legitimate settlement scheme. Most of its members intended to take up land in the purchase and to establish their homes in the west. The plan for settlement coincided with the Ordinance of 1787, which established the framework of government in the Northwest Territory, and the early history of the Ohio Company's activities in Ohio is closely related to the first civil government under United States jurisdiction beyond the Appalachians. It would have been difficult for either enterprise to succeed without the other, and the speedy settlement of the west with the orderly formation of territorial and then state government was due in considerable measure to the Ohio Company and its leaders.

The planning of the chief city in the territory received early attention. A map of Ohio attributed to Manassah Cutler and probably dating from 1788 shows an inset plan of the "City to be built on the Muskingum River," although its details differ somewhat from those described in the proceedings of the Ohio Company at its meeting of August 30, 1787, the day after its members learned of congressional approval of their land purchase proposal. At that time the directors resolved to set aside nearly 6,000 acres at the mouth of the Muskingum River for "a City & Commons." They further directed,

"That within the said Tract and in the most eligible situation there be appropriated for a City, sixty squares of three hundred &

sixty feet by three hundred & sixty feet each, in an oblong form. . . .

"That four of said squares, be reserved for public uses, and the remaining fifty-six divided into house Lots. That each square contain twelve house lots of sixty feet front, and One hundred feet depth. . . .

"That contiguous to, and in the vicinity of the above tract there be laid off one Thousand Lots of Sixty-four acres each . . . which as the city lots, shall be considered a part of each proprietary share."[6]

At a later meeting the size of the city lots was increased to 90 by 180 feet. Provision was also made for 10-foot alleys through each block, and the central street was directed to be laid out with a width of 150 feet. These details were to be modified later when the actual site was selected.

Early in April 1788 an advance party led by Rufus Putnam arrived at the mouth of the Muskingum River on the Ohio. Like many other locations throughout Ohio, the spot had previously been occupied by the early mound-building Indians. Along the high ground parallel to the Muskingum stretched two great quadrangles and other geometrical earthworks, including a high circular mound. Connecting the largest of the rectangular enclosures with the river ran a broad, straight, avenue-like processional way.

In designing the city, Putnam incorporated some of the mound constructions in a most interesting manner, indicating his sensitivity to the strange remains built by the site's earlier occupants (Fig. 94).

[6] A. B. Hulbert, ed., *The Records of the Original Proceedings of the Ohio Company*, Ohio Company Series, Vol. I, Marietta, 1917, pp. 15-16.

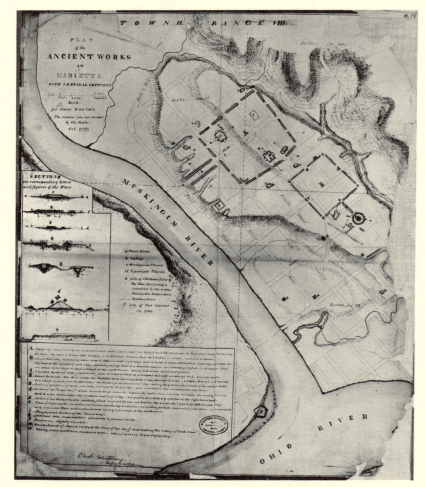

Figure 94. Plan of Marietta, Ohio: 1837

An early plan of Marietta, as the town was named, shows how Putnam and his helpers adapted the general directions of the Ohio Company to the peculiarities of the site. The street pattern followed the axis of the large rectangular mounds. The conical mound was retained in an open square on the axis of a street leading to the river. The processional way of the Indians became a very wide street and was given the name of Sacra Via. Much of the land along the Muskingum was permanently reserved for public use.

This ambitious plan could not be carried out immediately. For the protection of the first settlers, Putnam's party set about the construction of the traditional fortified enclosure similar in nature to the frontier stations of Kentucky. At the top of the river bank, a block southeast of the Sacra Via, they built a stockade enclosing a number of structures. Putnam has left the following description in his memoirs:

"Campus Martius . . . consisted of four block houses of hewed or sawed timber, two story high (erected at the expense of the Company) the upper stories on two sides projected two feet with loop holes in the projection to take the sides of the lower stories. Two of the block houses had two rooms on a floor, & the other two three rooms. The block houses were so placed as to form bastions of a regular square and flank the curtains of the work, which was proposed to consist of private houses, also to be made of hewed or sawed timber and two story high—leaving a clear area within of 144 feet square."[7]

[7] Rufus Putnam, *Memoirs*, Boston, 1903, p. 105.

On two sides of the Campus Martius and in the adjacent block, gardens were laid out for the use of those living within the stockade. The Company assigned lots within the enclosure for twenty years only and specified that in the event of attack all persons in the community were to be given shelter in these dwellings. Putnam's own house was located here, adjacent to one of the corner blockhouses, and it still stands on its original site, now enclosed by the Marietta Historical Museum.

Most of the land reserved for public use in the original plan still remains, including a broad stretch of park extending along the banks of the Muskingum. The common land mentioned in the early records of the Company, however, no longer surrounds the town. As at Savannah this was apparently regarded as land to be disposed of to later arrivals. The city is one of the most attractive in the old Northwest Territory, combining some of the charm and openness of older New England communities with the regularity of more conventionally planned towns in the middle west. In the ranks of urban planners of pioneer America, Rufus Putnam deserves recognition as a skilled practitioner of the art of civic design.

While Marietta grew and other settlements were laid out by the Ohio Company, Duer and his associates of the Scioto speculation were attempting to unload their vast holdings at a profit. Their "title" to the land consisted of a contract to take over a portion of what amounted to a land option held by the Ohio Company on the 5-million-acre tract. Their plan seems to have been to make sales of large areas abroad for cash and to use the funds in exercising their rights under the contract. Joel Barlow was sent to Europe as their agent with operations centered in France. Unable to find buyers for large tracts of land, he established a French subsidiary to "buy" land from the parent company on installments. To persons buying shares in the French company he guaranteed land title and the right to immediate settlement of Ohio land in proportion to their share holdings. Barlow met with considerable success in this questionable venture, and in 1790 some 500 Frenchmen arrived in Alexandria, Virginia, believing that they would be transported to Ohio by the Scioto Company and there would find a great city in which they could live in comfort.

Barlow's claims for the state of civilization in Ohio were highly exaggerated, and Duer and his friends, who were not prepared to spend a penny on improvements in their domain, made almost no arrangements to care for these new settlers. Nor were the French at all suited to life on the rugged American frontier. The group included such oddly assorted persons as a dancing master, doctors, lawyers, jewelers, and assorted exiled nobles. As a final touch to this fiasco, Barlow, through error or design, had sold land for the settlement in territory actually belonging to the Ohio Company. Duer finally contracted with the Ohio Company to lay out a town for the French, and Major John Burnham was sent down the Ohio to clear some land, plan a town, and construct some cabins for the settlers. Gallipolis was the result, with a great square opening to the river much like the earlier French colonial towns and having a linear gridiron street system parallel to the river (Fig. 95).

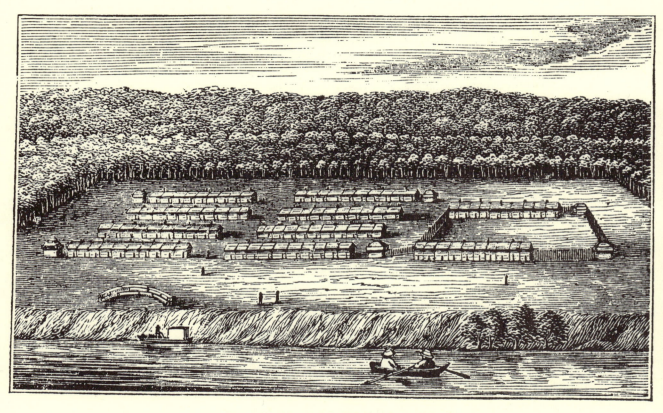

Figure 95. View of Gallipolis, Ohio: 1791

The first houses were small huts built in compact rows in the square, intended, like the Campus Martius at Marietta, for temporary accommodations. These miserable dwellings only gradually were replaced by more suitable houses that eventually dotted the streets of the new town. When the Comte de Volney visited the little settlement in 1796 two rows of log houses originally built in the central square were still occupied by the unfortunate French. Many of the original settlers drifted away from Gallipolis when it became evident, after the collapse of the Scioto Company, that they had no legal title to the lands they occupied. In 1795 Congress recognized their plight and granted 24,000 acres of land near the mouth of the Scioto for distribution to the residents of Gallipolis. In that same year the Ohio Company agreed to sell the land occupied by Gallipolis for a small amount, making an outright donation of the improvements which had been made at Company expense.

Towns of Southern and Central Ohio

In the same year that saw the establishment of the Ohio Company and the planning of Marietta, Congress approved another wholesale land purchase in the Northwest Territory. This lay between the Little and Great Miami rivers in what is now southwestern Ohio. The purchaser, John Cleves Symmes, served as a member of Congress from New Jersey. Asking for 2 million acres, he later reduced his request by half and paid down $82,000, with the remainder to follow in seven installments. Before these negotiations were concluded Symmes departed for the west leaving his associates, Elias Boudinot, formerly President of the Continental Congress, and Jonathan Dayton, later to become Speaker of the House of Representatives, to work out the details.

Several towns were founded in Symmes' Purchase. The first was Columbia, located just east of the mouth of the Little Miami River. Here, in November 1788, Benjamin Stites laid out a little town on land purchased from Symmes. Two months later Symmes himself established the settlement of North Bend near the mouth of the Great Miami River at the western end of his purchase.

A third community on the north bank of the Ohio opposite the mouth of the Licking River soon outstripped both of the earlier towns. Symmes had sold this site to Matthias Denman, a New Jersey land speculator, who in turn sold equal interests to Robert Patterson and John Filson. Filson and Israel Ludlow planned the town in December 1788, giving it the name Losantiville. Filson created this verbal patchwork to indicate that it was the city (*ville*) opposite (*anti*) the mouth (*os*) of the Licking (*L*). Governor Arthur St. Clair soon renamed the community in honor of the military order formed after the Revolution, and Cincinnati it became. With the establishment of Hamilton County and the designation of Cincinnati as its county seat and the location of Fort Washington, the future of the town was assured.

A plan of Cincinnati in 1815 reveals nothing very remarkable (Fig. 96). Indeed, it shows every indication of being laid out by its proprietors as a speculative enterprise and little more. In its design it resembled hundreds of similar towns that were soon to spring up

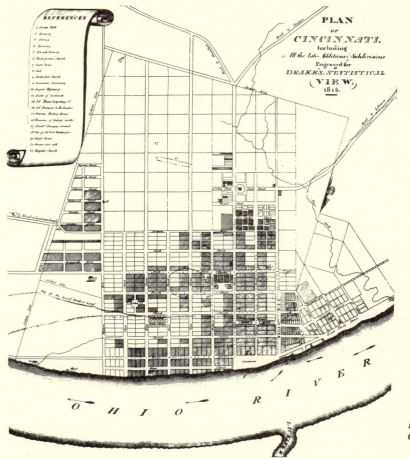

Figure 96. Plan of Cincinnati, Ohio: 1815

throughout southern and central Ohio as the region began to attract land hungry settlers from the east. Soon a brisk trade developed in Cincinnati town lots and adjacent outlots. Symmes, realizing that the town was destined to grow, platted a small addition to the city in 1790 on land owned by him at its eastern boundary.

The other major city founded in Symmes' Purchase was Dayton, planned in 1795 on land purchased by St. Clair, Jonathan Dayton, Israel Ludlow, and James Wilkinson. While Symmes had represented himself as the owner of this land, he did not in fact possess clear title. Eventually the new residents were forced to repurchase their property at standard land office prices, but the city of Dayton grew nonetheless as the fertile valleys of the new territory began to fill with settlers and the need developed for trading and governmental centers.

The development of towns in central Ohio lagged somewhat behind the Ohio River communities because of the lack of adequate transportation routes. Recognizing this problem, Congress in 1796 authorized Ebenezer Zane to build a road from Wheeling, West Virginia, through a portion of central and southern Ohio. Zane's payment consisted of the right to use his military land warrants to locate land not otherwise patented by others. On one of these sites, near the falls of the Muskingum, he planned a town in 1799. Zanesville became a thriving community and for a time was the state capital. With its wide streets, riverside common land, and unique Y-shaped bridge, the town received many favorable comments from early visitors. Nearby, Newark was laid out by General William Schenck in 1802 and named for his home in New Jersey. The streets were so wide and in rainy weather so muddy that some of the local citizens claimed that strangers sometimes were swallowed up in the mud and never seen again. The condition doubtless was shared by other frontier towns, for under the primitive conditions that prevailed it was many years before streets were properly filled and graded.

Other cities on Zane's Trace included Lancaster and Chillicothe, both important communities in the early development of Ohio. Chillicothe served as the seat of government of the Northwest Territory for a time, and the government located its land office there. During the first years of statehood Chillicothe was designated as the capital of Ohio, but in 1812 the state legislature directed Joel Wright to plan a new capital city on the site of the present Columbus. This land was already in private ownership, but the proprietors agreed to surrender their rights in exchange for substantial tracts of land in the new town.

Wright's plan for Columbus took the usual gridiron form (Fig. 97). Two rectangular reservations of ten acres each were set aside for the governmental buildings and a penitentiary. Between the town proper and the outlots lay the tier of large blocks reconveyed to the original proprietors. The Columbus plan is a dull, uninteresting one, lacking any distinctive features to distinguish it from dozens of others founded for private gain. Among the planned capital cities of the United States it is probably the least inspiring. Rather different, however, was the capital of Ohio's neighbor to the west.

In 1816 Congress approved the admission of Indiana to the union. One section of the act passed in that year authorized the new state

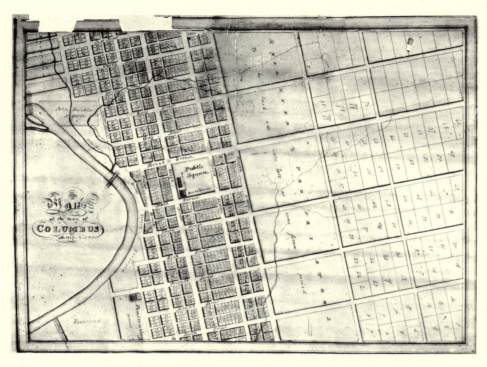

Figure 97. Plan of Columbus, Ohio: 1817

to select as a site for its capital a tract of four square miles not previously sold by the government land office. In 1820 the state legislature appointed a commission of ten men to locate a suitable site. After a series of preliminary surveys the commission reported favorably on a central location near the junction of the White River and Fall Creek. The legislature accepted the recommendations and appointed a second commission to prepare the town plan. Alexander Ralston, who had been one of the surveyors under L'Enfant and Ellicott at Washington, was retained by the commission as its planner.

Ralston's plan for Indianapolis in 1821 was an ambitious one (Fig. 98). From the corners of a mile-square gridiron he laid out four diagonal avenues which converged to the intersections of four streets near the center of the city. Within this smaller square he located the site for the governor's house in a circle some 300 feet in diameter. Three squares lying in the paths of the diagonals were set aside for religious purposes, market places were reserved, and two complete city blocks were retained for a capitol building and the courthouse. The influence of the Washington plan of 1792 shows not only in the pattern of streets but in the names given to them honoring other states in the union.

Ralston had the good sense not to bring the diagonals together at the center but to terminate them some distance apart. Nor was his plan surveyed without regard to topography. Along Fall Creek in the southeastern part of the city Ralston departed from the otherwise symmetrical pattern and planned two streets paralleling the creek. Doubtless he intended this area as a site for mills and other industries requiring water power or a place for waste disposal.

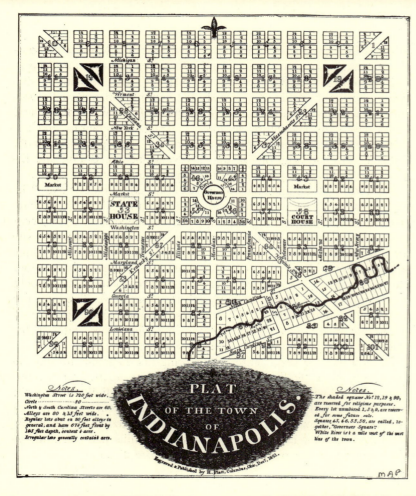

Figure 98. Plan of Indianapolis, Indiana: 1821

His plan was less satisfactory where the diagonals crossed the intersections of the gridiron streets. Instead of cutting back the sharply pointed lots at this point or providing smaller circles or squares as L'Enfant had done, Ralston retained the precise corners resulting from the geometrical pattern. Some of the city's present traffic problems stem from this failure to modify the scheme at these intersections. It might also have been more in keeping with the concept of Baroque planning to leave open at least a portion of the blocks surrounding the central circle. The governor's mansion, started in 1827, must have been invisible from the diagonal approaches as the lots surrounding the circle were built on. A more satisfactory solution from the visual standpoint has resulted in modern times with the erection of the Soldiers' and Sailors' Monument standing over 300 feet high on the site of the old governor's residence. Here at least is a visual exclamation point marking the center of the city and, very nearly, the center of the state itself.

Jeffersonville and Marietta were not the only early towns of the Ohio valley with distinctive plans. Perhaps the most unusual was that for the county seat of Pickaway County, Ohio. The county had been created by the legislature in 1810, and three commissioners were appointed to select a site for its administrative center. In their search they came across another of the mound-building Indians' strange creations—a circle tangent to a square. They chose this unique site, and Daniel Driesbach, who was directed to prepare the plan for the town, imaginatively conceived of a design that would utilize the circular mounds as the right-of-way for the principal street (Fig. 99). He

BIRD'S EYE VIEW OF CIRCLEVILLE, OHIO, IN 1836, LOOKING SOUTH.

Court House.
County Officers.
County Jail and Sheriff's Dwelling.
Market House.
Presbyterian Church.
Episcopal Church.
Lutheran Church.
Methodist Church.
District School.
Academy.
Henry House.
Morgan's Tavern.
Red Lion Tavern, by Jacob Try.
Canal Hotel, by Cradlebaugh.

15, National House.
16, Rogers & Martin's Warehouse.
17, Wilkes & Wareh's Lumber Yard.
18, Finley's Warehouse.
19, J. & H. Smart's Provision Store.
20, Block built by James Bell.
21, Block built by M. M'Crea.
22, Block built by N. S. Gregg.
23, Block built by Sam. Rogers.
24, Block built by Francis Kinnear.
25, Bank of C——, H. Lawrence, Chr.
26, Wolfley & Duncan's Grocery.
27, M. Bright's Tin Shop.
28, Howard's Hat Store.

29, Westenhover's Grocery and Bakery.
30, Samuel Rogers' Store.
31, C. B. Crouse's Store.
32, Jacob Lutz's Store.
33, Francis Kinnear's Store.
34, Mrs. Jackson's Residence.
35, M. M. Gren's Residence.
36, Gossler's Tavern.
37, De. E. B. Olds' Drug Store.
38, Huston's Residence.
39, Diffenderfer's Grocery.
40, Hurst's Store.
41, H. Sage's Jewelry Store.
42, Jenkin's Grocery.

43, Israel Darst's Residence.
44, H. Sage's Residence.
45, Dr. Luckey's Office.
46, Dr. Luckey's Residence.
47, Geo. C. Gephart's Residence.
48, Wm. McLane Cabinet Shop.
49, Geo. W. Doane's Res. and Office.
50, W. B. Thrall's Residence.
51, Michael May's Residence.
52, W. M'Culloch's Residence.
53, S. Diffenderfer's Residence.
54, S. Marfield's Residence.
55, Dr. E. B. Olds' Residence.
56, Gen. Green's Residence.

57, Wm. P. Darst's Residence.
58, Thos. Pedrick's Residence.
59, Joseph Olds' Residence.
60, James Bell's Residence.
61, James Bell's Tannery.
62, Jos. Johnson's Residence.
63, Hy. Foresman's Residence.
64, Religious Telescope Office.
65, Circleville Herald Office.
66, F. G. Whittick's Book Bindery.
67, M. Myer's Chairshop and Res.
68, Wilkes' Brewery.
69, F. Williamson's Residence.
70, Hays' Residence.

71, H. Lawrence's Residence.
72, Tanus Crouse's Residence.
73, H. Robbins' Residence.
74, Thos. Wilkes' Residence.
75, T. Darst's Foundry.
76, Parts of Circular Ditch.
77, Mount Gilboa.
78, Lutheran Graveyard.
79, M. Arthur's Block, in progress.
80, Ohio Canal.

Figure 99. View of Circleville, Ohio: 1836

laid out eight other streets radiating outward from a central open space set aside for the courthouse. The name of the town was almost inevitable, and Circleville it became. In fact, the circular portion of the town was actually a double octagon, thus permitting all properties to be bounded by straight, rather than curved lines.

But, like that of Jeffersonville, the plan of Circleville had but a brief life. Some of the more enterprising residents concluded that its design wasted otherwise valuable urban land between the circle and the enclosing square. There were complaints, too, that the open area about the courthouse had become a foraging spot for local swine. These persons approached the state legislature with a request to permit the replanning of the town, and in 1837 an act was passed authorizing the replatting of the circular portions of the town with the consent of the property owners concerned. The legislature also created what was doubtless America's first private redevelopment corporation to carry out this task. The name chosen for this concern indicates that its founders did not lack an appreciation for the humorous aspects of their proposed project, for they were chartered as "a body corporate and politic . . . by the name and style of the 'Circleville Squaring Company.'"

The old order had its adherents, and the company secured the necessary consents from owners of land in only two quadrants of the city. For eleven years company activities hung suspended while the town remained half square and half circular. Not until 1849 did landowners in the northeast quarter of the town capitulate. Then once again several years were to pass while negotiations took place with

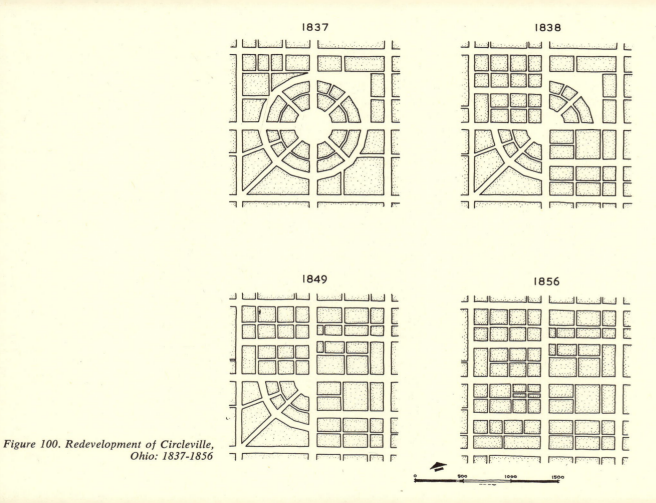

1837   1838

1849   1856

Figure 100. Redevelopment of Circleville,
Ohio: 1837-1856

0 500 1000 1500

the remaining supporters of the original plan. Finally, in March 1856, the new plan was accepted. The squaring of Circleville had been achieved (Fig. 100).

Thus, gradually, the Ohio Valley was settled by pioneers for whom town life was an important aspect of a developing culture. The difficulties were many and the hardships great. Not all of the towns laid out by these settlers were particularly attractive, but many, like Marietta, have much of the charm of the still unspoiled New England communities of an earlier era. Some attempts at real urban elegance failed completely, as at Hygeia. Other unusual plans of both interest and merit were replaced by conventional designs, as in Jeffersonville and Circleville. There still remains impressive evidence that these early colonizers of a great internal land empire were not unaware of the values of urban beauty and the amenities of town life. These features of town planning were submerged in the later 19th century under the tide of speculation. Land came to be regarded as a commodity for personal enrichment rather than a resource to be managed wisely by the citizens and their governmental institutions. What remains of the original townscape deserves the utmost efforts by present residents to protect and preserve this unique heritage of the pioneers who first pushed beyond the eastern mountains and established the early frontier towns in the pleasant rolling lands of the Ohio Valley.

Following the Revolutionary War Americans resumed the settlement of a continent and the building of towns. Typically, the promoters of such towns chose a suitable site, reached some kind of agreement with the land owners or themselves acquired the title, had the site surveyed into streets, blocks, and lots, and, with a handsomely printed map and brochure describing the unique advantages of the town, proceeded to sell building plots to anyone with cash for a down payment.

In 1791 just such a town was planned by an enterprising group on the banks of the Potomac River. It was unique in a number of respects. In size the new town dwarfed all others that had heretofore been projected. Its highly unusual plan introduced to America new concepts of city design. It was a city intended as the center of a great enterprise, the eventual scope of which could not be foreseen even by its founders. And, finally, its promoters were no mere real estate speculators interested in private enrichment but included such towering figures as George Washington, James Madison, and Thomas Jefferson, who in this capacity acted as trustees for an entire nation. For this was Washington on the Potomac, the future capital of an ambitious and confident government, intended to express the glory and power that the new nation would surely attain.

During the long, dark years of the war the Continental Congress had conducted its affairs in Philadelphia, Baltimore, Lancaster, and York. Nor did the peace of 1783 bring stability. The capital moved from Philadelphia to Princeton, Annapolis, Trenton, and New York. The prospect of a permanent home for the infant government seemed elusive. The southern states were reluctant to agree to a location in the north, while those of the north were equally unwilling to approve a southern site.

Debates on the subject grew heated as each faction pressed the other to give in. But there were moments of humor as well. Francis Hopkinson records that at one point a member of the Congress proposed "that there should be *two* places of *alternate*, *permanent* residence . . . and but *one* federal town; which town should be built upon a large platform mounted on a great number of wheels, and drawn by a great number of horses. This . . . would be productive of many great conveniences. . . . It would save much precious time, inasmuch as there would be no interruption of their proceedings; for the business of the house might be going on, whilst the house itself *was going on*; and motions not only be made in the house, but the house itself *make motions. . . .*"[1]

The Constitutional Convention in 1787 adopted a provision which gave Congress the power to "exercise exclusive legislation" over an area not to exceed ten miles square which might be ceded for that

[1] Francis Hopkinson, *The Miscellaneous Essays and Occasional Writings of Francis Hopkinson, Esq.*, Vol. 1 (Philadelphia, 1792), as quoted in U.S. Library of Congress, *Sesquicentennial of the Establishment of the Permanent Seat of the Government*, Washington, 1950, p. 7.

purpose by one or more of the states. It said nothing about planning a town in the federal district, and it avoided entirely the question of location. With the meeting of the first Congress under the new constitution in 1789 the debates over a site for the capital city began anew. Finally, in 1790, as a result of a political compromise by which southern congressmen agreed to back Alexander Hamilton's fiscal policy in exchange for his support for a capital site in the south, the Residence Act received approval.

This law specified that the President was to select the exact location on the Potomac River somewhere within an eighty-mile distance from the mouth of its "East Branch," or Anacostia River. It also authorized presidential appointment of three commissioners "to provide suitable buildings for the accommodation of Congress and of the President and for the public offices of the United States" by the first Monday in December 1800. Until that date the seat of government was to be in Philadelphia.

In October, President Washington began his inspection of the territory, although all the evidence indicates that he had already decided on the southernmost location near the existing towns of Alexandria and Georgetown. Citizens of each village and hamlet along his route welcomed him and presented statements and petitions advocating their particular location as the most desirable for the new city. The following month he conferred with Thomas Jefferson, who, as Secretary of State, had prepared a memorandum late in August setting forth his views on how the Residence Act should be implemented. This was supplemented by a report to the President two weeks later.

Jefferson pointed out that while the Act did not specify that a new town should be laid out, he had "no doubt it is the wish, & perhaps expectation" of Congress that this should be done. He also had no doubt that for effective planning it would be necessary for the government to acquire all the land needed for the new city, and he suggested two possible methods of bringing this about. One was to purchase the land, or to take it by eminent domain if necessary at double the present value, "estimated as . . . [it] . . . would have been had there been no thought of bringing the federal seat into their neighborhood." The other was to induce each proprietor to "cede one half his lands to the public, to be sold to raise money." It was a variation of this last suggestion that the President was later to work out with the owners of the land.

It is worth noting that in this recommendation to acquire the entire site, an idea immediately endorsed by the President, Jefferson was following an old tradition in Virginia and Maryland used for well over 100 years in the establishment of provincial capitals, county seats, and port towns. Williamsburg, Annapolis, and Norfolk, among others, owed their origins to this approach. It was also a procedure which was to be followed later in many states when the time came to found new communities under public auspices to serve as capital cities. Among the state capitals planned on land purchased or acquired by eminent domain or located on land already in public ownership are Columbia, South Carolina; Jefferson City, Missouri; Lincoln, Nebraska; Raleigh, North Carolina; Tallahassee, Florida; Jackson, Mississippi; Austin, Texas; Columbus, Ohio; and Indianapolis, Indiana. This aspect of the influence on American planning exerted by the procedure for planning adopted by Washington and Jefferson for the national capital has not been adequately appreciated.

By January 1791 the President was ready to act. He appointed the three commissioners called for in the statute, and he informed the Congress that after "mature consideration" he had selected a site near Georgetown. He requested, and Congress quickly approved, a minor change in the law, which permitted the inclusion of a small amount of land south of the Anacostia. To secure an accurate survey of the new district, Washington appointed Andrew Ellicott to run the bounds of the area and to report on its major topographic features.

The Grand Plan for the Capital City

On March 9 Ellicott was joined by Major Pierre Charles L'Enfant. L'Enfant at that time was directed only to study the site and recommend the best locations for the principal buildings. He was not asked to prepare the city plan. Yet this may have been understood, and it seems likely that Washington or some emissary must have conferred with L'Enfant prior to this appointment. We do know that a year and a half earlier L'Enfant had written to Washington offering his services in planning the new capital. He had been the architect in charge of remodeling the New York city hall for use by the Congress in 1789. As a volunteer Frenchman who had become an American officer in the Revolution under Washington, as the designer of the insignia for the Society of the Cincinnati, of which Washington was President-General, and as a person for whom Washington evidently felt affection and admiration, L'Enfant, with his Paris training as an artist and with his military experience as an engineer, was a natural choice for the assignment.

While Ellicott continued his surveys of the district's boundaries, L'Enfant began to explore the territory along the East Branch. He was assigned first to the land farthest from Georgetown in an effort to obtain lower prices for land immediately adjacent to that town. For on the day of his proclamation of the Federal District the President entered into confidential correspondence with friends of his in Georgetown asking them to begin negotiations for land in the vicinity. He shrewdly reasoned that the sight of L'Enfant working elsewhere would persuade the owners of land along the Potomac to be more reasonable in their demands.

It was obvious to all that the city would be located along one of the rivers. Two small towns already had been platted—Hamburg, half way between Georgetown and Goose or Tiber Creek, and Carrollsburg, at the juncture of the Potomac and the Anacostia (Fig. 101). These towns were largely paper communities, but among the owners an intense rivalry developed over the location of the new city.

On March 28 Washington arrived in Georgetown for a meeting with the commissioners, Ellicott and L'Enfant. The next evening he called the proprietors of land to his rooms and discussed with them possible terms of land settlement. Agreement was reached the following day, and Washington jubilantly wrote Jefferson:

"The terms . . . are That all the land from Rock-creek . . . to the

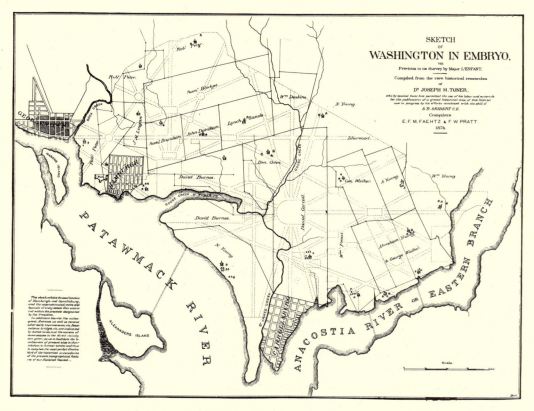

Figure 101. Division of Land on the Site of the National Capital: 1791

eastern-branch and . . . upwards . . . including a breadth of about a mile and a half, the whole containing from three to five thousand acres, is ceded to the public, on condition that, when the whole shall be surveyed and laid off as a city . . . the present Proprietors shall retain every other lot, and for such part of the land as may be taken for public use . . . they shall be allowed at the rate of Twenty five pounds per acre. . . . No compensation is to be made for the ground that may be occupied as streets or alleys."[2]

Thus, not only did Washington settle the difficulties with the landowners, but he also obtained a site far larger than anyone had contemplated, L'Enfant possibly excepted.

At the meeting in Georgetown L'Enfant presented Washington with his site analysis. In it he identified Jenkins' Hill as the most advantageous site for public buildings, now the location of the capitol, and described the general topography and site possibilities elsewhere. Then, turning to the point obviously of the most immediate interest to him, he stated:

"In viewing the intended establishment . . . and considering how in process of time a city so happily situated will extend over a large surface of ground, much deliberation is necessary . . . to determine on a plan for the total distribution and . . . that plan [should be conceived] on [such] a system . . . as to render the place commodious and agreeable to the first settler, [while] it may be capable of . . . [being] en-

---

[2] Letter from Washington to Jefferson, March 31, 1791, in Saul Padover, *Thomas Jefferson and the National Capital*, Washington, 1946, p. 54.

larged by progressive improvement . . . [all] which should be foreseen in the first delineation in a grand plan of the whole city. . . ."[3]

These views evidently coincided with those of Washington, and L'Enfant was directed to proceed with the "grand plan" for the capital city. Washington may not have then specified the terms of the appointment, or, equally likely, L'Enfant may have been too animated to understand that he was to be subordinate to the commissioners. Misunderstanding on this point was later to prove troublesome, but in March 1791 there were no signs of the future difficulties that were to stem from this situation. L'Enfant's appointment was regarded as an excellent, almost inevitable, choice, and it was with high hopes and every expectation of success that Washington left L'Enfant to proceed with the task the Frenchman had so ardently desired.

Already, in examining the site, L'Enfant's agile mind had undoubtedly begun to conceive the broad pattern of his eventual scheme. He was, however, not the first to project a plan for a capital city layout on the Potomac site; that honor belongs to Thomas Jefferson. Both the circumstances and the plan are of considerable interest.

We first find Jefferson setting down his thoughts on the capital city in his memorandum and report to the President in August and September 1790. In his memorandum of August 29 he advocated a gridiron plan with streets 100 feet wide and blocks at least 600 feet square. He listed the sites that would be needed for major buildings

[3] Elizabeth S. Kite, *L'Enfant and Washington 1791-1792*, Baltimore, 1929, pp. 43-48.

and also suggested nine blocks for "public walks." At the end of his report on September 14 he included a little sketch for the site then occupied by Carrollsburg—a grid town four blocks deep by thirteen blocks long stretching along the Anacostia (Fig. 102).

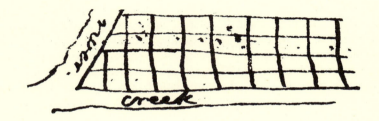

Figure 102. Jefferson's Plan for a Capital City on the Site of Carrollsburg, District of Columbia: 1790

Later he shifted his attention to the land along Tiber Creek. In March 1791 he prepared a draft for a presidential proclamation that would have designated the land from Georgetown to Hamburg as the capital city site. With this draft was found a plan for the city that was evidently given to Washington before his meeting in Georgetown with the proprietors.

Jefferson's plan shows many of the features first described in his earlier studies but now transferred to the site along the Tiber. The little gridiron town appears three blocks deep and eleven blocks long, with three of the blocks consolidated for the President's house and gardens and an equal area for the capitol building to the east (Fig. 103). Connecting these two sites Jefferson showed a stretch along the Tiber as a public walk. Here, perhaps, is the genesis of the present mall as well as the eventual relationship of the White House and Capitol.

Jefferson's notes on the map indicate that the squares shown around the public buildings would be platted immediately and "sold in the first instance." Surrounding this area of initial settlement are dots showing the intersections of streets, with the notation, "to be laid off in future." Roughly 2,000 acres are included in the whole area. Jefferson's plan, it should be emphasized, was prepared before the much larger area negotiated by Washington became available.

The President did send a copy of Jefferson's plan to L'Enfant for his information. It could not have been received with much approval, for only a few days before L'Enfant had roundly condemned the rectangular plan concept in his site analysis presented to President Washington, asserting,

". . . it is not the regular assemblage of houses laid out in squares and forming streets all parallel and uniform that . . . is so necessary, for such a plan could only do on a level plain and where no surrounding object being interesting it becomes indifferent which way the opening of streets may be directed.

"But on any other ground, a plan of this sort must be defective, and it never would answer for any of the spots proposed for the Federal City, and on that held here as the most eligible it would absolutely

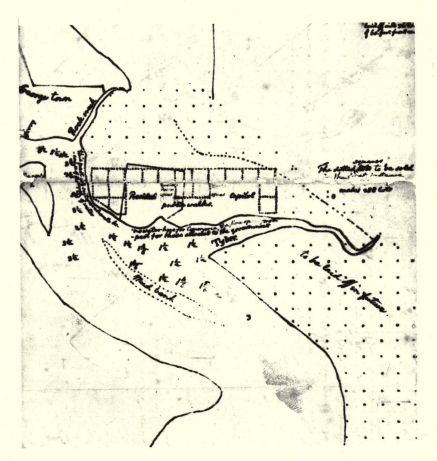

Figure 103. Jefferson's Plan of Washington, D.C.: 1791

annihilate every of the advantages enumerated and . . . alone injure the success of the undertaking."[4]

Jefferson, of course, had read this report and could hardly escape the conclusion that he and L'Enfant were at opposite poles in their ideas of city planning. Yet he did not allow this to color his relationship with L'Enfant. He sent him part of his collection of European city maps, congratulated him on his appointment, and referred to his own plan of the new city as an idea submitted to Washington to be made use of only in such manner as the President wished.

So, L'Enfant was left with complete freedom to develop his own ideas of a plan for the capital. During April, May, and June of 1791 he busied himself with his surveys and designs, spurred on by the confidence shown in his abilities and excited by the unique opportunity that lay before him. As early as the third week in April his earlier ideas had been refined and tentative locations selected for some of the major features. By the end of June, when Washington was again in Georgetown to arrange for the deed of trust from the proprietors, a preliminary plan was ready. Washington himself, as his diary records, "went out with Major L'Enfant and Mr. Ellicot to take more perfect view of the ground in order to decide finally on the spot on which to place the public buildings. . . ." Then, on June 29, the proprietors gathered with the President; the diary entry reads,

[4] Undated communication by L'Enfant, "Note relative to the ground lying on the eastern branch of the river Potomac and being intended to parallel the several positions proposed within the limits between the branch and Georgetown for the seat of the Federal City," in Kite, *L'Enfant*, pp. 47-48.

"A plan was also laid before them of the city; but they were told that some alterations, deviations from it, would take place, particularly in the diagonal streets or avenues, which would not be so numerous, and in the removal of the President's house more westerly, for the advantage of higher ground. They were also told that a Townhouse or Exchange would be placed on some convenient ground between the spots designed for the public buildings before mentioned, and it was with much pleasure that a general approbation of the measure seemed to pervade the whole."[5]

This plan has not survived, and in describing and discussing L'Enfant's planning concepts and proposals we must refer to his revised scheme which was submitted to the President two months later on August 19 (Fig. 104). From the lengthy explanation on that drawing and from an explanatory memorandum submitted to Washington with the preliminary plan in June, we can piece together L'Enfant's objectives, methods, and results.

The June memorandum is an important and interesting document. Both L'Enfant's enthusiasm for and technical understanding of his unique assignment are apparent as he began the explanation for his illustrious client:

"Having determined some principal points to which I wished to make the others subordinate, I made the distribution regular with every street at right angles, . . . and afterwards opened some in differ-

[5] Joseph A. Hoskins, ed., *President Washington's Diaries, 1791 to 1799*, Summerfield, N.C., 1921, entry for June 29, 1791, p. 52.

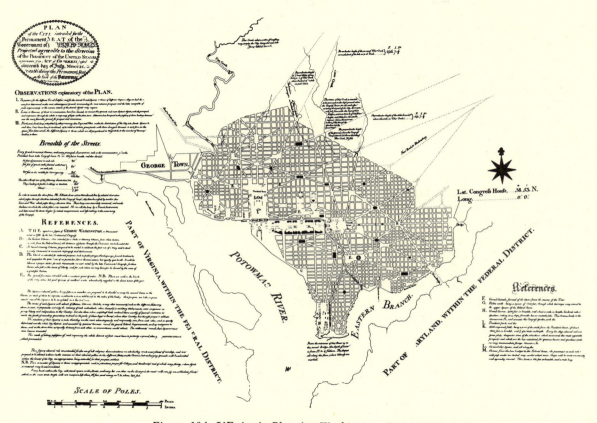

Figure 104. L'Enfant's Plan for Washington, D.C.: 1791

ent directions, as avenues to and from every principal place, wishing thereby not merely to [contrast] with the general regularity, nor to afford a greater variety of seats with pleasant prospects . . . but principally to connect each part of the city, if I may so express it, by making the real distance less from place to place, by giving to them reciprocity of sight and by making them thus seemingly connected, promote a rapid settlement over the whole extent, rendering those even of the most remote parts an addition to the principal. . . ."[6]

L'Enfant planned extremely broad avenues; roadways of 80 feet, an additional 30 feet on each side "for a walk under a double row of trees," and with a further 10 feet beyond between the trees and the houses. L'Enfant described the principal avenue as the one leading from the crossing of the Anacostia to Georgetown by way of the Capitol and the President's house—the present Pennsylvania Avenue. The house for the President, with its "garden park and other improvements," L'Enfant faced toward the Tiber near the western end of the city. Jenkins' Hill, which L'Enfant had already previously remarked as a commanding site, was reserved for the Capitol. Here, said L'Enfant, was a spot that "stands really as a pedestal waiting for a superstructure," and no other location "could bear a competition with this."

The memorandum took up one by one many of the other features of the plan. There were the "public walks" that would connect the presidential gardens with the grounds of the Capitol; a monument

[6] Undated report by L'Enfant to Washington, the text of which appears in Kite, *L'Enfant*, pp. 52-58.

at the intersection of the axis of the presidential grounds and the mall; and executive buildings in close proximity to the house of the President. One proposal was not to be realized. This was a great cascade of water to issue from the base of the Capitol and to tumble down an incline 40 feet high and 100 feet wide. The water would then flow into the Tiber, which was to be straightened, deepened, and confined to an east-west channel running along the north side of the mall. Near the cascade it was to turn south and then branch into two canals before its entry into the Anacostia. It was along this canal, which was eventually constructed, that L'Enfant proposed the initial development of the city. Even at this early stage of planning he was searching for a land development policy that would promote rapid growth. In his memorandum he suggested that building "should be begun at various points equi-distant as possible from the center; not merely because settlements of this sort are likely to diffuse an equality of advantages over the whole territory allotted, and consequently to reflect benefit from an increase of the value of property, but because each of these settlements by a natural jealousy will most tend to stimulate establishments on each of the opposed extremes. . . ."

In this manner, these individual nodes of settlement would quickly become joined, and the city would soon begin to take form. The canal was intended to provide lateral communication between these points, guide development in the proper direction, and speed the rate of growth.

L'Enfant's revised plan of August 1791 incorporated another feature to further this policy. Fifteen squares were designated, one for each of the states, to be embellished with "Statues, Columns, Obelisks, or any other ornament." Each state was expected to make "improvements around the Square to be completed in a limited time," and he assumed that "The Settlements round those Squares must soon become connected."

Other open spaces were proposed. One was to be occupied by a church, "intended for national purposes, such as public prayer, thanksgiving, funeral orations, etc." While this was to be a non-denominational church, other church sites were marked out to be distributed on the same basis as the squares of the states. The remaining undesignated squares were to be used as sites for "Colleges and Academies" or societies "whose object is national."

The new capital was to be a city of beauty. In addition to the cascade, "five grand fountains intended with a constant spout of water" appear on the plan. Three important monuments were described: an equestrian statue of Washington at the intersection of the axes of mall and President's gardens; a column in what is now Lincoln Square one mile east of the Capitol from which all distances on the continent were to be measured; and a column in honor of the navy directly south of the national church on the Potomac. For what we now know as the Mall, L'Enfant proposed a "Grand Avenue," 400 feet wide with gardens on each side leading from the Capitol to the Potomac.

The memorandum and the second plan's marginal comments also indicated the general arrangement of principal uses of land. "Mercantile interests should be pushed with the greatest activity" along the banks of the canal. Shops were to be located in two areas: along "the streets from the grand avenue to the palace and towards the canal" and along the street running directly east from the Capitol. In this latter area we are told that the sidewalk "on each side will pass under an Arched way, under whose cover Shops will be most conveniently and agreeably situated."

L'Enfant stated to the President his wish "to delineate a plan wholly new." Certainly in its magnitude, its clever fitting of a generally symmetrical design to irregular topography, and its generous provision of a variety of open spaces, the plan for Washington must stand as one of the great city planning efforts of all time. At least as remarkable is the speed with which L'Enfant prepared and revised his basic plan. Site surveys, first sketch, finished plan—all were carried out in less than six months. Clearly this would have been impossible for anyone less a genius or one less familiar with the design idioms that comprise this vast essay in civic planning. In this respect, then, the plan was not "wholly new"—for L'Enfant used the familiar devices of European Baroque designers in devising his grand plan. To say this is not to minimize L'Enfant's accomplishment but merely to assert the obvious—that he was a product of his age and the instrument through which certain principles of urban design that had been developed in western Europe found expression on the Potomac River.

Where had L'Enfant learned this design vocabulary? The answer seems clear. As a young lad L'Enfant had explored the gardens of Versailles, that great landscape composition of Le Nôtre's, where his father was a court painter. Later, as a student in Paris at the Royal

Academy of Painting and Sculpture, he came to know intimately another monumental axial composition of similar scale: the Tuileries Gardens, the Place de la Concorde, the beginnings of today's Avenue des Champs-Élysées, and the *rond point* in an apple orchard that is the modern Place de l'Étoile.

In these and similar Baroque designs we can see the same concern with axial treatment of building masses and open spaces, the same delight in sweeping diagonal avenues, and the same studied use of monuments or important buildings to close streets with terminal vistas that L'Enfant employed in his plan of Washington. This was the language of civic design that came most naturally to him, and he spoke it fluently and with conviction.

It is ironic that this method of expression had, by the time L'Enfant employed it in America, already become slightly archaic in Europe where it had first gained currency. And it was doubly ironic that the new nation which boasted rather loudly of its democracy and freedom should have employed for its capital city the plan forms that were the very symbols of autocratic rule and aristocratic elegance. The sophisticated Jefferson may have perceived these contradictions; in all of his voluminous writings about the capital city and its buildings there is not one word of praise for L'Enfant's plan.

This great essay in urban planning was not without its faults. Perhaps most serious is the over-long distance between its two major focal points, the Capitol and the White House. Even before the Treasury building was interposed between the two it must have been obvious that the view down Pennsylvania Avenue to the presidential residence was much too long for the building which terminated that vista. Quite aside from this visual shortcoming, the widely spaced public buildings created in effect a series of separate communities scattered through the Federal District. While L'Enfant consciously adopted this device as part of his intended policy to promote more rapid development of the city, its practical effect for almost a century was to inhibit contiguous growth and the appearance of a unified city.

Moreover, the combination of two systems of streets—the underlying grid and the bold pattern of radials—created dozens of awkward intersections and strangely shaped building sites. While in later years many of these have been utilized for attractive small parks or sites for monuments, for the first few decades of the city's existence most of them lay idle and vacant. And to the extent that a capital city plan should somehow reflect the basic pattern of government of which it is the seat, the plan of Washington exhibits a major defect. L'Enfant failed to provide for the third branch of government, the judicial, a site equal in prominence or important to the locations assigned for the legislative and the executive. He mentioned only once a site for the "Judiciary Court," but did not specifically locate it, and it is obvious (and understandable) that he never conceived of the potential importance of the Supreme Court or the symbolic importance of locating it in a commanding spot within the city.

Yet L'Enfant's magnificent achievement in a few short months of study must be stressed. He created a design for a new city on a scale never before attempted. Perhaps St. Petersburg was Washington's closest rival in this respect. It must be understood, too, that the plan of Washington was no mere abstract design conceived in ignorance or disregard for the natural conditions of the site. L'Enfant's descriptions of the basis for the street pattern plainly indicate that he first located the major functions and buildings and then provided direct connections through the system of diagonal boulevards. He was thus ahead of his time in attempting differentiation in street design on the basis of functional requirements in a desire to separate purely local and service traffic on the grid streets from longer journeys via the major connecting radials.

Perhaps most important, L'Enfant aimed at the creation of a city of beauty and monumentality, characteristics notably lacking until that time on the American urban scene. The great central Mall, intended as a unifying, formal open space, was a major device to achieve this end. Each major building was integrated with the street system to provide the maximum number of vistas, and located throughout the city were numerous formal open spaces, squares, or circles to provide visual punctuation. With all its flaws the plan of Washington stands as one of the great accomplishments of all time in urban planning.

L'Enfant Terrible

With the plan completed, thoughts now turned toward its implementation. L'Enfant strongly opposed the early sale of lots in the new city, which everyone else concerned with the project had planned. He pointed out that if lots of greatest potential value—those near the President's house—were put up for sale first, as was the intention, they would fail to bring their true value. It would be far better, he maintained, to complete many of the streets and public buildings first, since then the lots would appear more attractive and yield greater revenue. He advocated mortgaging property located at the edge of the city, completing many improvements, and then placing a limited number of lots on the market. With the proceeds the loan could be repaid, and decisions on timing and location of development would be made independent of immediate concern with raising funds.

To this suggestion Washington could not agree, nor did Jefferson or the commissioners. They were under extreme pressure to show immediate results in the development of the city. For at this time, before any plan had been exhibited and when far weightier problems faced the new nation, many persons appeared skeptical that a suitable city could be created. Moreover, Washington and Jefferson had already reported that the first lands would be available for sale soon, and to abandon this policy in favor of long negotiations over loans would simply give the enemies of the new city additional grounds for criticism. Finally, L'Enfant apparently overlooked the fact that half of the lots in the city belonged to the original proprietors, and they would be able to meet any foreseeable demand for building sites, thus obtaining for private landowners profits that might otherwise accrue to the government.

October 17 was fixed as the date for the first sale of lots at public auction. L'Enfant, then in Philadelphia, was requested to have 10,000 copies of the city plan printed for distribution. L'Enfant disregarded this instruction; moreover he even refused to permit the display of his drawings at the auction itself. The only maps available were the plats of individual blocks, and prospective purchasers were unable to determine their exact location within the city.

This was but the first of a series of incidents that led to L'Enfant's downfall. The next was more serious. One of the proprietors, Daniel Carroll, had begun the construction of his house south of the Capitol building site. When the surveys of New Jersey Avenue were run in August it was found that the house extended into the avenue by some seven feet. According to L'Enfant he directed Carroll to remove the house, and when this was not done he simply ordered his workmen to demolish it. A brisk exchange of correspondence followed. Washington curtly ordered L'Enfant to "touch no man's property without his consent, or the previous order of the Commissioners," and reminded him that he was subordinate to the commissioners and should conduct himself accordingly.

Other frictions between L'Enfant and the commissioners developed, but it was his continued procrastination over engraving the plan that brought on the final crisis. When L'Enfant continued to offer excuses, Washington in exasperation directed Ellicott to take over this assignment and see that a map was printed. L'Enfant even refused to turn over the original drawing, but Ellicott informed the commissioners that he would use the survey data in his possession for the engraving, and stated his belief that "the plan which we have furnished . . . will be found to answer the ground better than the large one in the Major's hands."

Two engravings were finally made early in 1792, one printed in Boston and the other, by Thackara and Vallance, in Philadelphia (Fig. 105). They are substantially identical in what they reveal of the plan, and both show changes from the revised L'Enfant design of the previous fall. Some of these changes originated with Jefferson, with the consent or at least the knowledge of the President. It is also possible that Ellicott on his own initiative may have modified the L'Enfant plan. Since he lacked the details of the drawings withheld by L'Enfant, some of his modifications may have been inadvertent, resulting from an attempt to reconstruct from memory the details of the original.

The most obvious difference is the change in direction and alignment of Massachusetts Avenue, which in the Ellicott version was considerably straightened. Other changes were numerous but certainly less drastic. One feature suppressed from the original drawing, which justifiably angered L'Enfant, was any mention of the designer's name. Only Ellicott's appears on the printed version.

L'Enfant charged that his plan had been "most unmercifully spoiled and altered . . . to a degree indeed evidently tending to disgrace me and ridicule the very undertaking," and in a bitter letter written to the President's secretary placed the blame squarely on Ellicott. He also delivered a long tirade against the commissioners, accusing them of incompetence, laxity, and favoritism and declining to submit himself to their control. Washington made one last attempt to retain L'Enfant's services, dispatching his secretary, Tobias Lear, to talk with him. L'Enfant brusquely dismissed Lear, saying "that he had al-

Figure 105. Ellicott's Plan for Washington, D.C.: 1792

ready heard enough of this matter." The next day Washington, Jefferson, and Madison met and decided that L'Enfant should be notified that his appointment was terminated.

So ended L'Enfant's brief career as planner of the city of Washington. For many years, however, he was to be seen about the city observing the progress of construction and doubtless offering his observations to anyone who might listen. In typical fashion he had rejected the payment of "500 guineas and a lot in a good part of the city" offered him by the commissioners at Washington's suggestion. In 1800 he sent to Congress the first of three memorials requesting compensation for his services, claiming $95,500. This was disapproved. The earlier offer was renewed in 1804 but apparently a creditor secured a judgment against this sum. Finally, in 1810 Congress authorized another payment totalling $1,394.20. Most of this, too, went to his creditors. L'Enfant died in 1825 at the age of seventy. In 1909 his body was moved from its burial place in Maryland to the Capitol rotunda. Following a memorial service it was reburied at the National Cemetery at Arlington. From the tomb the City of Washington can be seen across the Potomac. On the slab of Tennessee marble marking his grave there is a replica of the plan that L'Enfant devised for his beloved city.

The City of Magnificent Distances

During the early years of its existence Washington grew with such slowness that renewed doubts arose about the transfer of the capital from Philadelphia. The site of the city must have presented a strange picture during this period (Fig. 106). When Thomas Twining visited

Figure 106. View of Washington, D.C.: 1800

the Federal District in April 1796 he tells us that he "entered a large wood through which a very imperfect road had been made, principally by removing the trees, or rather the upper parts of them. . . . After some time this indistinct way assumed more the appearance of a regular avenue, the trees here having been cut down in a straight line. Although no habitation of any kind was visible, I had no doubt but I was now riding along one of the streets of the metropolitan city. I continued in this spacious avenue for half a mile, and then came out upon a large spot, cleared of wood, in the centre of which I saw two buildings on an extensive scale."[7]

Twining expressed surprise at seeing the city in such a "sylvan state," since he had seen maps and read descriptions which led him to believe that much more progress had been made. As was usual in the real estate promotional literature of the time, the wildest claims were advanced of the advantages of the site and the important buildings that were under construction.

In that same year Francis Baily recorded his impressions of the embryonic city. He admired the President's house, the Capitol, and the view from the point where the Potomac and Anacostia join. But, there was little in the way of a city to be seen, as Baily informs us: "The private buildings go on but slowly. There are about twenty or thirty houses built near the Point, as well as a few in South Capitol Street and about a hundred others scattered over in other places . . . and these constitute the great city of Washington. The truth is,

[7] Thomas Twining, *Travels in America 100 Years Ago*, New York, 1894, p. 100.

that not much more than one-half the city is *cleared*:—the rest is *in woods*; and most of the streets which are laid out are cut through these woods and have a much more pleasing effect now than I think they will have when they shall be built. . . ."[8]

Morris Birkbeck, who visited the city in 1817, reacted similarly. He mentions that most of the streets could be distinguished only with difficulty, mainly by the rows of poplars planted along their edges. He was disdainful of the marble capitals brought over from Italy to be used on the Capitol, which showed in his words "how *un*-American is the whole plan." And he sourly observed, "This embryo metropolis, with its foreign decorations, should have set a better example to the young republic, by surrounding itself first with good roads and substantial bridges, in lieu of those inconvenient wooden structures and dangerous roads, over which the legislators must now pass to their duty. I think too, that good taste would have preferred native decoration for the seat of the legislature."[9]

Birkbeck was one of the first in a long succession of Europeans, chiefly English, who dutifully visited the capital and almost invariably mocked the pretensions of future grandeur embodied in its elaborate plan. The Minister from Portugal referred to Washington derisively as "The City of Magnificent Distances"; Charles Dickens a few decades later changed this to "The City of Magnificent Intentions." Pennsyl-

[8] Francis Baily, *Journal of a Tour in Unsettled Parts of North America in 1796 & 1797*, London, 1856, pp. 127-28.

[9] Morris Birkbeck, *Notes on a Journey in America from the Coast of Virginia to the Territory of Illinois*, 3rd edn., London, 1818, p. 29.

vania Avenue was referred to as "the great Serbonian Bog," the Capitol as "the palace in the wilderness." While Georgetown, it was said, was "a city of houses without streets," Washington was "a city of streets without houses."

Nor were these epithets inaccurate, as views of the city in the middle of the last century reveal (Fig. 107). The Mall resembled a pasture more than the intended formal avenue lined with monumental buildings, many of the squares were planted as vegetable gardens, and crops were set out within the street lines on the outskirts of the city. The city had not become the contiguous settlement that L'Enfant envisaged. It was more a collection of detached villages, each one clustered around one of the major public buildings.

The bucolic appearance of the city moved the Irish poet, Thomas Moore, to write these lines following his visit in 1804:

> This embryo capital, where Fancy sees
> Squares in morasses, obelisks in trees;
> Which second-sighted seers, ev'n now, adorn
> With shrines unbuilt, and heroes yet unborn,
> Though now but woods and J——n they see,
> Where streets should run and sages *ought* to be.[10]

Strangely enough, Mrs. Frances Trollope, who found little else to admire of America, perceived the underlying merit of building a great city on a preconceived plan when she visited Washington in 1830:

[10] Thomas Moore, "To Thomas Hume, Esq., M.D. from the City of Washington," *Poetical Works*, New York, 1868, p. 178.

Figure 107. View of Washington, D.C.: 1850

"I was delighted with the whole aspect of Washington. . . . It has been laughed at by foreigners, and even by natives, because the original plan of the city was upon an enormous scale, and but a very small part of it has been as yet executed. But I confess I see nothing in the least ridiculous about it; the original design, which was as beautiful as it was extensive, has been in no way departed from, and all that has been done has been done well. . . . To a person who has been travelling much through the country, and marked the immense quantities of new manufactories, new canals, new rail-roads, new towns, and new cities, which are springing, as it were, from the earth in every part of it, the appearance of the metropolis rising gradually into life and splendour, is a spectacle of high historic interest."[11]

Members of Congress who arrived in 1800 to meet for the first time in the new capital were less ecstatic. Representative John Cotton Smith of Connecticut, for example, found the city in a primitive state and recorded his disappointment in these words: "One wing of the Capitol only had been erected, which, with the President's house, a mile distant from it, both constructed with white sandstone, were shining objects in dismal contrast with the scene around them. Instead of recognizing the avenues and streets portrayed on the plan of the city, not one was visible, unless we except a road with two buildings on each side of it, called the New Jersey avenue. The Pennsylvania

[11] Frances Trollope, *Domestic Manners of the Americans*, 4th edn., London, 1832, p. 176.

[avenue] . . . was then nearly the whole distance a deep morass, covered with alder bushes. . . ."[12]

Smith described a row of six houses between the President's house and Georgetown, two other groups of two or three dwellings, and a number of isolated houses, the intervening spaces "being covered with shrub oak bushes on the higher grounds, and on the marshy soil either trees or some sort of shrubbery." He commented as well on the muddy and unimproved streets and on the sidewalk built of chips from scraps of stone used for the Capitol which cut the shoes of those who chanced to walk on its surfaces. Yet Smith felt strongly that the site chosen for the city held great promise and that President Washington's action in selecting this location "affords a striking exhibition of the discernment, wisdom, and forecast which characterized that illustrious man." And, Smith added, during his six years in Congress he had always opposed the frequent attempts by northern members of Congress to move the seat of government to some more prosperous and developed community.

One final observation of the city's planning, development, and appearance in the early years of its existence is of particular interest because of its source. Benjamin H. Latrobe, who had come to America in 1796, became Surveyor of Public Buildings in 1803. A designer of refinement and skill, he soon found himself involved in numerous projects intended to improve the city. In a letter written to an Italian friend in 1806 he put down frankly his observations about

[12] As quoted in John B. Ellis, *The Sights and Secrets of the National Capital*, New York, 1869, p. 42.

the city's plan, the circumstances of its founding, and the difficulties encountered in promoting its growth:

"The establishment of the Federal City was one of the offsprings of that revolutionary enthusiasm which elevated the American mind far above the aera in the life of our nation, then present. It has been said that the idea of creating a new city . . . was the favorite folly of General Washington. Its existence at last was due to a compromise of interests between the Eastern and Western States. After the law had established that there should be a city, General Washington seems to have thought that everything had been done towards making it. He himself built two indifferent houses in it. Everything else was badly planned and conducted. L'Enfant's plan has in its contrivance everything that could prevent the growth of the city. The distribution of the public buildings over a space five miles in length and three in breadth prevents the possibility of concentration. The proprietors of the soil, on which the town is to be spread, are rivals and enemies and each opposes every project which appears more advantageous to his neighbor than to himself. Speculators, of all degrees of honesty and of desperation, made a game of hazard of the scheme. . . . The plans of the public buildings were obtained by public advertisement, offering a reward for that most approved by General Washington. General Washington knew how to give liberty to his country but was wholly ignorant of art. It is therefore not to be wondered, that the design of a physician, who was very ignorant of architecture was adopted for the Capitol and of a carpenter for the President's house. The latter is not even original, but a mutilated copy of a badly designed building near Dublin. If these buildings are badly designed, they are still more indifferently executed."[13]

Improvements in the city came slowly. One of Jefferson's principal contributions was the planting of rows of poplars along Pennsylvania Avenue. These trees, much more than the scattered and isolated buildings built facing this intended monumental and ceremonial route, served to confine and direct views along the great diagonal boulevard connecting the Capitol with the residence of the President (Fig. 108).

The Washington Canal, which L'Enfant's plan showed as replacing Tiber Creek and running along the north edge of the Mall and then southward to the Anacostia River, had been temporarily abandoned by the commissioners because of lack of funds. A private company obtained a Congressional charter for its construction, but it was not started until 1810, opening five years later. Although this project was supposed to bring commercial prosperity to the city, its value for shipping turned out to be largely an illusion, and its stagnant waters served chiefly as a handy dumping place for filth and garbage. It was thus not only a menace to health but a source of noxious odors that stifled development along its banks except for woodyards, local industries of various types, and other unsightly uses. The Center Market, which was built later between 7th and 9th streets along the canal,

[13] Letter from B. H. Latrobe to Signor Mazzei, May 29, 1806, John H. B. Latrobe, "Construction of the Public Buildings in Washington," *Maryland Historical Magazine*, Vol. 11, No. 3 (September 1909), pp. 222-23.

Figure 108. View of Washington, D.C.: ca. 1837

still further added to the confusion, odor, noise, and filth that was to characterize this part of the city until well into the next century.

But the city continued to grow and change. With the Civil War and the re-establishment of the Union, the importance of the central government increased. Without industry of major importance and little but local trade, Washington gradually developed the economic base that sustains it today—the vast bureaucracy of the Federal establishment. Substantial improvements and dreadful mistakes alternated with one another during the latter half of the 19th century. "Boss" Shepherd, head of the newly constituted Board of Public Works, in 1871 transformed the muddy, poorly graded streets of the city into modern thoroughfares. He filled open sewers, including the Tiber Canal, and extended water service to most of the community.

Yet in 1872 the Congress authorized the Baltimore and Potomac Railway to lay its tracks across the Mall and construct its station at the southwest corner of what is now Constitution Avenue and 6th Street. A quarter of a century earlier the Smithsonian Institution and then the old Agriculture building had been located almost in the center of the Mall, and this new action seemed to eliminate for all time any possibility that this central open space of the capital city would ever take form as provided in the original plan. A view of the central part of the city from the south in 1882 shows the conditions at that time (Fig. 109). Its perspective is somewhat distorted, since it fails to reveal the extent to which the Agriculture and Smithsonian structures encroached on the Mall, but its depiction of the railway station and the old central market shows the extent to which public care-

1. Capitol. 2. Botanical Garden. 3. Columbian Armory (where first Troops arriving in 1861 were quartered). 4. National Museum. 5. Smithsonian Institution. 6. Agricultural Department. 7. Washington Monument. 8. State, War, and Navy Departments. 9. White House. 10. Treasury Department. 11. Army Medical and Surgical Museum (Ford's Theatre, where President Lincoln was shot).
12. Young Men's Christian Association. 13. General Post-Office. 14. Patent-Office. 15. Centre Market. 16. Baltimore and Potomac Depôt (where President Garfield was shot). 17. City Hall (Place of Guiteau's Trial). 18. Baltimore and Ohio Depôt. 19. Government Printing-Office.
20. Mount Vernon Square. 21. Franklin Square. 22. Stephen Asylum. 23. Howard University. 24. Columbian College. 25. Soldiers' Home (Summer abode of several Presidents).

OUR NATIONAL CAPITAL, VIEWED FROM THE SOUTH.—Drawn by Theo. R. Davis, from photographs by W. H. Jackson.

Figure 109. View of Washington, D.C.: 1882

lessness had nearly destroyed a major feature of the L'Enfant plan.

But this proved to be a turning point in Washington history. Perhaps appalled by the appearance of the city, townspeople and legislators alike soon found themselves engaged in a search for ways of improving conditions. In the last decade of the century a dozen or more plans for the central area were put forward. Finally, in 1901, with the appointment of the Senate Park Commission through the efforts of Senator James McMillan, a comprehensive, official, and inspiring plan was produced which was to guide the growth of the part of the nation's capital for the next half century. It was thus that L'Enfant's visionary scheme was ultimately to be realized.[14]

[14] A full account of the replanning of the central portion of Washington in 1901 and 1902 can be found in my *Monumental Washington: The Planning and Development of the Capital Center*, Princeton, 1967, which also traces in detail the founding and early development of the city.

Following the Revolution a great period of internal colonization began in the United States as western lands became available for settlement. One route of migration to the west extended from Philadelphia to Pittsburgh and then either by road or river to the valleys of the Ohio and Mississippi rivers. Another, of equal importance, was somewhat longer, but it avoided the difficult journey through the Appalachian Mountains. This route followed the Hudson River north to Albany, then west through the Mohawk Valley to Lake Erie. From here the remainder of the trip west could be made by water or along the level land route of the southern shore of Lake Erie. We have already explored some of the towns that developed in the Ohio Valley, and we now turn to those settlements that were made along the northerly of these two great trails to the inland empire of America.

Hope on the Hudson

The basis for urban settlement along the Hudson River had been established early in the 17th century by the Dutch. Albany, for example, never lost its dominant position as the chief city of the upper Hudson Valley. But as New York began to fill up with settlers following the Revolution, new towns were needed. Hudson, on the eastern bank of the river from which the town took its name, was one of these new trading and mercantile communities. It had come into existence in 1783 when it was settled by a band of New Englanders, many of them Quakers from Nantucket, who had found it impossible to continue their fishing activities because of the war. The plan of Hudson included two open squares as part of the gridiron street plan that sloped downward to the river from higher ground to the east. In these features Hudson resembled most of the inland communities that came into existence later as the result of a speculative town promotion activities by individual proprietors of advantageous sites.

Not all these cities were so conventional in design. One, at least, was quite exotic. This was Esperanza, founded on the west bank of the river opposite the city of Hudson by a distinguished group of New Yorkers headed by Edward Livingston, whose career included service as a congressman from New York, mayor of New York City, senator from Louisiana, U.S. Secretary of State, and minister to France (Fig. 110).

Hudson's intended rival was laid out to tap the trade from the western part of the state, first by a land route and ultimately, it was hoped, by a canal. The proprietors hoped that eventually the state capital would be moved to their city. Land was purchased in 1794, and shortly thereafter a plan was prepared and circulated to prospective settlers.

The street pattern and the names given the streets are curious. Liberty and Equality streets suggest the influence of the French Revolution, and the portion of the town to the northwest, with its circular and radial boulevards, also calls to mind the grand plan of French Baroque tradition. This was, of course, immediately after Washington had been planned, and it is likely that the Livingston group at-

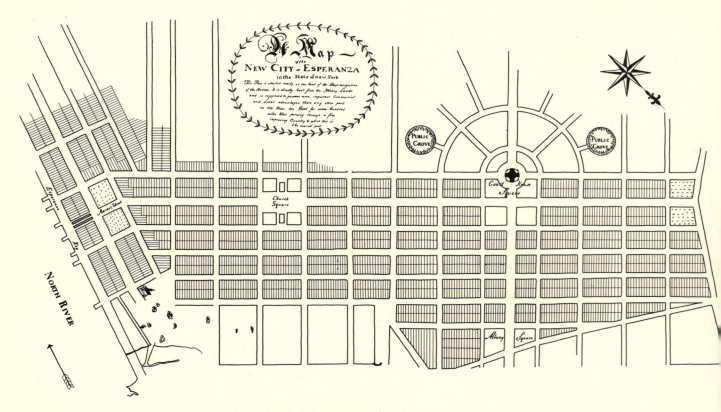

Figure 110. Plan of Esperanza, New York: ca. 1794

tempted to imitate some of the features of the new national capital. There were interesting paired streets: Love and Happiness; Beer and Cider; Meal and Bread; Art and Science; and Wheat and Rice, with a Corn Street also added.

With its squares for a market, churches, courthouse, and with reserved common land and sites for "groves." Esperanza seemingly was well equipped to become a great city. But despite the prediction of its sponsors that "this infant town, will beyond all doubt, experience a considerable increase," Esperanza failed to develop. As late as 1867 a map of the township in which it was located showed the paper streets and squares in all their elegance, but today there is no trace of this speculative enterprise, which, as its name signified, was a city built only on hope.

The Empire State at Wholesale

There were many other individual speculations in towns elsewhere along the Hudson and the Mohawk valleys, but the bulk of the western portion of the state was bought, subdivided, and sold by quite a different method. Here wholesale land development replaced the smaller scale operations centered on individual towns.

Two great land companies commenced operations in western New York shortly after the Revolution. This was territory claimed by Massachusetts, but in 1786 the two states agreed that New York would acquire sovereignty and that Massachusetts would retain ownership of the land lying west of a north-south line running through Seneca Lake. Massachusetts sold these lands, some 6 million acres, to Oliver Phelps and Nathaniel Gorham in 1787, subject to their acquisition of the title from the Indians. Phelps and Gorham were able to buy only the eastern one-third of this vast tract, and the remainder reverted to Massachusetts. In 1791 Robert Morris purchased this reverted land, and in turn sold it along with other territory he had previously acquired to two land companies. The largest portion, about 3 1/2 million acres of the western part of the Morris Purchase, was bought by a group of Dutch bankers who formed the Holland Land Company in 1793. The remaining tract Morris sold to a group of English speculators headed by Sir William Pulteney.

Development of the Pulteney Purchase was entrusted to Captain Charles Williamson who opened his land office at Bath in 1793. Williamson was lavish in his expenditures aimed at developing the land and attracting settlers. He built a road connecting Williamsport, Pennsylvania with Williamsburg, New York, on the Genesee River. A number of town sites were surveyed, including Williamsburg, Geneva, and Great Sodus.

But it was at Bath that Williamson laid out "a handsome progressive city" designed to be the great metropolis of western New York. He built a theater and a hotel, started a weekly newspaper, and laid out a race track. In order to promote land sales in the town he held a series of fairs, with horse races, dances, and theatrical performances. This enterprise attracted wide attention, and when La Rochefoucauld visited Bath in June 1795 he reported its progress with obvious admiration: "Mr. Williamson is, at present building a school, in Bath. This he intends to endow with some hundred acres of land, and to take upon himself the maintenance of the master. . . . He is also building a sessions-house and a prison. The present inn was likewise built by him. . . . Near Bath . . . he has erected a cornmill, and two sawmills."[1] However, he added, only "about twenty houses compose, as yet, the whole of the town of Bath."

The following year "A Farmer," in a letter to the *Wilkesbarre Gazette* described the fever of speculation with which his son had become afflicted at Bath:

"He has been to Bath, the celebrated Bath, and has returned both a speculator and a gentleman, having spent his money, swapped away my horse, caught the fever and ague, and what is infinitely worse, that horrid disorder which some call the 'terraphobia.'

"We hear nothing from the poor creature now (in his ravings) but . . . of ranges, of townships, number, thousands, hundreds, acres, Bath, fairs, races, heats . . . etc., etc. My son has part of a township for sale, and it's diverting enough to hear him narrate its pedigree, qualities, and situation. In fine, it lies near Bath. . . . It cost my son but five dollars per acre. . . . One thing is very much in my boy's favor —he has six years' credit. Another thing is still more so—he is not worth a sou, and never will be, at this rate. . . ."[2]

Bath, as planned by Williamson, was an elegant little town by fron-

---

[1] Duke de La Rochefoucauld-Liancourt, *Travels Through the United States of North America*, London, 2nd edn., 1800, I, 233.

[2] As quoted in Isaac Weld, *Travels Through North America and Canada*, London, 4th edn., 1799, II, 336-37.

tier standards. It had two squares connected by a short, wide street. These squares were perhaps intended to resemble those laid out in its Georgian namesake in western England. But the location of Bath was unfavorable for any large development, and the wave of western settlement washed on beyond to more advantageous sites in the Ohio Valley or along the shores of the Great Lakes. Bath never became more than a large village, and the unrealistic expectations of the Pulteneys were never to be achieved.

The city planning activities of the Holland Land Company were more successful and of greater interest. Not only did its chief town become one of America's great cities but the planning concepts employed there reflect the influence of L'Enfant's plan for Washington a few years earlier. There was, in fact, a direct connection between the Washington plan and that used for New Amsterdam, later renamed Buffalo. The land agent for the Holland Land Company in western New York was Joseph Ellicott, the brother of Andrew Ellicott, who succeeded L'Enfant as planner for the federal city. Joseph Ellicott was familiar with the plan of Washington and determined to use some of its features in his own work.

Ellicott liked the future site of New Amsterdam at the eastern end of Lake Erie from the beginning. As early as 1798 he described its beauty and strategic location to his superiors. But it was not until 1802 that he received authorization to lay out the town. In the summer of 1803 he was busy with site surveys, and a year later he could report to the general agent of the company in Philadelphia that the survey work was "in such a state for forwardness as to enable me to forward to you in the course of 10 or 15 days a complete plan of this Village. . . ."

Ellicott's plan reveals to what extent he followed the diagonal street pattern used at Washington (Fig. 111). From the corners of the central square four of these radial avenues extended to the edges of the city. Another pair of diagonal streets focused on a semi-circular open space located along one of the main streets. It is doubtful, however, that Ellicott had much of a feeling for the architectural treatment of buildings placed to close the vistas from these radial roadways. We do know, however, that he intended to build his own house on a projection of land extending into the eastern side of the semi-circular space. From here he would have had views up and down the street and in two directions along the paired diagonals to the waterfront. This intention was thwarted in 1809 by the town highway commission, and Ellicott, in retaliation, moved the land office of the company to Batavia, an inland town that he had planned in 1801.

Ellicott's plan also shows the pattern of outlots varying in size from five to twenty acres that extended to the east beyond the town proper. This was similar to the land system employed elsewhere in the west. Ellicott also followed the practice usual in other speculative towns of reserving choice lots for the company. This was an obvious device to increase land values and thus maximize profits when the reserved lots were put up for sale later. Ellicott was paid partly in land, and he chose for himself the most desirable town lot and a very large outlot immediately adjacent.

The Holland Land Company was responsible for other cities, al-

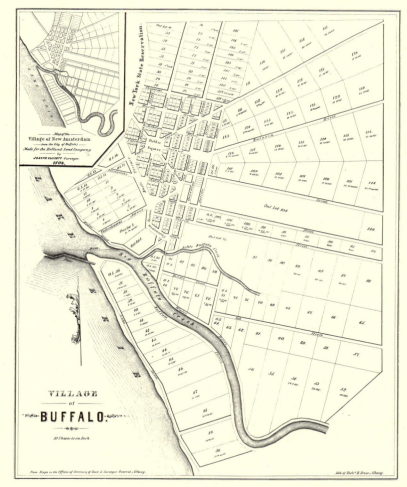

Figure 111. Plan of Buffalo, New York: 1851

though none of them rivalled Buffalo in importance after the initial years of that lake port's development. Cazenovia was one of these towns, planned as early as 1793 on an isolated tract owned by the company many miles east of its main holdings. This was a little grid plan with a single square in the center. Mayvil, planned in 1804, was another of the company settlements. In all cases, sale of town lots provided only one source of income. The entire Holland Purchase was surveyed into rectangular townships and farm tracts, and much of Ellicott's efforts went into the promotion of these lands. The towns were described as providing market facilities and as sources of supplies needed by farmers.

The Holland Land Company also acted as a wholesaler of land. In 1804, after protracted negotiations, Ellicott sold some 20,000 acres of land at the head of navigation on the Allegheny River to Adam Hoops, a protégé of Robert Morris and former *aide de camp* to Alexander Hamilton. Hoops laid out a town, calling it first Hamilton and then Olean. Olean, like Bath, was never successful as a large-scale promotion, and Hoops was eventually forced to relinquish his land when his investment proved unrewarding.

Little New England in Frontier Ohio

When Connecticut waived its claims to all the land between extensions of its northern and southern boundaries west to the Mississippi it reserved a generous tract of land in northeastern Ohio. The bounds of this 3 1/2 million-acre domain extended 120 miles west of the Pennsylvania boundary between Lake Erie and the 41st parallel. The General Assembly of the state determined to dispose of the entire tract at once rather than become involved in piecemeal sales. Only the western twelve miles of the reserve, called the Firelands, were set aside to be granted to residents of certain Connecticut shore towns whose property had been destroyed during the war. Proceeds from the sale of the remaining land were to constitute a perpetual fund, with the interest devoted to support the public schools of the State of Connecticut.

In the fall of 1795 a sale agreement for $1,200,000 was concluded with a syndicate called the Connecticut Land Company. The company received a deed to this still unsurveyed wilderness, posting a bond and a mortgage on the land with the state treasurer. The property was then conveyed in trust to three persons until the tract could be surveyed. When the survey was completed and the Indian title extinguished, the members of the syndicate would then receive land in proportion to their financial contributions, and the location of the land so distributed was to be decided by lot. The land was to be divided into townships five miles square, similar to although smaller than the congressional townships specified by the Land Ordinance of 1785.

A survey party under the direction of General Moses Cleaveland set out for Ohio in 1796. Their initial task was to lay out the township grid as far west as the mouth of the Cuyahoga River and to select a site for and plan a city as the "capital" of the Western Reserve. While some of his surveyors followed the Pennsylvania line south to the southeast corner of the Reserve, Cleaveland moved westward along the shore of Lake Erie. When he reached the mouth of the

Cuyahoga River, roughly in the center of the tract, he selected a site on the bluff overlooking the lake and marked out the town.

The drawing by Seth Pease, one of the surveyors, shows the original plan (Fig. 112). The public square, a characteristic of most of the settlements of the Reserve, included some ten acres of ground. From the sides of the square ran streets 99 and 132 feet wide. Other streets parallel and perpendicular to these formed a familiar grid pattern except for the irregular roads leading down the bluff to the river's bank. Town lots of two acres and outlots up to 100 acres were then laid out.

Certainly Cleaveland, who thought that his city might someday be "as large as Old Windham" in his native Connecticut, never envisaged the true future of the city. The Cleveland plan of 1796 is simply a New England village transplanted to northern Ohio, in the process gaining something in regularity but perhaps losing part of its charm. The town during its early years did indeed retain the peaceful atmosphere of a remote country village. A plan of Cleveland in 1835 shows the community, not much larger than its original size, just as the canals and then the railroads began transforming it into a bustling transportation and industrial center and lake port (Fig. 113).

While Cleveland began under company sponsorship, the other communities in the Western Reserve owe their origins to individual proprietors who received their shares of land when the surveys were complete and townships and fractional townships were distributed by lot. Almost every landowner, whether one of the original proprietors or a later purchaser, seemed to interest himself in town planning. Be-

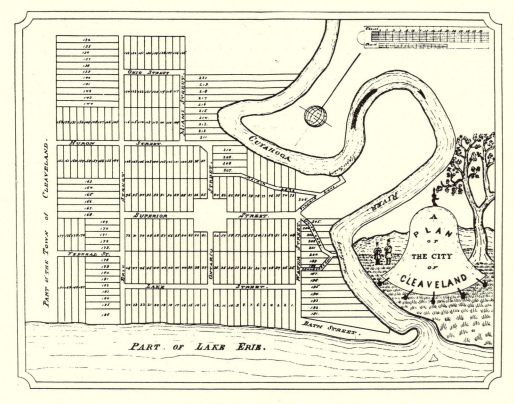

Figure 112. Plan of Cleveland, Ohio: 1796

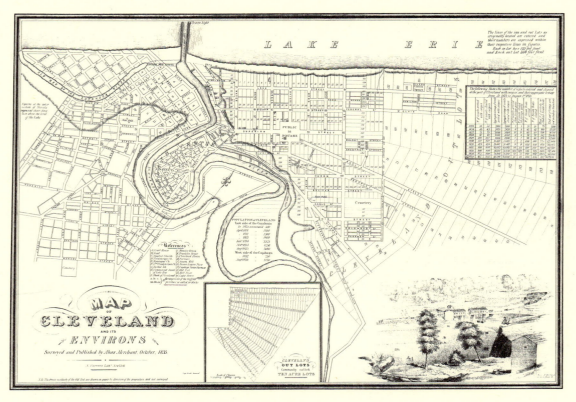

Figure 113. Plan of Cleveland, Ohio: 1835

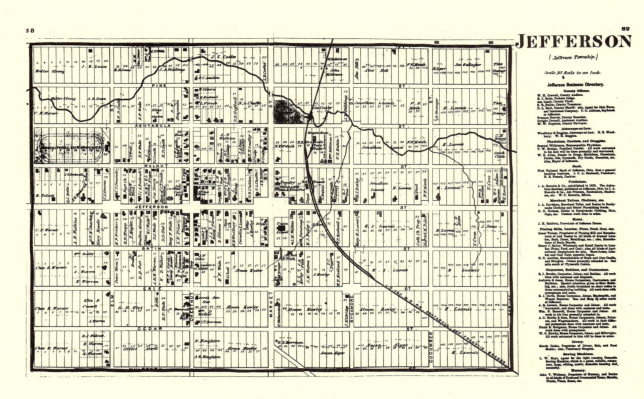

Figure 114. Plan of Jefferson, Ohio: 1874

cause of the diverse backgrounds, resources, and intentions of the owners, these towns varied in form and size. Yet if there was variation in details there was nevertheless a similarity of atmosphere pervading these communities. Most towns in the Reserve share certain characteristics: a system of outlots and house lots of ample size, one or more central greens, wide streets, moderate size, and a general air of order and repose. The resemblance to New England communities is as unmistakable as it is understandable. The settlers came mainly from Connecticut and the other New England states, and in this wilderness they attempted to recreate the community pattern they knew best.

A sampling from the rich treasure of town planning experience in this area may serve to demonstrate the wealth of material that exists. One of the earliest and most ambitious plans was for Jefferson, laid out by Gideon Granger, Postmaster General of the United States, in 1805 (Fig. 114). The plan of the town as it existed in 1874 was described as follows:

"Mr. Granger prepared a draft . . . of his townsite and designated streets, which as yet had an existence only on paper. Nine large avenues running east and west and crossing at right angles, seven others running north and south, with several squares at the crossing of the streets, one of these in the center of the plat being 38 rods from east to west by 22 rods from north to south. . . . It required only a vivid imagination, and lo! here was a magnificent city of palatial residences and churches whose spires pointed heavenward, but the sober fact is that the town plat was recorded when only a solitary cabin occupied the townsite. . . ."[3]

The central square and portions of three others have survived, but the remainder were used as building sites when Jefferson failed to live up to the glorious expectations of its proprietor.

Canfield is located near the southeastern corner of the Western Reserve. The plan does not convey the beauty and serenity of this lovely village (Fig. 115). The great central green measures 600 by 2,200 feet, sloping gently upward to the south. Facing it on lots of generous size stand some of the most impressive houses in the Reserve. As in New England, the plan forms are deceptive and fail to reveal the true quality of the third dimension of architecture. Chardon, planned in 1808 by Peter Chardon Brooks and offered by him as the seat of Geauga County on condition that it be given his middle name, is of similar charm and scale. The rectangular green occupies the crest of a modest hill. Streets enter at the center and the ends of its shorter sides. Around the village a kind of ring road serves as a link between village and the surrounding farmlands.

Twenty miles west of Cleveland, where the two forks of the Black River come together, Herman Ely, son of one of the original company shareholders, planned his town of Elyria in 1817 (Fig. 116). The attractive site lay on a narrow strip of high ground formed by the looping rivers. At the highest point above the river Ely placed an open space in the form of an elongated rectangle. He laid out the main

[3] Williams Brothers, *History of Ashtabula County, Ohio*, Philadelphia, 1878, p. 147.

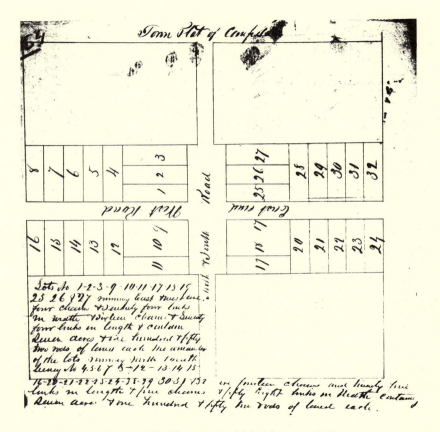

Figure 115. Plan of Canfield, Ohio: ca. 1800

Figure 116. View of Elyria, Ohio: 1868

street to run southward from one corner of the central "square." Other streets were surveyed parallel and at right angles to this principal axis. A perspective view of 1868 reveals the details of one of the most successful of all the Reserve towns in its adaption to natural site conditions and its adaptability to modern requirements.

Treatment of the green or public square received careful attention from the planners of the Reserve's communities. The rectangle at Sharon Center, the ellipse at Leroy, the parallelogram at Madison, and the variations on these shapes in other communities probably represent attempts by the proprietors to be a bit different from then existing nearby towns, or, it may simply have resulted from imitations of the home communities of the planners in New England. But to a considerable extent these diverse patterns indicate efforts to experiment with different forms in the search for a better plan, a more livable town, a more attractive and impressive site for a church, or a town hall or a county courthouse.

Of great interest because of its break with the gridiron pattern is Tallmadge, now a suburb of and almost engulfed by the city of Akron. The Reverend David Bacon purchased the township in 1807 with the idea of establishing a kind of religious commonwealth. Although this aspect of the community was never fully carried out, Bacon's plan for the township and the village at its center was evidently based on his belief that all settlers should be in close communication and that the church in the village should be the focus of the entire settlement.

He had the township divided into sixteen squares of 1,000 acres, each with 66-foot wide roads at the boundaries of these mile and a quarter square sections. Then he boldly ran four roads diagonally from the corners of the township toward the center, where they met at the village. From the rectangular village square, four other roads ran north, south, east, and west. Town hall and church inside the oval green in the center of the square completed the composition (Fig. 117).

Perhaps the most interesting of all the cities of the Western Reserve was Sandusky, located in the Firelands section and planned in 1818. A settlement of sorts had existed on Sandusky Bay for some years before. One Isaac Mills became owner of a portion of the site and had it laid out by Major Hector Kilbourn (Fig. 118). A local legend, which has never been verified but seems plausible, is that Kilbourn's plan for the city's streets and open spaces duplicated the Masonic emblem of an open Bible, mason's square, and open compass. In the plan, Washington Square is supposed to represent the Bible, and the two pairs of interlocking diagonal streets resemble the square and compass. It is known that Kilbourn was an avid Mason and the master of the first Masonic lodge in Sandusky.

Whatever the inspiration for the plan, it resulted in generous allotments of open spaces in the central portion of the modern city. There are three large triangular parks and several smaller spaces of similar shape in addition to the large central open space. While Sandusky developed an air of quiet prosperity and dignity, the essential failure of its plan as an essay in grand design must be noted. The two chief diagonals were planned, strangely enough, to terminate at open spaces

Figure 117. View of the green in Tallmadge, Ohio: 1874

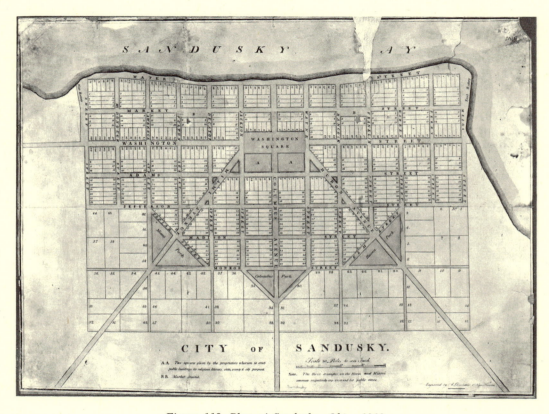

Figure 118. Plan of Sandusky, Ohio: 1818

rather than at the sites designated for public buildings. A splendid opportunity to create a little regional capital with something of the elegance of a Williamsburg was lost. Instead, mere eccentricity of design resulted from the use of the motifs of the grand plan without a clear concept of their function in emphasizing the importance of strategic building sites.

Thus, gradually, the northern part of Ohio filled with settlers from the New England states who planned for the future of their communities with intelligence and skill. The difficulties were many and the hardships great. These courageous pioneers and their predecessors throughout Kentucky and Ohio left a rich legacy of planning experience.

West and north of the Western Reserve lay the territory of Michigan, the setting for one of the more bizarre episodes of American planning. It was here, on June 11, 1805, that a fire swept through the frontier outpost of Detroit, just a few days before Michigan was to achieve territorial status and its new leaders were to take office. Under the system of territorial government three judges formed the judiciary, and a governor and the judges constituted the legislative board. President Jefferson had appointed General William Hull, a veteran of the Revolution, as governor and, as one of the judges, Augustus Brevoort Woodward.

Woodward was an ambitious young man of thirty-one, learned, precocious, and a trifle eccentric. He had lived in Washington, where he knew both L'Enfant and Jefferson, and possibly he already had begun to form some ideas about city planning when he arrived in

Detroit only to find the city completely destroyed. Woodward convinced Governor Hull that a new plan should be prepared, and Hull appointed Woodward a committee of one to carry this out.

Lots in the new town were then put up for sale. Owners of land in the old town were entitled to equal amounts of land under the new plan. Most of the new lots, however, were larger, and the owner was required to pay for the extra area. No money was actually accepted, however, pending the approval by Congress of the action taken by the new government. The plan of 1805 has not survived, but it seems likely that it was essentially the same as the one which gained official sanction the following year.

That winter both Hull and Woodward traveled to Washington seeking congressional approval of their activities. In this they succeeded, and in April 1806 the President put his signature to an act authorizing the governor and judges "to lay out a town, including the whole of the old Town of Detroit, and ten thousand acres adjacent" and to adjust all claims for land under a provision granting a lot of not more than 5,000 square feet to every resident of the city over seventeen at the time of the fire.

During the summer Woodward prepared a new plan for this extensive area, aided by Abijah Hull, a relative of the governor's. By September this work was complete, and the legislative board then gave official approval to one of the most unusual city plans ever devised (Fig. 119). The law adopted by the board specified "that the bases of the town of Detroit shall be an equilateral triangle, having each side of the length of four thousand feet, and having every angle

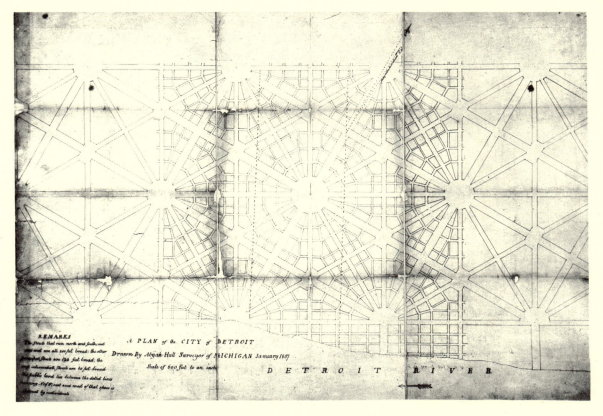

Figure 119. Plan of Detroit, Michigan: 1807

bisected by a perpendicular line upon the opposite side, such parts being excepted, as from the approximation of . . . [the] . . . river Detroit, or other unavoidable circumstances, may require partial deviation."[4]

The "perpendicular lines" divided each equilateral triangle into six right-angle triangles. Each of these was to be known as a "section." Section 1 was described by metes and bounds in the act, which then specified that other sections of identical size were to be laid out from time to time as the plan was extended. At this time 3,000 of the 10,000 acres of land were planned into a vast honeycomb pattern made up of the basic triangles. Principal avenues were laid out north-south and east-west with widths of 200 feet. Other main streets were 120 feet wide, while minor streets were given the generous width of 60 feet. Every lot was afforded rear access from an ingenious system of alleys (Fig. 120).

Woodward employed two repeating units of open space. At the intersection of twelve avenues he designed a circular space of five and a half acres. To avoid sharp points at the street entrances he cut back the blocks to provide lots of more normal shape. Smaller rectangular open spaces appear at every intersection of six avenues and were treated in similar fashion. The central portion of each triangular section of land was left open "for public wells and pumps, for markets, for public schools, for houses for the reception of engines or other articles for the extinction of fires, and the preservation of the

[4] An Act Concerning the Town of Detroit, *Laws of the Territory of Michigan*, 1807.

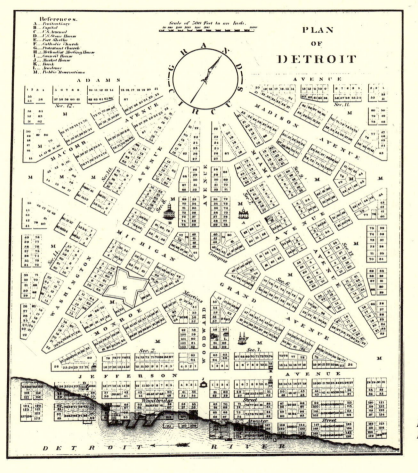

Figure 120. Plan of the Central Portion of Detroit, Michigan: 1807

property of the inhabitants, for houses for the meeting of religious, moral, literary, or political societies, or other useful associations, and generally, for such purposes of utility or ornament, as the city council of Detroit may, at any time, by law, provide. . . ."[5]

The same law provided for double lines of trees on both sides of the 120-foot avenues, and for trees in "clumps or groves to be of an elliptical shape" on both sides of the 200-foot avenues. Spaces for walks and front yards and porches were also defined in this statute. Judge Woodward and his colleagues were clearly concerned with beauty as well as utility.

Woodward's Detroit was no mere copy of the Washington plan, to which it has been frequently compared. It is true that both plans were on a heroic scale, both utilized diagonal streets, and both made frequent use of symmetrical open spaces as terminal features for broad avenues. The underlying concepts, however, were different. Where Washington really combined two types of street systems, one superimposed on the other, the Detroit plan used a single integrated pattern. Detroit lacked, however, a clearly articulated focal point, such as the Washington plan provided in the relationship between Capitol and the President's house and the Mall.

The citizens of Detroit appeared much less interested in Woodward's vision of a great metropolis than in obtaining clear and immediate title to property in the new town. As soon as the terms of the congressional act of 1806 became known, demands for "donation"

[5] An additional Act Concerning the Town of Detroit, *Laws of the Territory of Michigan,* 1807.

lots were presented to the board. Those who had purchased lots under the scheme of the previous year understandably felt that such lots now should be awarded them without payment. What should have been a straightforward procedure of land allocation became mired in a bog of conflict and dissension. Moreover, members of the legislative board frequently disagreed violently among themselves.

Whatever Hull's original attitude was toward Woodward as a person and town planner, he soon came to regard the judge with suspicion and hostility. These two men of opposite temperament and interests were often at odds. In 1807 they clashed over plans for fortifying the town, a disagreement that continued into the next year. That fall Woodward left for Washington. In his absence Hull attempted to scrap the triangular plan for Detroit, ordering James McCloskey, a surveyor, to prepare a revised plan using the traditional gridiron pattern. A few months later the legislative board repealed the act of 1806 which had established the triangular system of land division. Woodward was successful in having these actions nullified on his return, but the board remained hopelessly split, and the people of Detroit became increasingly dissatisfied under its rule.

In the autumn of 1813 Lewis Cass succeeded Hull. For a time the affairs of Detroit seemed to move more smoothly, the new governor declining to identify himself with either faction of the board. However, with the increase in Detroit's population following the War of 1812, mounting opposition developed to the extension of the triangular system of land subdivision throughout the 10,000 acres surrounding the area of original settlement. Many requests came before the legislative board for the purchase of this reserve land in rectangular farms of 160 acres. To prevent such action from interfering with the city plan, Woodward introduced a resolution reaffirming the triangular system of land division.

In the fall of 1817 the judge was again absent in Washington. Cass and Judges Witherell and Griffin began the survey of rectangular farms in the tract of reserve land. As a personal affront to their absent colleague, the name of Woodward Avenue below the Grand Circus was changed to Market Street, its extension to the northwest was narrowed from 120 feet to 66 feet, and it was renamed Witherell Avenue. Land sales under this new system were to begin on June 1, 1818. On that day Woodward submitted to the governor and his fellow judges a truly remarkable document attacking the new proposal as illegal on a number of grounds. He did not confine his arguments to the legal issues involved but continued with a number of persuasive statements on the necessity of planning as an essential element of policy to be followed in a rapidly developing nation. And he correctly pointed out Detroit's future as a great metropolis. But this forceful appeal was of no avail. Land sales were begun, and the opportunity to extend the original plan was lost for all time. The judge was soon to leave the territory, for in 1824 his term of office expired, and he was not reappointed.

During the 1820's Detroit grew on the familiar grid pattern (Fig. 121). Some of the diagonal streets were narrowed; many were abandoned completely. The military tract where the fort had stood was turned over to city authorities and promptly platted in checkerboard

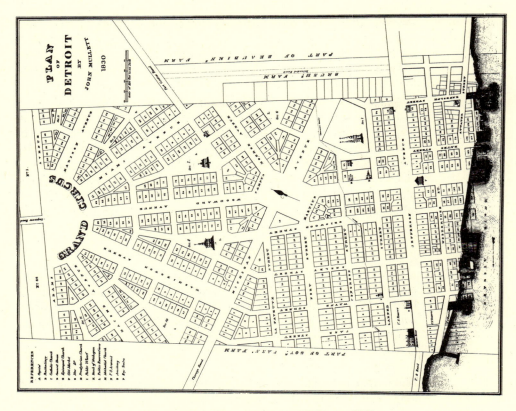

Figure 121. Plan of Detroit, Michigan: 1830

fashion. Only a few of the original streets, the Campus Martius, and half of the Grand Circus, were retained. Planning was forgotten in the haste for expansion and land speculation.

What would Detroit be like if Woodward's vision had been followed? Would it have been a workable plan for a modern city? Perhaps the plan, with its intricate triangular pattern, was too abstract and complicated. Modern planners might shudder at the maze of diagonal streets and confusing intersections. One thing is certain. If Detroit's growth through the years had been guided by men approaching Woodward in vision and determination and with the additional characteristics of technical ability and flexibility of mind, Detroit's planners of today would be facing an easier and more enviable task of adjusting the pattern of a complicated metropolis to meet the demands of contemporary life.

Section 9, Township 39, Range 14

New York was a city of 200,000 and had already filled in a good part of the commissioners' grid when civil engineer James Thompson filed his plat of Chicago in 1830. Here on the shore of Lake Michigan another of America's numerous gridiron cities began its development. Chicago owed its origins and its growth to transportation. Where now it is the railroads, the airlines, and the St. Lawrence Seaway, in the beginning a canal that was to connect the Great Lakes with the Mississippi furnished the main impetus to growth. Such a canal had long been a subject of comment. Joliet, after his visit to the site in 1673, mentioned the possibility of the project in his reports to his superiors. In 1808 Gallatin recommended its construction in his program of internal improvements. Finally, in 1822 Congress authorized the young state of Illinois to survey and acquire a 90-foot swath of land for this purpose.

There were conflicts over the exact location for the canal, and the state faced serious difficulties over its financing. In 1826 the Illinois legislature requested, and Congress a year later approved, federal aid in the form of a land grant. Under the act the state was to receive title to alternate sections of land for five miles on each side of the canal's route. By 1829 three canal commissioners were appointed, a route was selected, and in the following year the commissioners retained James Thompson to lay out a town in Section 9, Township 39, Range 14, so that a few lots might be sold in order to meet current expenses. Chicago thus had its origins in a speculative real estate transaction, an event to be endlessly repeated in the early years of the growth of the second largest metropolis of the nation.

A map of the city in 1834 shows the original "canal lots" of the 1830 survey in a six- by ten-block grid at the forks of the Chicago River (Fig. 122). The other streets and blocks, including those in the tract set aside to be sold for the support of schools, had been laid out in the intervening six years. Although in 1839 the town council purchased two acres of land for park purposes, at the time of this map the only public reservation was the land at the mouth of the river where Fort Dearborn was located. Land for the present Grant Park along the lake was, however, set aside at about this time, an example of foresight all the more commendable because of the pressure to

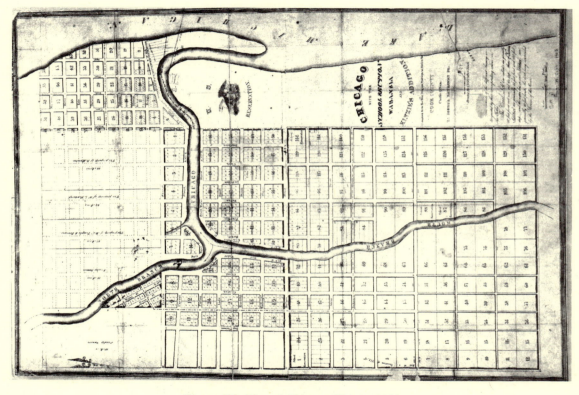

Figure 122. Plan of Chicago, Illinois: 1834

subdivide all available building sites. The beginnings of the vast grid-iron that is modern Chicago are clearly to be seen. With each succeeding addition to the town new streets were laid out connecting with or parallel to Thompson's original grid system.

Construction on the canal did not begin until 1836 and was not completed for a dozen years, but the promise of this project was enough to draw settlers and to stimulate a lively speculation in city lots. Evidently Chicago has always been a city of optimists, for it must have required a sturdy faith in the future to survive the discomforts in this pioneer city. That faith was strengthened by the knowledge of the prosperity the Grand Erie Canal had brought to the cities of upstate New York.

The boom began in 1833, and in that year 200 houses were built. The population then was under 400. In 1834 this had increased to 1,800, and at the height of the boom in 1836 there were about 4,000 persons living in the city. The mania for buying and selling town lots that was then sweeping the country was nowhere wilder than at Chicago. Harriet Martineau, who visited the city in 1836, recorded these impressions: "I never saw a busier place than Chicago was at the time of our arrival. The streets were crowded with land speculators, hurrying from one sale to another. A negro dressed up in scarlet bearing a scarlet flag and riding a white horse with housings of scarlet announced the time of sale. At every street corner where he stopped the crowd gathered around him; and it seemed as if some prevalent mania infected the whole people. As the gentlemen of our party walked the streets, storekeepers hailed them from their doors with offers of farms and all manner of land lots, advising them to speculate before the price of land rose higher."[6]

Land prices soared. James Silk Buckingham reported that some lots changed hands ten times in a single day and that the "evening purchaser" paid at least "ten times as much as the price paid by the morning buyer for the same spot!" The school section, which in 1833 sold for $38,000, was valued at $1,200,000 in 1836. Land in the present city limits worth $168,000 in 1830 rose in value to more than $10,000,000 at the peak of the boom. Most of this "value" was fictitious since it was not based on cash sales but on purchases with extremely liberal credit.

In the rush to lay out new subdivisions, sites beyond the immediate area of Chicago were not overlooked. As one participant later recalled, "The prairies of Illinois, the forests of Wisconsin, and the sandhills of Michigan, presented a chain almost unbroken of supposititious villages and cities. The whole land seemed staked out and peopled on paper. . . . Often was a fictitious streamlet seen to wind its romantic course through the heart of an ideal city, thus creating water lots, and water privileges. But where a *real* stream, however, diminutive, did find its way to the shore of the lake . . . the miserable waste of sand and fens which lay unconscious of its glory on the shore of the lake, was suddenly elevated into a mighty city, with a projected harbor and lighthouse, railroads and canals. . . . Not the puniest

[6] As quoted in Homer Hoyt, *One Hundred Years of Land Values in Chicago*, Chicago, 1933, p. 30.

brook on the shore of Lake Michigan was suffered to remain without a city at its mouth. . . ."[7]

The Chicago land boom collapsed, as it did in every other American city, with the panic of 1837. Growth would begin anew, and with the opening of the long-delayed canal in 1848 the city would attain a population of 20,000. By this time the canal would be obsolete, soon to be outstripped in importance by the railroads. By the beginning of the Civil War the city was the focal point of ten rail lines, its population was approaching 100,000, and its rate of growth was steadily increasing. The next years were to witness perhaps the most rapid increase in population of any large American city. In 1865 the population was about 180,000. This had doubled by 1872 and quadrupled by 1885. The primitive, formative years of the city lay behind, but the later city was merely an enormously enlarged version of the original modest gridiron. Only in a few suburbs could one find relief from the relentless pattern of Chicago's oppressive grid, magnificent only in its scale and in the tenacity with which this pattern was followed by successive generations.

[7] Joseph N. Balestier, *The Annals of Chicago: A Lecture Delivered Before the Chicago Lyceum, January 21, 1840*, Chicago, 1876, pp. 27-29.

Almost from the beginning of settlement America attracted a variety of reformers, utopians, and pariah religious sects whose restless quest for kingdoms of paradise on mortal earth sometimes produced communities substantially different in character from those planned by more practical men of affairs. These dedicated, often fanatical, groups shunned existing cities with their temptations and distractions, preferring to create settlements in harmony with their religious, economic, or social convictions. Not all of them succeeded in developing towns that matched in interest and variety their often strange and complicated philosophical doctrines, but many of the utopian communities are of great interest and possess a distinctive character.

Homes for Heretics: The Huguenots

Two religious groups of colonial times stand out as planners of towns—the Huguenots and the Moravians. The Huguenots, French Protestants, had long been persecuted by the Catholics. Exclusion from public office and academic honors, heavy fines, loss of property, and tortures and executions were imposed by the authorities in an attempt to stamp out their heretical beliefs. It is little wonder that from the middle of the 16th century Huguenots sought refuge abroad, including the New World.

Under the sponsorship of Admiral Gaspard de Coligny, one expedition set out for Brazil in 1555 and succeeded in establishing a small settlement on the site of Rio de Janeiro. But this was broken up in 1560 by the Portuguese, and Huguenot eyes turned northward to the virtually unknown coast of Florida and the Carolinas.

In 1562, following renewed violence against them in France, a second Huguenot expedition under Jean Ribaut first landed at the mouth of the St. John's River in Florida, then proceeded northward along the coast to Port Royal harbor in what is now South Carolina. Here they built a small fortress, which they named Charlesfort. Ribaut, leaving a small group behind, returned to France to obtain reinforcements and additional supplies. At home the country was virtually in a civil war over the massacre of a group of Protestants in Champagne, and Ribaut found it impossible to organize a new expedition for Carolina. The tiny Charlesfort garrison meanwhile had quarreled among themselves, murdered their leader, constructed a small sailing vessel, and finally managed to reach France after a voyage of unbelievable hardships.

Coligny managed to organize still a third settlement group which, with three ships and commanded by René de Laudonnière, was able to find the mouth of the St. John's River a second time. This little band established Fort Caroline on a site six miles inland. A drawing of this Florida fortress town shows a triangular stockade enclosing the houses of the settlers and the barracks for the soldiers (Fig. 123). This little settlement enjoyed but a brief existence. The Spanish, alarmed by this invasion of land claimed by them, quickly eliminated

Figure 123. View of Fort Caroline, Florida: 1671

the band of Huguenots by striking from their hurriedly founded base at St. Augustine. Virtually all the French were brutally put to death, and Huguenot settlement of this part of America came to an end.

Huguenot interest shifted to other parts of North America. The first successful colonization of Canada was by the Sieur de Monts, a wealthy Huguenot who secured his grant from the former Huguenot leader, Henry IV. As we have seen, this group established the first settlements in New France, first at Ste. Croix Island, then Port Royal, and finally at Quebec. The revocation of de Monts' exclusive trading rights, the assassination of Henry IV, and the early interest of the Jesuits and other Catholic orders in colonization brought an end to Huguenot influence in French America.

Much the same history was written in the founding of New Amsterdam. In the years following the bloody St. Bartholomew's Day massacres in 1572, thousands of Huguenots fled abroad. Among them were the Walloons from northeastern France. Most of them went to Holland seeking freedom from religious tyranny, many of them settling in Leiden. Here in the early years of the 17th century they met another group searching for religious freedom, the Brownists or, as we know them, the Puritans. Doubtless the Walloons watched with envy as the Puritans departed for America in 1620, and a year later the Walloon leaders petitioned the English ambassador at The Hague for similar settlement rights. Although this request was denied, in 1622 the Dutch government agreed that the Walloons should take part in the colonization attempt of the newly formed Dutch West India Company. So it was that these refugees from French religious persecutions were largely responsible for the founding and early growth of New Amsterdam. Other Walloon and French Huguenot émigrés found their way to the Dutch colony during the ensuing years and added to the development not only of New Amsterdam but the other settlements along the Hudson and on Long Island.

Huguenot migration continued throughout the 17th century, but its volume sharply increased following the revocation of the Edict of Nantes in 1685. This formally eliminated the protection, more honored in the breach than in the observance, which had been extended to French Protestants by Henry IV in 1598. Estimates of the number of migrants from France following this action vary, but certainly 200,-000 and possibly 400,000 persons fled the homeland during the years of renewed and now official persecutions. It was only natural that many should come to America.

Oxford, Massachusetts, was one of the earliest of the Huguenot communities to be established in this period, dating from 1687. Here in south-central Massachusetts under the leadership of Daniel Bondet, a group of Huguenot refugees recently arrived from England established a settlement. The little town that resulted apparently closely resembled the other settlements of frontier New England, with a cluster of houses forming the village and with the farm and pasture lots lying beyond.

Aside from New York and Albany, which attracted substantial numbers of Huguenot settlers, two new communities were founded by these religious refugees. One was New Paltz, which remained quite small and relatively unimportant. The other was New Rochelle, named for the last great stronghold of Huguenot strength in France. New Rochelle was begun in 1688 by a group of Huguenot merchants in New York as a place of settlement for new arrivals from France. The new community lay along the Boston Post Road. Home lots were surveyed in a tract between the road and the shore of Long Island Sound. Apparently these were fairly large, and the village took on a linear appearance, with the houses rather widely spaced. New Rochelle was strategically located, and the frugal French succeeded in creating an attractive community. Many additional houses were constructed, most of them in stone, and when Sarah Knight visited the place in 1704 she wrote these favorable comments: "This is a very pretty place well compact, and good handsome houses, clean, good and passable Rodes . . . which caused in me a Love to the place, wch I could have been content to live in it. Here wee Ridd over a Bridge made of one entire stone of such a Breadth that a cart might pass with safety. . . . Here are three fine Taverns within call of each other, very good provision for Travailers."[1]

Virginia also received Huguenot refugees, and one of the settlements in that colony—Manakin—is of special interest because of its unusual plan. In the summer of 1700 a party of 200 Huguenots arrived in Virginia. Governor Francis Nicholson arranged for a tract of 10,000 acres on the James River, and William Byrd I escorted them to the site where cleared lands of the departed Manakin Indians provided favorable settlement conditions.

[1] Journal of Sarah Knight, December 22, 1704, as quoted in Herbert B. Nichols, *Historic New Rochelle*. New Rochelle, 1938, p. 22.

The only known plan of the town is something of a puzzle (Fig. 124). No scale is indicated, and its author is unknown. The great square in the middle is named for Governor Nicholson, who may have been responsible for the design of the settlement. If the tiny rectangles represent individual houses, the inside of the square would measure something like 800 feet across. This would also mean that Byrd Street would have a width of some 150 feet. All this is on the assumption that each house might be on the order of only 10 feet square. On the other hand the larger, only partially enclosed rectangles may be intended to represent houses, with the very small rectangles the chimneys. Unfortunately Byrd's report on the state of the settlement in May 1701 sheds no light on its design.

According to the drawing the four corners of the square were reserved for public uses: hospital, church, laundry, and town house and school. Gardens were provided between the double rows of houses on two sides of the square and fronting the woods and the river on the other two sides. Farm fields evidently stretched along the James River on both sides of the settlement. Some 500 Huguenots eventually lived in and around Manakin and for many years spoke only their own language. But as the danger from Indians passed and the Huguenots became familiar with their new surroundings the original compact settlement gradually broke up and within a short time had disappeared altogether.

Huguenots also settled in South Carolina. North of Charleston on the Santee River one group laid out the town of Jamestown in January 1705. The smallest lots fronted directly on the town common

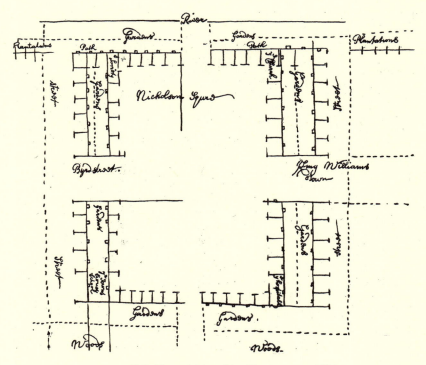

Figure 124. Plan of Manakin, Virginia: ca. 1700

bordering the river. Larger lots extended back from the Santee. The common contained sites for church and cemetery. The town was not much of a success, and by 1720 apparently was almost abandoned. Much later, in 1764, another group of Huguenots founded a settlement a hundred miles up the Savannah River. Patrick Calhoun, grandfather of John C. Calhoun, helped the Frenchmen lay out a township, in the center of which a tract of 800 acres was reserved for the village of New Bordeaux, vineyards, commons, and church glebelands. Village lots of two and a half acres and vineyard lots of four acres were surveyed, and sites were allotted for a fort, church, parsonage, market place, and parade ground.

Homes for Heretics: The Moravians

The Huguenot settlements in America did not last long as closed communities. Either their inhabitants drifted away or the original settlements opened their doors to outsiders. While Huguenot religious beliefs were strongly held, religious communalism was not contemplated. Quite different in this respect were the towns planned by that remarkable sect, the Unitas Fratrum, the Church of the United Brethren, or, as it is usually referred to in America, the Moravian Church. Less numerous than the Huguenots and later in beginning their settlement activities, the Moravian communities nevertheless are of greater interest. A consistent policy governed their planning, and church doctrines and settlement forms were considered to be closely related.

The Moravians originated in Bohemia in the 15th century. Early in the 18th century they emigrated to Saxony and founded the town of Herrnhut in 1722 on the lands of Count Zinzendorf. In 1734 a few Moravians embarked on the long journey to America, landing in Philadelphia. Others came to Georgia and then moved northward to Pennsylvania. In 1741, on a site about fifty miles northwest of Philadelphia on the Lehigh River, work was begun on the town of Bethlehem (Fig. 125).

All of the buildings constructed at Bethlehem were located only after careful deliberation. The first structure, the *Gemeinhaus*, still stands, although in somewhat altered form. Designed as a community center, this building also served as church, town hall, hospice, and church office. Two years later a large dormitory for single men was built, several small houses were completed, and gradually the town began to take form.

By 1757 Bethlehem was a busy, thriving community with a wide variety of local industries. A bakery, tailor shop, shoemaker, spinning and weaving establishment, grist mill, carpentry shop, blacksmith, potter, and other crafts were all represented. All worked under general church direction in a communal form of organization. Schools, dormitories for single members of the congregation, a tavern, and other buildings completed the town. Isaac Weld was deeply impressed by Bethlehem and included a view of the city and the following description in his informative book of travels in America:

"The town is regularly laid out and contains about eighty strong built stone dwelling houses and a large church. Three of the dwelling houses are very spacious buildings, and are appropriated respectively to the accommodation of the unmarried females, and of the widows. . . .

Figure 125. View of Bethlehem, Pennsylvania: 1798

"Attached to the young men's and to the young women's houses there are boarding schools for boys and girls. . . . These schools are in great repute. . . .

"Situated upon the creek, which skirts the town, there is a flour mill, a saw mill, an oil mill, a fulling mill, a mill for grinding bark and dye stuff, a tan yard, a currier's yard; and on the . . . River an extensive brewery, at which very good malt liquor is manufactured. These mills, &c. belong to the society at large, and the profits arising from them . . . are paid into the public fund. . . . The fund thus raised is employed in relieving the distressed brethren of the society in other parts of the world, in forming new settlements, and in defraying the expense of the missions for the purpose of propagating the gospel among the heathens."[2]

Other Moravian towns followed the initial settlement at Bethlehem. In Pennsylvania, Nazareth was founded in 1742 and Lititz in 1757. Their patterns were essentially similar to Bethlehem's, and, like all Moravian settlements, they were designed as congregation towns with permanent residents limited to members of the church.

The Moravians established a second series of towns in North Carolina, where they had acquired a 100,000-acre tract in 1753. The first of the Carolina towns was Bethabara, for which at least two preliminary plans were prepared. A plan of the town in 1766 shows that remarkable progress had been made and that within a few years the

[2] Isaac Weld, *Travels Through the States of North America.* London, 4th edn., 1807, II, 355-59.

town contained all of the traditional Moravian structures and uses (Fig. 126). A second town, Bethania, was begun in 1759, planned by Christian Gottlieb Reuter, a surveyor who had also laid out Lititz (Fig. 127). The plans of Bethania and Bethabara were more regular than those of Bethlehem, each having a rectangular town square located at the intersection of two main streets. The farm fields surrounding these villages were also perfectly regular in outline and location.

The most important of the Moravian towns in Carolina dates from 1766. Here, at Salem, all the accumulated Moravian experience in city planning was brought into use (Fig. 128). Here, too, we have the clearest and most detailed statement by church authorities of the principles that the Moravians held most important in the development of towns.

Christian Reuter laid out the town, but he was guided by a remarkable set of instructions and a model plan sent from Bethlehem in 1765 by Friedrich Marshall. Marshall's instructions began by pointing out that Moravian "congregation towns" were closely knit socially. This, said Marshall, "must be considered in deciding the form of the Town Plan."[3]

Close buildings or tall apartments seemed unsuitable. "Not more than two houses should be built side by side," and each family should

[3] This and other quotations are from Friedrich Marshall, "Remarks concerning the Laying Out of the new Congregation Town in the Center of Wachovia" (Bethlehem, July 1765), in Adelaide L. Fries, ed., *Records of the Moravians in North Carolina*. Raleigh, 1922, I, 313-15.

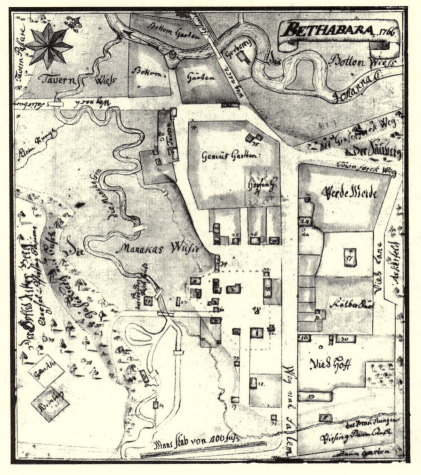

Figure 126. Plan of Bethabara, North Carolina: 1766

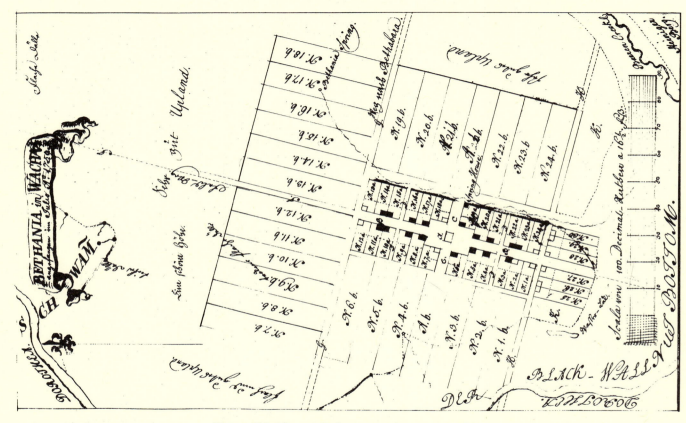

Figure 127. Plan of Bethania, North Carolina: 1759

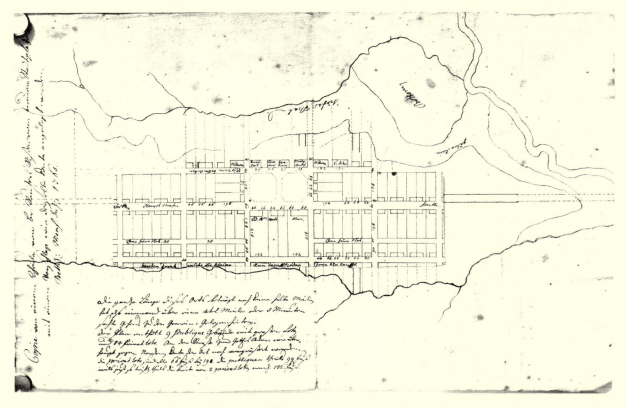

Figure 128. Plan of Winston-Salem, North Carolina: 1765

have its separate house. This latter instruction reflected some dissatisfactions with communal living which had developed among the Moravians.

Marshall advocated lots large enough so that each family could have its own yard and garden in the rear of the house, adding that this was "particularly good for the children, who can thereby have room for their recreations under oversight." But lots should not be so large that the settlement would sprawl. "The inconvenience of a widespread town is that the Brethren and Sisters can not so often attend the evening services or those of a day when there are many meetings, and the daily life of the Congregation, as one large family, cannot be so well supervised by the Ministers and other Congregation officers."

Having stated these and other general principles to be observed, Marshall described many details of town layout to be followed, stating that he had prepared several plans but "of them all the enclosed has received the most approbation." This plan which, with a few minor changes, governed the design of the town was further described in Marshall's communication: "Br. Reuter considers it important that the main street runs in a straight line from the . . . [river] . . . through the town, and beyond it. . . . I have made it 60 ft. wide, as in Lititz where the main street was originally only 40 ft. but that was found to be too narrow . . .; the other streets are 40 ft."

Marshall then described the sites and buildings facing on the open square: "The Gemein Haus, Saal [place of worship], Boys' and Girls' School, their kitchens and gardens are all together; then the Widows'

House, and the House for the Single Sisters. . . . On the other side will be the Widowers' House, or whatever of that kind of building may be needed. A Single Brothers' House is a manufacturing center, and an important business feature of the Congregation, and may well stand beside the Widowers' House, and keep all the business together; it would not be well to put these things among the family houses. . . . In order to keep the plan symmetrical the Store might be placed on the lower corner, since it also is larger than a family house."

The instructions explained that Salem was not intended as an agricultural village "but for those with trades." However, until village industry and handicrafts could develop, each family was to be furnished with farm lots so that they could provide their own food. Marshall also suggested that the town lots not immediately used for building might be cultivated for a few years to make food production easier for residents.

Salem, like Bethlehem, became the center of Moravian activity in its region. But the Moravians were not passive Christians; they were dedicated missionaries who carried the Gospel to the Indians, even those tribes living beyond the frontier of white settlement. The profits from church-directed industrial and craft activities in such towns as Bethlehem and Salem supported missionary endeavors. In these efforts to convert the Indians the Moravian missionaries employed some of the town planning skills developed in Pennsylvania and Carolina.

The most interesting and best documented example is Schoenbrunn in eastern Ohio (Fig. 129). Here, far beyond the scattered settlements in western Pennsylvania, the Reverend David Zeisberger gained the confidence of the Delaware Indians. In 1772 he laid out the little settlement of Schoenbrunn ("beautiful spring"), and a year later, ten miles to the south, a second community named Gnadenhutten. At Schoenbrunn the plan took the appropriate form of a cross, with the church at the center. The school building stood across the street at one corner. Along the two streets stood the houses of the Indians. The cemetery, or "God's Acre," was at one end of the village near the foot of the cross.

The Moravians built well. In Bethlehem and other Pennsylvania towns and in Salem their simple, sturdy buildings may still be seen. Modern restoration efforts have begun to recreate some of the original character and atmosphere these towns once possessed. Designed for a limited population and for a closed society, these Moravian communities were admirably suited for their purpose. They are also ruggedly handsome towns, the result of careful consideration of the relationships of architectural design to the plan forms employed. America produced few towns that excelled those of the Moravians in the qualities of community that are more important than size and financial power.

George Rapp and his Towns of Harmony and Economy

The Lutheran province of Wurtemburg in Germany gave birth to at least two religious groups that ultimately planned towns in North America. The earliest of these and the one responsible for no less than three towns was the Harmony Society led by George Rapp. Rapp became the leader of a small band of dissidents from the

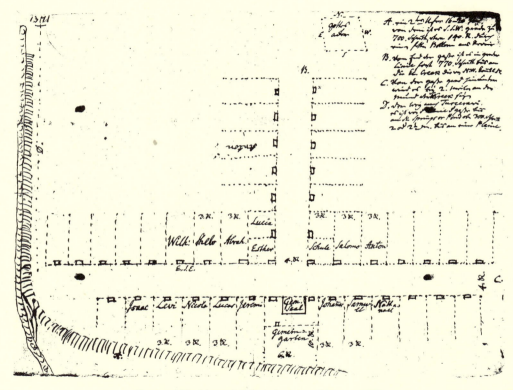

Figure 129. Plan of Schoenbrunn, Ohio: ca. 1772

Lutheran Church who migrated to America to find freedom of worship. In 1803 he and a few disciples purchased a 5,000-acre tract of land in western Pennsylvania, where they made their first settlement, calling the little town Harmony.

The plan of Harmony, like the later communities of the Harmony Society, was a simple grid (Fig. 130). In the center was an elongated square, perhaps intended to serve as a market place. Along the streets of the town the Harmonists began to construct their simple but sturdy and dignified buildings, many of which still remain. Soon the village became the center of a successful farming community. New settlers were attracted from Germany, and within a few years the group decided to move farther west, where they hoped to find more suitable soil for raising grapes and where additional land could be obtained to accommodate their growing numbers.

In 1814 they sold their village and its surrounding land, and with the proceeds purchased 30,000 acres along the Wabash River in Indiana. Within ten years they succeeded in building a thriving community, New Harmony, which attracted considerable attention.

But in the mid-1820's, the Harmonists decided to return to Pennsylvania and sold their Indiana holdings to Robert Owen. On the banks of the Ohio twenty miles north of Pittsburgh they laid out the town of Economy (Fig. 131). While there was nothing whatever remarkable about its simple grid layout, the buildings that lined these streets had a quiet elegance about them that set the Rappite community apart from most other American towns of the period. Charles Nordhoff,

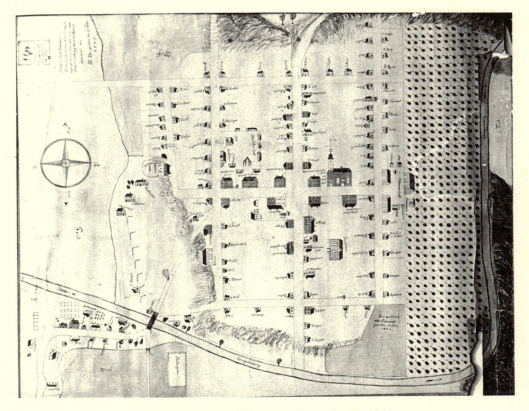

Figure 130. Plan of Harmony, Pennsylvania: 1815

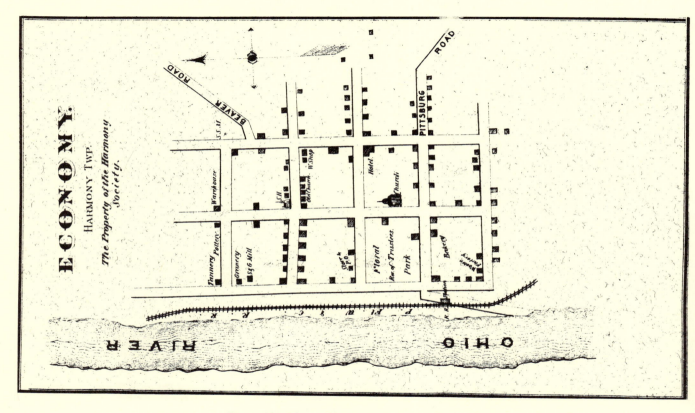

Figure 131. Plan of Economy, Pennsylvania: 1876

who visited Economy in the early 1870's, furnishes these impressions of the attractive little community:

"The town begins on the edge of the bluff; and under the shade-trees there benches are arranged, where doubtless the Harmonists take their comfort on summer evenings, in view of the river below and of the village on the opposite shore. Streets proceed at right angles with the river's course; and each street is lined with neat frame or brick houses, surrounding a square in such a manner that within each household has a sufficient garden. The broad streets have neat foot-pavements of brick; the houses, substantially built but unpretentious, are beautiful by a singular arrangement of grape-vines, which are trained to espaliers fixed to cover the space between the top of the lower and the bottom of the upper windows. This manner of training vines gives the town quite a peculiar look, as though the houses had been crowned with green."[4]

The modern visitor may inspect Economy, substantial portions of which have been preserved and reconstructed by the state, and form his own opinion of the quality in town building achieved by the Harmonists. It is unlikely that he will fail to be impressed by the dignity, the excellent sense of proportion and scale, and the true urban character of the remaining buildings. The Harmony Society came to an end in the early years of the present century, and although plans for a

[4] Charles Nordhoff, *The Communistic Societies of the United States.* New York, 1875, p. 64.

fourth city were under consideration these were unfortunately abandoned.

Robert Owen's New View of Society in
Theory and Practice

The Indiana settlement of Rapp and his followers—New Harmony—was taken over by Robert Owen in 1825. Here Owen expected to begin his transformation of modern industrial society in America. Owen was a self-made man who had become a textile manufacturer of some renown in his native Britain. At his mills in New Lanark near Glasgow he introduced a number of labor reforms. Soon his interests centered on national, social, and economic problems. In 1817 he proposed the creation of a great many new towns in England as a measure to reduce unemployment and to provide a more humane setting for manufacturing activities. Because this type of community is what Owen evidently had in mind when he came to America, his ideas on the design of these new towns are worth reviewing.

Owen believed that each town should contain about 1,200 persons in a quadrangle-like enclosure some 1,000 feet on each side. He was quite specific about the arrangement of buildings and uses within the town:

"Within the squares are public buildings, which divide them into parallelograms.

"The central building contains a public kitchen, mess-rooms, and all the accommodations necessary to economical and comfortable cooking and eating.

"To the right of this is a building, of which the ground-floor will form the infant school, and the other a lecture-room and a place of worship.

"The building to the left contains a school for the elder children, and a committee-room on the ground floor; above, a library and a room for adults.

"In the vacant space within the squares, are enclosed grounds for exercise and recreation: these enclosures are supposed to have trees planted in them."[5]

On three sides of each square were to be the family lodgings. On the other side would be a dormitory for all children "exceeding two in a family" or more than three years old. Manufacturing buildings were to be located outside the quadrangle to one side, where also would be placed stables and farm buildings. Beyond would be the agricultural lands. In this rural-urban unit the residents would be almost self-sufficient and would produce goods necessary for the good life under a cooperative economic system.

Owen undoubtedly expected to carry out this plan in America. Stedman Whitwell prepared an elaborate drawing for him showing a perspective view of the proposed community (Fig. 132). But Owen's

[5] Robert Owen, "Report to the Committee of the Association for the Relief of the Manufacturing Poor" (March 1817), in Robert Owen, *The Life of Robert Owen*, London, 1858, Appendix I.

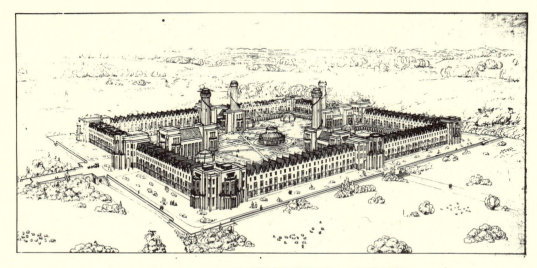

A BIRD'S EYE VIEW OF ONE OF THE NEW COMMUNITIES AT HARMONY.
IN THE STATE OF INDIANA NORTH AMERICA.
AN ASSOCIATION OF TWO THOUSAND PERSONS FORMED UPON THE PRINCIPLES ADVOCATED BY

ROBERT OWEN
STEDMAN WHITWELL, ARCHITECT.

THE SCITE IS NEARLY IN THE CENTRE OF AN AREA OF 2000 ACRES POSSESSED BY THE COMMUNITY, SITUATED UPON HIGH LAND, ABOUT THREE MILES FROM THE EASTERN SHORE OF THE GREAT WABASH RIVER, AND TWELVE MILES FROM THE TOWN OF MOUNT VERNON, ON THE RIVER OHIO. BOTH THESE RIVERS ARE NAVIGATED BY STEAM BOATS OF CONSIDERABLE BURTHEN, WHICH MAINTAIN A COMMUNICATION BETWEEN NEW-ORLEANS IN THE GULPH OF MEXICO ON THE SOUTH AND PITTSBURGH IN THE EASTERN STATES ON THE ATLANTIC. THE GENERAL ARRANGEMENT OF THE BUILDINGS IS A SQUARE, EACH SIDE OF WHICH IS 1000 FEET. THE CENTRES & THE EXTREMITIES ARE OCCUPIED BY THE PUBLIC BUILDINGS. THE PARTS BETWEEN THEM ARE THE DWELLINGS OF THE MEMBERS ; IN THE INTERIOR OF THE SQUARE ARE THE BOTANICAL & OTHER GARDENS, THE EXERCISE GROUNDS &c. THE WHOLE IS RAISED ABOVE THE LEVEL OF THE NATURAL SURFACE, AND SURROUNDED BY AN ESPLANADE. THE DESCENT TO THE OFFICES IS UPON THE OUTSIDE OF THE WHOLE. — ONE OF THE DIAGONALS OF THE SQUARE COINCIDES WITH A MERIDIAN, AND THE DISPOSITION OF EACH OTHER PART IS SO REGULATED BY A CAREFUL ATTENTION TO THE MOST IMPORTANT DISCOVERIES & FACTS IN SCIENCE, AS TO FORM A NEW COMBINATION OF CIRCUMSTANCES, CAPABLE OF PRODUCING PERMANENT GREATER PHYSICAL, MORAL, AND INTELLECTUAL ADVANTAGES TO EVERY INDIVIDUAL, THAN HAVE EVER YET BEEN REALISED IN ANY AGE OR COUNTRY.

INGREY & MADELEY, LITHO. 230. STRAND.

Figure 132. View of New Harmony, Indiana: ca. 1825

visionary plans were never to be realized. At the start, with the purchase of Rapp's village, Owen lost his chance to introduce his quadrangle town to America, and no further opportunity presented itself. Dissensions developed, and the Owenites soon came to realize that the perfect society was more easily talked about in the lecture hall than actually created on the Indiana frontier. Within two or three years the experiment was over, several splinter societies had been formed, and many of the original members of the group departed for more conventional communities. Owen himself, however, remained convinced of the validity of his ideas, and he continued to lecture and write until his death in 1858.

Owen's proposal for a secular utopia was, if not the first, one of the earliest in America. It was to be followed by a great many more similar attempts, including many with novel ideas for town building. The followers of the Frenchman, Charles Fourier, had no more success, nor did the disciples of another French utopian, Etienne Cabet. The climate for secular utopianism was not propitious. Seemingly only those bound together by religious faith could endure the hardships inherent in the founding of a new community without abandoning the doctrines of their leaders.

The shattering of the visions of Fourier and Cabet on the hard realities of American 19th-century society was duplicated dozens of times. With few exceptions, the more bizarre the doctrine of the groups attempting to found a new community life, the greater was the incidence of failure. Those which succeeded, or at least were able to maintain some kind of existence, were those which diverged least from the established pattern of the world. Thus, a Fairhope, Alabama, could prosper because, except for its Georgian doctrine of the single tax, it resembled an ordinary industrial and real estate promotion. But for every Fairhope there were a hundred Owenite New Harmonys. Frontier America may have been the great proving ground for liberty and initiative, but in this respect at least it also proved too stern a test for most nonconformists, especially those with a secular basis.

The Mormon Cities of Zion

The year 1830 saw the birth of a new religion, one among the dozens spawned in the backwaters left by the advancing waves of the frontier. This Church of Jesus Christ of Latter-Day Saints—or the Mormons, as they soon were called—became the most successful city builder of all the religious and utopian societies.

From Fayette, in upstate New York, Joseph Smith and his followers began their much-interrupted march to the west; this march was not to end for many years and until a thousand miles and more had been covered. Their first move was to Kirtland, Ohio, a town in the old Western Reserve northeast of Cleveland, where they built the first Mormon temple and established a base from which to grow.

The Mormon religion included a belief in divine revelation to God's chosen people. In July 1831 the prophet Joseph announced that God had revealed to him that the future center of the Mormon kingdom was to be Jackson County, Missouri. From this spot near the center of the continent the Mormon doctrine would spread

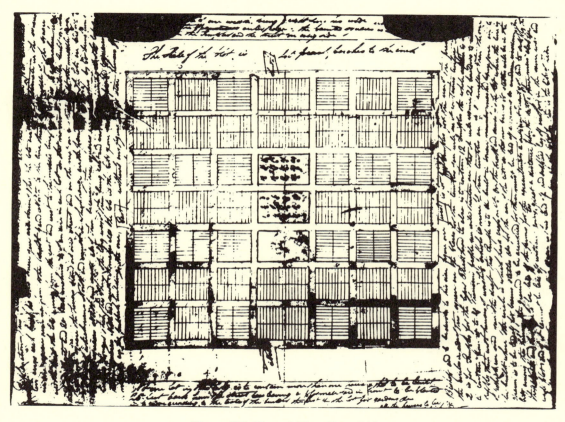

Figure 133. Plan of Zion City: 1833

the south and north to the line through the center of the square; and in the next, the lots run from the east and west to the center line. Each lot is four perches [66 feet] in front, and twenty [330 feet] back, making one-half of an acre in each lot, so that no one street will be built on entirely through the street; but on one square the houses will stand on one street, and on the next one, another, except the middle range of squares, which run north and south. . . ."[6]

All streets were to be 132 feet wide, and the houses were to be set-back 25 feet from the street lines. Smith further specified that all houses were to be built of brick and stone; he obviously wished to create a spacious and impressive headquarters for his new religion. He also evidently had in mind some kind of permanent agricultural belt around the city which would limit its ultimate growth. After mentioning that the farm lands should be laid out beyond the town boundaries, he added, "When this square is thus laid off and supplied, lay off another in the same way, and so fill up the world in these last days; and let every man live in the city for this is the City of Zion."

Acting under these instructions the church leaders in Missouri planned the city of Far West on a one-mile-square tract of land. The only surviving map of the town shows a uniform grid of streets and lots, extending well beyond the one-mile limits. Perhaps these were the farm lands, or it may have been necessary to expand the original settlement as more and more of the Saints made the long journey from Kirtland and as new church members were recruited. Not

[6] Kate B. Carter, *The Mormon Village*, Salt Lake City: Daughters of Utah Pioneers, 1954, Lesson for November, pp. 133-34.

all of the streets met the specifications of the City of Zion plat, since some of them were platted only 82 1/2 feet wide. It is not known whether the alternating lot orientation system was used at Far West. Whatever advantages this pattern may have had remain obscure, and it is possible that this prescription, too, was modified when the town was actually laid out.

The Mormons had been driven to Far West, in Caldwell County, Missouri, by the older residents of Independence and other towns in Jackson County who resented the Mormon influx. Nor was Far West to remain for long a permanent resting place for these persecuted people. Once again they were driven away, this time eastward to the banks of the Mississippi in Illinois. Here, at a place they called Nauvoo ("the beautiful"), a great new city was planned. Plans and views of Nauvoo show a gridiron street system with streets 50 feet wide enclosing blocks divided into four parcels of land each about 100 feet square (Fig. 134). On the bluff above the bend in the river towered the great temple overlooking the town and the river valley.

Nauvoo prospered and soon became the largest town in the state. It received a charter from the legislature, a university was organized, and it appeared that the Mormons had at last found a permanent resting place. However, once again their neighbors began a systematic series of persecutions which soon developed into full-scale warfare. After the brutal shooting of Joseph Smith by a mob which stormed the jail where he and a few companions had been thrown, the Mormons resolved to abandon Nauvoo and begin once again their quest for a new kingdom.

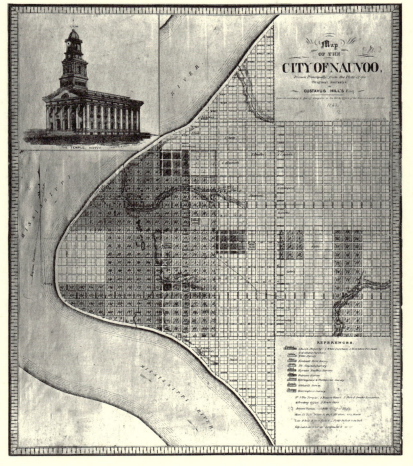

Figure 134. Plan of Nauvoo, Illinois: ca. 1842

By the winter of 1847 many of them moved to the west bank of the Missouri River in Nebraska. Even here, at the temporary settlement they called Winter Quarters, the Mormons laid out a regular city. Their new leader, Brigham Young, described the town in a letter written that February: "Winter Quarters is platted in 41 blocks, numbering 20 lots to a block, 4 rods by 10 [66 by 165 feet] covered by about 700 houses divided into 22 wards, with 22 bishops and counsellers over whom preside a municipal High Council of 12 High Priests."[7]

In the spring the long trek westward began. Up the valley of the Platte and into the mountain passes the Mormons wound their way until Young, looking out over the valley of the Great Salt Lake, uttered his famous words, "This is the place." In what they called the Territory of Deseret the Mormons began to plan and build their great city of the Salt Lake.

The initial years were hard, and the town was anything but elegant. On his way to the gold fields of California one forty-niner recorded these impressions: "The buildings are mostly small; they are built some of logs, but mostly of what they call dobies. . . . When the Mormons first settled here, they put their buildings in the shape of a fort; they built two rows of buildings three-fourths of a mile in length and [a] fourth of a mile apart, and shut up the ends by buildings across; inside of this they had three rows of buildings at equal distances across, forming four hollow squares, into which they could

---

[7] As quoted in Ray West, *Kingdom of the Saints*, New York, 1957, p. 172.

take all their cattle, wagons, etc., if they should be attacked by Indians. . . ."[8]

Howard Stansbury, who spent the winter of 1849-50 in Salt Lake City during his official government survey of the Salt Lake valley, estimated that by that spring 8,000 Mormons lived in the new city. A temporary temple with an enormous roof supported by posts had been erected in one of the central squares, planned according to the earlier specifications of Joseph Smith. Stansbury describes the plan of the city as following in most of its details the City of Zion plat except for its larger size and the dimensions of the lots:

"A city had been laid out upon a magnificent scale, being nearly four miles in length and three in breadth; the streets at angles with each other, eight rods or one hundred and thirty-two feet wide, with sidewalks of twenty feet; the blocks forty rods [660 feet] square, divided into eight lots, each of which contains an acre and a quarter of ground. By an ordinance of the city, each house is to be placed twenty feet back from the front line of the lot, the intervening space being designed for shrubbery and trees. The site for the city is most beautiful; it lies at the western base of the Wahsatch mountains, in a curve formed by the projection westward from the main range, of a lofty spur which forms its southern boundary."[9]

[8] Letter by A. P. Josselyn, July 15, 1849. Reprinted in William Mulder and A. Russell Mortensen, *Among the Mormons: Historic Accounts by Contemporary Observers*, New York, 1958, p. 236.
[9] Howard Stansbury, *Exploration and Survey of the Valley of the Great Salt Lake of Utah*, Washington, 1853, p. 128.

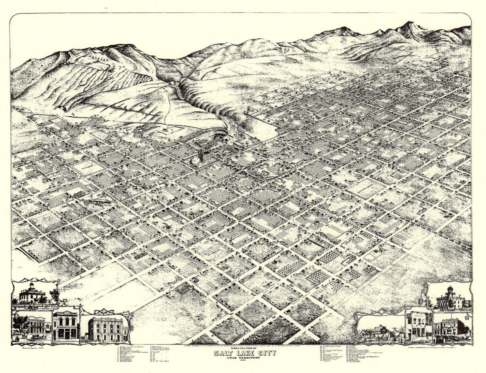

Figure 135. View of Salt Lake City, Utah: 1870

Within twenty years of its founding Salt Lake City was of impressive size and appearance. A bird's eye view published in 1870 shows the great new city against its imposing mountain setting (Fig. 135). Beyond the city proper stretch the garden and farm parcels, also planned in geometric order, an ultimate realization of the vision of Joseph Smith.

Salt Lake City was by no means the only city planned by the Mormons. Dozens of communities throughout Utah were soon laid out. While not all of them adhered to the strict order of the City of Zion scheme, they were all planned in the spirit of this original concept. One curious feature may still be observed in many of these towns. Square blocks are divided into four building sites of generous size. The houses, instead of being located near the middle of the plots, are grouped in fours at the street intersections with each house built near the corner of its site formed by the two intersecting street lines.

This method of siting houses probably developed to allow greater use of the remaining land for gardens and also to promote a feeling of neighborliness among the four families living in close proximity to one another. The origins of the City of Zion plat are somewhat less obvious. Smith was, of course, a student of the Bible and no doubt was familiar with the description of both the city of the Levites mentioned in Numbers 35: 1-5 and Leviticus 25 and the proposals by Ezekiel for the building of Jerusalem. Both called for square cities set in the middle of their agricultural lands and thus comprising the kind of rural-urban unit or city-state that Smith envisaged and Brigham Young later provided. The inspiration for the curious method of lot orientation advocated by Smith remains obscure. Perhaps it was mere whimsical variation from conventional patterns designed to set Mormon towns apart from secular communities. Whatever the reason, this feature was seldom followed. Its most consistent use is found in Kirtland, Ohio, where in an addition to that older town the Mormons employed this system.

The number of utopian groups in America was almost endless. Only a few of those responsible for the founding of communities in the formative years of American settlement have been described in the foregoing pages. There were many others with exotic names and peculiar doctrines: the Separatists of Zoar, the Inspirationists of Ebenezer and Amana, the Shakers, the Perfectionists of Oneida, the Labadists, the Society of the Woman in the Wilderness, the Ephrata Community, the Altruists, the Straight-Edgers, the Christian Catholic Church of Zion, and the Spirit Fruit Society, to name but a few.

Although these groups were numerous, their influence on American society was modest. The bulk of the nation stubbornly pursued its old sinful and materialistic ways, seemingly oblivious to the teachings of the new, self-appointed prophets who promised novel methods of spiritual or secular salvation. Their neighbors viewed these sects and their leaders either with outright hostility or with the pity usually reserved for the dim-witted or the helpless. The physical impact of the utopians remained equally slight. With the exception of the Moravians and the Mormons no one of these groups made any significant impression on the pattern of towns in its region or in the nation as a whole. Perhaps this is why we value all the more such artifacts as have survived in Economy, Zoar, New Harmony, and Amana.

But if the heritage of bricks and mortar is meager, the utopians at least left a rich legacy of hopes and dreams. One should not be too harsh in judging what, with the advantage of a lengthened perspective, now appear as ludicrous or wildly impractical schemes to reconstruct society. The modern city planner, who himself must be something of a utopian if he is to maintain his idealism and sanity in an increasingly ugly and chaotic world, may appear equally absurd a century hence.

By the middle of the 19th century the basic pattern of urban settlement east of the Mississippi had been established. Virtually all of what were to become the major cities of an increasingly urban nation had begun as planned communities: Boston, New York, Philadelphia, Baltimore, Washington, Pittsburgh, Buffalo, Cleveland, Detroit, Chicago, Cincinnati, Indianapolis, St. Louis, and New Orleans. Not all had been planned with skill, and in every case the explosive growth of these urban centers was soon to outrun the bounds of their original borders. In each of these, as well as in dozens of planned cities of smaller size, something of the heritage of its planned beginnings remains. In many, indeed most, the character and quality of the first settlement forms prescribed by their founders exceeds in merit the accretions of the later 19th century and of our own era.

We are now entering a new period of American urbanization. By the year 2000 current projections indicate that we will develop as much additional land for urban purposes as we did in the first 400 years of city building from 1565 to 1965. In addition, we are setting about the complex task of reconstructing the blighted and congested centers of our existing cities. Increasingly the effort to create a better life will focus on the issues of city growth and control of the urban environment, along with attempts to grapple with the nagging social problems of poverty and racial segregation.

The American philosopher George Santayana once observed that those who are ignorant of history are condemned to re-live it. What are the lessons to be learned from our planning experience during the first period of frontier development as we approach the new frontier of making our cities habitable for ourselves and succeeding generations? Let us try to sum up our failures and our achievements during that remarkable era of our history when we laid the foundation for an urban civilization.

We must not let national pride warp our perspective. The North Atlantic proved a major barrier to the transplanting of town planning techniques and concepts which were highly developed in Europe at the beginning of colonization and which continued to advance and change in the centuries to follow. The resources of colonial settlers pitted against the difficulties of a harsh and often hostile environment permitted little more than the minimum requirements of town life let alone the amenities or embellishments which were commonplace in 17th- and 18th-century Europe.

Compare, for example, the Quebec of Champlain with the Charleville of its founder, Duke Charles III. Both date from 1608. Quebec consisted of Champlain's crude "Habitation" and a tiny grid of streets hugging the banks of the St. Lawrence River. Charleville embodied all the theories of Renaissance formal planning, with its elaborate hierarchy of streets and open squares on which fronted carefully scaled buildings all making up a sophisticated composition in civic design. Not until 1791, with L'Enfant's Baroque plan for Washington, did American urban planners produce a large-scale example of what had long been established as a standard plan form in Europe.

Or, contrast the development pattern of the West End of London in the mid-18th century with the plan of Savannah and its multiple squares. While the plan forms are essentially similar, the differences between them in the third dimension were striking. Fronting the London squares stood elegant and restrained terrace houses of urbane dignity and harmonious proportions. Lining the squares of frontier Savannah were the simplest of huts and cabins. Not for nearly a century did Savannah attain something of the character of even the least imposing of Georgian London's squares. The lag between city planning practice in Europe and what occurred in the colonial empires of North America was thus substantial.

The reasons for these differences between colony and mother country are readily understandable. The strangeness of the environment, the slowness of communications, the absence of traditions, the lack of institutional patterns, and the necessity to create anew even the most elementary of urban services and facilities—all contributed to prevent the speedy and complete transfer to the New World of what had been learned about city planning in the old. Today these inhibiting factors have vanished, yet one can argue that in comparison with such remarkably well-ordered European cities as Stockholm and Amsterdam we still lag far behind European practice in urban planning. No longer do we have the excuse of limited physical resources; indeed, their very abundance may contribute to our urban physical disarray. Yet in a sense we still act like primitive colonials, helpless to put into practice the latest lessons of how to arrange cities in patterns which are both functional and beautiful.

Our failure to achieve an urban order fitting for the time and within our capabilities may well stem from attitudes toward the city developed in our swaddling years. America was peopled by Europeans who were hungry for land. In a seemingly limitless continent the most insatiable appetites could be satisfied. For a time fear of Indian attack combined with old habits of settlement to promote the development of compact agricultural villages. But when the natives were overcome and when the boundless extent of the land became apparent, the old associations of village and town life gave way to a quite different agricultural settlement pattern of isolated farmsteads. As early as 1623 in Plymouth Governor Bradford regretfully described these events:

"For now as their stocks increased . . . there was no longer any holding them together, but now they must of necessitie goe to their great lots; they could not other wise keep their katle; and having oxen growne, they must have land for plowing and tillage. And no man now thought he could live, except he had catle and a great deale of ground to keep them; all striving to increase their stocks. By which means they were scatered all over the bay, quickly, and the town, in which they lived compactly till now, was left very thine, and in a short time allmost desolate. . . . And this, I fear, will be the ruine of New-England."[1]

For a good many Americans it was rural life which represented the ideal. The town was something from which to escape. The Jeffer-

[1] William Bradford, *History of Plymouth Plantation*, W. T. David, ed., New York, 1908, pp. 293-94.

sonian notion of an agrarian democracy represents an old and deep feeling in American culture which has its manifestation today in the attempt to find in endless suburbia the freedoms which our ancestors sought on the western frontier of settlement. It is perhaps a permissible exaggeration to state that today's urban sprawl began in 17th-century Plymouth.

One feature of American planning in the frontier era is the almost total absence of three-dimensional design. This is not to say that effective bits of townscape were unknown—countless New England villages testify to the care taken by early settlers in the siting of individual buildings. For the most part, however, towns were conceived of in only two dimensions. The example of Williamsburg is virtually unique. Here was a town in which the plan of streets and building sites was developed as part of a larger vision of the future which included the location, size, and elevational treatment of its major structures. This approach to total urban design is the great lesson which Williamsburg has to teach—not the plan itself, the architectural style of its buildings, or the layout of its gardens. These belong to another era, and mere imitation of their dimensions and appearance is an insult to the integrity of colonial designers. Many of the shortcomings of the nation's cities today have resulted from earlier failures to realize that the third dimension of architecture is a vital ingredient of urban planning.

Another characteristic of American town planning was the widespread use of the gridiron or checkerboard pattern. As in virtually all other periods of wholesale colonization in world history, early colonial and later frontier towns were planned mainly on a geometric pattern of rectangular blocks, straight streets, and right-angle intersections. As the plan form most economical to survey, quickest to build, and easiest to understand, it is not surprising that the orthogonal system prevailed. For European visitors this feature of the American scene was novel and, at first impression, desirable. Thus, Francis Baily, noting the "perfect regularity" of Philadelphia and Baltimore was moved to comment, "This is a plan of which the Americans are very fond, and I think with reason, as it is by far the best way of laying out a city. All the modern-built towns in America are on this principle." However, what may have at first seemed like a vision of a new world of urban rationality all too quickly blurred into an impression of sterile dullness. By the time Baily reached Cincinnati his infatuation with the grid had given way to disenchantment:

"I have taken occasion to express my approbation of the American mode of laying out their new towns, in a general way, in straight lines; but I think that oftentimes it is a sacrifice of beauty to prejudice, particularly when they persevere in making all their streets cross each other at right angles, *without any regard to the situation of the ground*, or the face of the surrounding country: whereas, these ought certainly to be taken into consideration, in order that a town may unite both utility and beauty; and, with a little attention to this, a town might still preserve the straight line, and yet avoid that disgusting appearance which many of the new towns in America make."[2]

[2] Francis Baily, *Journal of a Tour in Unsettled Parts of North America in 1796 & 1797*, London, 1856, pp. 105, 226-27.

The seeds of senseless mechanized and unimaginative town planning which was to characterize much of the 19th century were sown in colonial soil. Yet not all gridiron plans of the frontier era of American urban development were of this quality. One thinks of New Haven, with a generous one-ninth of the original town left as an open green; or of Savannah, with its multiple squares breaking the monotony of the grid; or of Jeffersonville, with its alternating pattern of open squares and building blocks. Even Philadelphia's original plan contained the five squares laid out by Penn, the largest intended as a town center and the four smaller as recreation grounds. And Williamsburg demonstrates that the orthogonal plan is not incompatible with an atmosphere of formality and dignity.

It was less the first gridiron plans, which, in most cases were too modest in size to be offensively dull, than the later extensions of cities that violated good sense in community planning. Without regard to topography or, more importantly, failing to include in the additions to the city some of the open spaces of the original design, these new areas mechanically repeated almost endlessly the grid street system without any relieving features. Savannah stands almost alone as an exception to this dreary tradition.

The reasons are not difficult to identify. Planning of towns and development of land, in the beginning a community enterprise, fell into the hands of individuals and corporations whose almost sole aim was private profit. Even if the proper skills and sensibilities had been present, there was little incentive to plan well when mediocre planning, or worse, yielded generous financial returns. Moreover, as most communities abandoned responsibility for town planning to individuals they failed to create adequate legal and administrative institutions for the public control of private land development.

Our present urban land policy has scarcely departed from this position. Most important decisions about the timing of development, its location, and its design remain in private hands, tempered only mildly by regulations supposedly intended to protect the public interest. Because memories are short and historical perspective lacking, our generation regards this as the American tradition. So it is, but it is not the only tradition of our town planning history, nor has it proved the most effective.

The examples of Annapolis, Williamsburg, Savannah, Washington, and many of the 19th-century planned state capital cities remind us that public initiative and investment for the planning of cities once served to create an urban environment superior in quality to that of the present when measured against available financial and intellectual resources. The history of modern American city planning since the turn of the century can be read as an attempt, faltering and so far largely ineffective, to recapture that earlier tradition which placed the planning of towns as a responsibility of the community at large.

If American urban history has anything to contribute to the modern world aside from mere antiquarian enjoyment it is that good cities—beautiful, as well as safe and efficient—will arise only when it is the city itself that assumes the obligation for its own destiny.

Notes on the Illustrations

This list contains bibliographic information about the illustrations reproduced in this work. The symbols indicating the source of these materials are shown at the end of this list.

Illustrations

1. *Vitry-le-François*. View of Vitry-le-François, France, from Nicolas Tassin, *Les Plans et Profils de Toutes les Principales Villes et Lieux Considerables de France*. Paris, 1634.A

2. *Palma*. Plan of Palma Nova, Italy, from Braun and Hogenburg, *Civitates Orbis Terrarum*. Cologne, 1598.A

3. *Plan Général de Montpazier (Dordogne)*. Plan of Monpazier, France, from Victor Didron Ainé, *Annales Archéologiques*, Vol. 12, Paris, 1852.CU-FA

4. *Charleville, sur le Bord de la Meuze dans la Principaute Souveraine Darches*. Plan of Charleville, France, from Martin Zeiller, *Topographia Galliae*. Frankfurt, 1656.A

5. Untitled vertical aerial photograph of Santa Fé, Spain, taken in 1958. Supplied by Arquitecto Valentin Picatoste, Madrid, Spain.A

6. *The Plat of the Cittie of Londonderrie*. . . . Plan of Londonderry, Northern Ireland, from Sir Thomas Phillips, *Londonderry and the London Companies, 1609-1629*. Belfast, 1928.LC-GC

7. *A Plan of London . . . Described by J. Evelyn. A Plan of the*

City of London . . . according to the design and proposal of Sr. Christopher Wren. Plans for the rebuilding of London in 1666 by John Evelyn and Christopher Wren, published by the London Antiquarian Society, 1748.A

8. *Partie du Plan Général de Paris.* Plan of Paris from Pierre Patte, *Monumens Érigés en France à la Gloire de Louis XV.* Paris, 1765.CU-O

9. *La Place Royale.* View of the Place Royale in Paris, from Israel Silvestre, *Recueil de Cent Vues Différentes . . . de la Ville de Paris.* Paris, 1652.BN

10. *Amsterdams Oudste Staat. . . .* Plan of Amsterdam by Isaac Tirion, from Jan Wagenaar, *Amsterdam.* Amsterdam, 1760.A

11. *Plan de Versailles.* Plan of Versailles by Abbé Delagrive. Paris, 1746.A

12. *Urbs Domingo in Hispaniola.* Plan of Santo Domingo, from Arnoldus Montanus, *De Nieuwe en Onbekende Weerld. . . .* Amsterdam, 1671.A

13. *Saint Augustine.* View of St. Augustine, from *Expeditio Francisci Draki Equitis Angli in Indias Occidentalis.* Leyden, 1588. NY-S

14. *St. Augustine the Capital of East Florida.* Plan of St. Augustine drawn by Thomas Jeffreys, from William Roberts, *An Account of the First Discovery and Natural History of Florida.* London, 1763.CU-O

15. *Plano dela Poblacion.* Plan of San Antonio, drawn by D. Joseph de Villaseñor, from a reproduction in Herbert E. Bolton,

Texas in the Middle Eighteenth Century. Berkeley, 1915.CU-O

16. *Carola Ignante, Urbem adifac amox, Galvez ad honoxem, nomen dedit que suum*. Unsigned manuscript plan of Galvez, Louisiana, drawn in 1778.LC-M

17. *A Plan of Pensacola and its Environs*. Manuscript plan of Pensacola drawn by Joseph Purcell in 1778.LC-M

18. *Plano Dela Villa de Santa Fee. . . .* Photocopy of a manuscript plan of Santa Fé in the British Museum, drawn by Joseph de Urrutia ca. 1766.LC-M

19. *The Presidio of San Francisco in 1820*. Manuscript copy of a plan of the Presidio of San Francisco made in 1905 from the original drawing of 1880.UC-BL

20. Untitled, undated manuscript copy of a plan showing Los Angeles, California, ca. 1781, prepared for Hubert Howe Bancroft in the nineteenth century from an early plan of unknown date.UC-BL

21. *Los Angeles*. View of Los Angeles by Charles Koppel, from U.S. War Department, *Reports of Explorations and Surveys. . . .* Washington, 1856.A

22. *Habitasion de l'iles Ste. croix*. View of the settlement on Sainte Croix (Douchet) Island, Maine, drawn by Samuel de Champlain. From a facsimile in Biggar, ed., *The Works of Samuel de Champlain*. Toronto, 1922.UC

23. *Abitation de Quebecq*. View of the first building at Quebec, drawn by Samuel de Champlain. From a facsimile in Biggar, ed., *The Works of Samuel de Champlain*. Toronto, 1922.UC

24. *A Plan of the City of Quebec.* Plan of Quebec, from Thomas Jefferys, *The Natural and Civil History of the French Dominions in North and South America.* London, 1760.CU-O

25. *A Plan of the City and Fortifications of Louisburg.* Plan of Louisburg, from Thomas Jefferys, *The Natural and Civil History of the French Dominions in North and South America.* London, 1760.CU-O

26. *Plan of the Town and Fortifications of Montreal or Ville Marie in Canada.* Plan of Montreal, from Thomas Jefferys, *The Natural and Civil History of the French Dominions in North and South America.* London, 1760.CU-O

27. Untitled, unsigned, and undated manuscript plan of Montreal, drawn ca. 1644 by Jehan Bourdon.McGL

28. *Plan du Fort du Détroit.* Plan of Detroit, from Bellin, *Le Petit Atlas Maritime.* Paris, 1764.CU-O

29. *A Plan of Cascaskies.* Plan of Kaskaskia, Illinois, drawn by Thomas Kitchin, from Philip Pittman, *The Present State of the European Settlements on the Missisippi.* London, 1770; reprinted, Cleveland, 1906.CU-O

30. *Saint Louis des Illinois.* Manuscript copy made in 1846 of a plan of St. Louis, drawn by Auguste Chouteau.MHS

31. *Plan de la Ville et Fort Louis de la Louisiane. . . .* Copy of the original manuscript plan of Mobile by the Sieur Cheuillot, from Peter J. Hamilton, *Colonial Mobile.* Boston, 1897.CU-O

32. *Plan de la Nouvelle Orleans.* Plan of New Orleans, from Bellin, *Le Petit Atlas Maritime.* Paris, 1764.CU-O

33. *Plan of the City and Suburbs of New Orleans*. Plan of New Orleans in 1815, drawn by I. Tanesse, published by Charles Del Vecchio and P. Maspero. New York, 1817.LC-M

34. *James Forte at Jamestowne*. Plan of Jamestown, Virginia, drawn by John Hull, published by the A. H. Robins Co., Inc. Richmond, 1957.A

35. *Virginiae Pars*. Map of the coast of Virginia and the James River, from Conrad Memmius, *Relations Historicae*. . . . Frankfurt, 1613.NY-R

36. *A Platt of the towne belonging to York County*. Manuscript plan of Yorktown, Virginia, drawn by Lawrence Smith in 1691.VSL

37. *Tappahanock Town: A Platt of fifty Acres of Land lying at Hob's hole in Essex County*. Manuscript plan of Tappahanock, Virginia, drawn by Harry Beverley in 1706.VSL

38. *The Town of Marlborough*. Manuscript plan of Marlborough, Virginia, drawn by John Savage in 1731 from the original survey of 1691 by William Buckner and Theodorick Bland. VSL

39. *The Mappe of Vienna Town*. . . . Unsigned and undated manuscript plan of Vienna Town, Maryland, drawn in 1706.MHR

40. *A Plan of Alexandria now Belhaven*. Unsigned, undated manuscript plan of Alexandria, Virginia, drawn by George Washington, ca. 1749.LC-M

41. Untitled, unsigned, and undated manuscript plan of Charlestown, Maryland, drawn in 1742.LC-M

42. *Eden in Virginia.* Map of Eden in Virginia with a plan of the proposed towns, from William Byrd, *New-gefundenes Eden.* Helvetischen Societät, 1737.JCB

43. *A Grand Plat of the City and Port of Annapolis.* Manuscript copy made in 1748 of a manuscript plan of Annapolis, drawn by James Stoddert in 1718.MHR

44. *Bird's Eye View of the City of Annapolis.* View of Annapolis, published by E. Sachse and Co., Baltimore, ca. 1860.PM

45. *Plan de la ville et environs de Williamsburg en virginie america.* Unsigned manuscript plan of Williamsburg, Virginia, drawn in 1782.CWML

46. *Wethersfield, Connecticut: 1640.* Manuscript redrawing by John Gibson in 1962 of a map of Wethersfield, Connecticut, in 1640, from Charles M. Andrews, *The River Towns of Connecticut.* Baltimore, 1889.CU-DP

47. *Salem, Massachusetts: 1670.* Manuscript redrawing by John Gibson in 1962 of a plan of Salem, Massachusetts, in 1670, from Sidney Perley, *The History of Salem, Massachusetts.* Salem, 1924, Vol.1.CU-DP

48. *Cambridge, Massachusetts: 1637.* Manuscript redrawing by John Gibson in 1962 of a plan of Cambridge, Massachusetts, in 1637, drawn by Erwin Raisz from data compiled by Albert P. Norris, in Samuel Eliot Morison, ·*The Founding of Harvard College.* Cambridge, 1935.CU-DP

49. *A Plan of the Town of New Haven With all the Buildings in*

1748. Plan of New Haven, Connecticut, drawn by William Lyon, published by T. Kensett, 1806.NYHS

50. *Hartford, Connecticut: 1640*. Manuscript redrawing by John Gibson in 1962 of a plan of Hartford, from DeLoss Love, *The Colonial History of Hartford*. Hartford, 1914.CU-DP

51. *Fairfield, Connecticut: 1640*. Manuscript redrawing by John Gibson in 1962 of a plan of Fairfield, Connecticut, from Elizabeth Schenck, *The History of Fairfield*. . . . New York, 1889, Vol. 1.CU-DP

52. *A Plan of the Compact Part of the Town of Exeter*. . . . Plan of Exeter, New Hampshire, in 1802, drawn by P. Merrill.DCL

53. *Woodstock*. Plan of Woodstock, Vermont, from Beers, Ellis, and Soule, *Atlas of Windsor County, Vermont*. New York, 1869.DCL

54. *Ipswich*. Plan of Ipswich, Massachusetts, from D. G. Beers and Company, *Atlas of Essex County, Massachusetts*. Philadelphia, 1872.CU-O

55. *Springfield, Massachusetts: 1640*. Manuscript redrawing by John Gibson in 1962 of a plan of Springfield, Massachusetts, from Henry M. Burt, *The First Century of the History of Springfield*. Springfield, 1898. Vol. 1.CU-DP

56. *Providence, Rhode Island: 1638*. Manuscript redrawing by John Gibson in 1962 of a plan of Providence, Rhode Island, from Cady, *The Civic and Architectural Development of Providence*. Providence, 1957.CU-DP

57. *Boston, Massachusetts: 1640*. Manuscript redrawing by John Gibson in 1962 of a reconstruction of street and property lines in Boston, prepared by Samuel C. Clough in 1927 and reproduced in Walter M. Whitehill, *Boston: A Topographical History*. Cambridge, 1959.CU-DP

58. *The Town of Boston in New England*. Plan of Boston, drawn by John Bonner, printed by Francis Dewing. Boston, 1722.NY-S

59. *A New Plan of Boston from Actual Surveys*. Plan of Boston, drawn by Osgood Carleton. Boston, 1800.NY-S

60. *Concept C. Het Fort; Concept A. Het plein van het Fort; Concept B. De Landen*. Conjectural reconstruction of Dutch plans for New Amsterdam, from F. C. Wieder, *De Stichting van New York en Juli 1625*. Amsterdam, 1925.CU-O

61. *Redraft of the Castello Plan. New Amsterdam in 1660*. Manuscript redrawing in 1916 by John Wolcott Adams and I. N. Phelps Stokes of the manuscript plan of New Amsterdam in the Medici Library, Florence, Italy, drawn in 1660.NY-S

62. *Kingstone*. Plan of Kingston, New York, from John Miller, *A Description of the Province and City of New-York*. London, 1843.CU-O

63. *Albany*. Plan of Albany, from John Miller, *A Description of the Province and City of New-York*. London, 1843.CU-O

64. *Plan of the City of New York*. Plan of New York City by Bernard Ratzer, surveyed in 1767, published by Jefferys and Faden. London, 1776.LC-M

65. *A New & Accurate Plan of the City of New York in the State*

of New York in North America. Plan of New York City, drawn by B. Taylor. New York, 1797.NY-S

66. *Map of the City of New York and Island of Manhattan.* Plan of New York City, from William Bridges, *Map of the City of New-York and Island of Manhattan; with Explanatory Remarks and References.* New York, 1811.NYHS

67. *Christina Shantz.* Manuscript plan of Fort Christina and Christinahamm, Delaware, drawn by Per Martensson Lindeström in 1654.SAS

68. *A Portraiture of the City of Philadelphia in The Province of Pennsylvania in America.* Plan of Philadelphia, Pennsylvania, drawn by Thomas Holme. From a restrike in John C. Lowber, *Ordinances of the City of Philadelphia, 1812.* Philadelphia, 1812.CU-O

69. *A Mapp of Ye Improved Part of Pensilvania in America.* Map of a portion of Pennsylvania and an insert plan of Philadelphia, drawn by Thomas Holme, published by Ino. Harris, ca. 1720. LC-M

70. *Philadelphia.* Plan of Philadelphia, drawn by Nicholas Scull. Philadelphia, 1762.LC-M

71. *Plan of the City and Suburbs of Philadelphia.* Plan of Philadelphia, drawn by A. P. Folie in 1794. LC-M

72. *A Plan of Charles Town from a survey of Edward Crisp.* Plan of Charleston, South Carolina, from David Ramsay, *The History of South Carolina*, Vol. 2. Charleston, 1809.CU-O

73. *The Ichnography of Charles-Town at High Water.* Plan of

Charleston, drawn by G.H., published by B. Roberts and W. H. Toms. London, 1739.LC-M

74. *Plan of the town of Willmington in New Hanover County North Carolina.* Manuscript plan of Wilmington, North Carolina, drawn by C. J. Sauthier in 1769.BM

75. *Plan of the Town of Newbern in Craven County North Carolina.* Manuscript plan of New Bern, North Carolina, drawn by C. J. Sauthier in 1769.BM

76. *A Plan of the Town & Port of Edenton in Chowan County North Carolina.* Manuscript plan of Edenton, North Carolina, drawn by C. J. Sauthier in 1769.BM

77. *A Plan representing the Form of Setling the Districts, or County Divisions in the Margravate of Azilia.* Proposed settlement plan for Georgia, from Sir Robert Mountgomery, *A Discourse Concerning the design'd Establishment of a New Colony to the South of Carolina.* London, 1717. Reprinted in George P. Humphrey, ed., *American Colonial Tracts*, No. 1. Rochester, 1897.CU-O

78. *A Map of the County of Savannah.* Map of Savannah and vicinity, from Samuel Urlsperger, *Ausführliche Nachricht von den Saltzburgischen Emigranten*, Vol. 1, Part 4. Halle, 1735.JCB

79. Untitled map of the Savannah common, garden, and farm lands ca. 1800. Drawn by John McKinnon, published privately by J. F. Minis. London, 1904.LC-M

80. *A View of Savannah as it stood the 29th of March, 1734.* View of Savannah, drawn by Peter Gordon. London, 1734.LC-P

81. *Plan Von Neu Ebenezer*. Plan of New Ebenezer, Georgia, drawn and published by Matthew Seutter. Augsburg, 1747.A

82. Untitled, unsigned, and undated manuscript map of St. Simons Island, Georgia, drawn by John Thomas ca. 1740. Photocopy of the original in the British Museum.LC-M

83. *Plan of London and Westminster*. Portion of a plan of London, surveyed and drawn by John Rocque in 1746, published by John Pine and John Tinney. London, 1746.A

84. Savannah, Georgia: 1733-1856. Manuscript plans of Savannah, drawn by John W. Reps in 1959.A

85. *Savannah Ga., 1855*. View of Savannah, drawn by J. W. Hill, published by Endicott & Co. New York, 1856.NYHS

86. *Plan of the Lots Laid out at Pittsburgh and the Coal Hill*. Manuscript plan of Pittsburgh, drawn by Tobin Mills. Philadelphia, 1787.LC-M

87. *Plan of Pittsburg and Adjacent Country*. Plan of Pittsburgh, drawn by William Darby, published by R. Patterson and William Darby. Pittsburgh, ca. 1815.LC-M

88. *Fort Boonesborough*. View of Fort Boonesborough, Kentucky, drawn by George Ranck after a plan by Judge Richard Henderson, from George Ranck, *Boonesborough*. Louisville, 1901. CU-O   CU-O

89. *Plan of Franklinville. Plan of Lystra*. Plans of Franklinville and Lystra, Kentucky, from William Winterbotham, *An Historical, Geographical, Commercial, and Philosophical View of the United States of America*. New York, 1796. Vol. 3.A

90. *Plan of a Proposed Rural Town, to be called Hygeia*. Plan of Hygeia, Kentucky, drawn by J. B. Papworth, from William Bullock, *Sketch of a Journey Through the Western States of North America*. London, 1827.CU-O
91. *Plan of Louisville 1779*. Photocopy of manuscript plan of Louisville, Kentucky, attributed to George Rogers Clark.FCL
92. *City of Louisville and its Enlargements*. Plan of Louisville, drawn by E. D. Hobbs, published by Gabriel Collins in 1836. LC-M
93. *Map of Jeffersonville as laid out after the plan suggested by President Jefferson*. Manuscript plan of Jeffersonville, Indiana, drawn by Jas. M. Van Hook in 1879 from a copy by J. W. Ray of the original plat of 1802.CCI
94. *Plan of the Ancient Works at Marietta*. Plan of Marietta, Ohio, drawn by Charles Whittlesey in 1837.WRHS
95. *Gallipolis in 1791*. View of Gallipolis, Ohio, from Henry Howe, *Historical Collections of Ohio*. Cincinnati, 1847.A
96. *Plan of Cincinnati, Including All the late Additions & Subdivisions*. Plan of Cincinnati, drawn by Thomas Darby, from Daniel Drake, *Natural and Statistical View, or Picture of Cincinnati and the Miami Country*. Cincinnati, 1815.DCL
97. *Map of the Town of Columbus*. Unsigned manuscript plan of Columbus, drawn in 1817.WRHS
98. *Plat of the Town of Indianapolis*. Plan of Indianapolis, published by H. Platt. Columbus, 1821.ISL
99. *Bird's Eye View of Circleville, Ohio, in 1836, Looking South*. View of Circleville, Ohio, from Williams Brothers, *The History*

of Franklin and Pickaway Counties, Ohio. Cleveland, 1880. CU-O

100. *Circleville, Ohio: 1837-1856*. Manuscript plans of Circleville, Ohio, drawn by John W. Reps in 1955.A

101. *Sketch of Washington in Embryo*. Map showing the division of land on the site of the national capital in 1791, drawn by E.F.M. Faehtz and F. W. Pratt, based on research by Dr. Joseph M. Toner. Washington, 1874.LC-M

102. Untitled manuscript marginal sketch by Thomas Jefferson from a report by him to George Washington, undated but probably September 14, 1790.LC-MS

103. Untitled, undated manuscript plan by Thomas Jefferson for the national capital, probably drawn in March, 1791.LC-MS

104. *Plan of the City Intended for the Permanent Seat of the Government of the United States*. Copy by the U.S. Coast and Geodetic Survey in 1887 of the manuscript plan for Washington, D.C., drawn by Pierre Charles L'Enfant in 1791.A

105. *Plan of the City of Washington in the Territory of Columbia. . . .* Plan of Washington, D.C., drawn by Andrew Ellicott, engraved by Thackara & Vallance. Philadelphia, 1792. Restrike in 1962 from the original plate.A

106. *The City of Washington in 1800*. View of Washington, D.C. drawn by Parkyns, published by Richard Phillips. London, 1804.LC-P

107. *View of Washington*. View of Washington, D.C. from the Capitol looking west, drawn and published by Robert P. Smith, 1850.LC-P

108. *View of the Capitol at Washington.* View of the Capitol and Pennsylvania Avenue in Washington, D.C. ca. 1837, drawn by W. H. Bartlett, from W. H. Bartlett, *The History of the United States of North America.* New York, 1856, Vol. 3.A

109. *Our National Capital, Viewed From the South.* View of Washington, D.C., drawn by Theo. R. Davis, from *Harper's Weekly,* May 20, 1882.A

110. *A Map of the New City of Esperanza in the State of New York.* Manuscript copy by John Gibson in 1962 of an undated and unsigned plan of Esperanza, New York, in the Green County, N.Y., records.CU-DP

111. *Village of Buffalo.* Plan of Buffalo, from E. B. O'Callaghan, ed., *The Documentary History of the State of New York.* Albany, 1851. Vol. 4.A

112. *A Plan of the City of Cleaveland.* Redrawing in 1855 by L. M. Pillsbury of the original plan of Cleveland by Seth Pease in 1796, from *Journal of the Association of Engineering Societies, Transactions,* Vol. 3, No. 10 (1884).LC-M

113. *Map of Cleveland and its Environs.* Plan of Cleveland, drawn and published by Ahaz Merchant. New York, 1835.LC-M

114. *Jefferson.* Plan of Jefferson, Ohio, from Titus, Simmons & Titus, *Atlas of Ashtabula County, Ohio.* Philadelphia, 1874.CU-O

115. *Town Plat of Canfield.* Unsigned, undated manuscript plan of Canfield, Ohio, ca. 1800.WRHS

116. *Bird's Eye View of the Town of Elyria.* View of Elyria, Ohio, drawn by A. Ruger in 1868.LC-M

117. *Tallmadge Center Park*. View of the central green in Tallmadge, Ohio, from Tackabury, Mead, and Moffett, *Combination Atlas Map of Summit County Ohio*. Philadelphia, 1874.CU-O

118. *City of Sandusky*. Plan of Sandusky, Ohio, drawn by A. Doolittle. New Haven, 1818.WRHS

119. *A Plan of the City of Detroit*. Manuscript plan of Detroit, drawn by Abijah Hull in January 1807.DP-BC

120. *Plan of Detroit*. Unsigned, undated plan of the central portion of Detroit as planned in 1807, from *American State Papers, Public Lands Series*, Vol. 6. Washington, 1860.CU-O

121. *Plan of Detroit*. Plan of Detroit in 1830, drawn by John Mullett, from *American State Papers*, Public Lands Series, Vol. 6.CU-O

122. *Chicago with the School Section, Wabansia, and Kinzie's Addition*. Plan of Chicago, Illinois, drawn by Joshua Hathway, Jr., in 1834.CHS

123. *Arx Carolina*. View of Fort Caroline, Florida, from Arnoldus Montanus, *De Nieuwe en Onbekende Weerld*. . . . Amsterdam, 1671.A

124. Untitled, unsigned, and undated manuscript plan of Manakin, Virginia, ca. 1700.VSL

125. *View of Bethlehem, a Moravian settlement*. View of Bethlehem, Pennsylvania in 1798, from Isaac Weld, *Travels Through the States of North America*. London, 4th edn., 1807, Vol. 2.CU-O

126. *Bethabara. 1766*. Unsigned manuscript plan of Bethabara, North Carolina.MAWS

127. *Bethania in Wacha*. Unsigned manuscript plan of Bethania, North Carolina, drawn in 1759.AMCB

128. *Copy of part of Br. Reuter's map of the new town site with a suggestion how it might be laid out* [title in German]. Manuscript plan of Salem, North Carolina, drawn by Christian Reuter in 1765.LC-M

129. Untitled, unsigned, and undated manuscript plan of Schoenbrunn, Ohio, ca. 1772.AMCB

130. *Die Stadt Harmonie.* . . . Manuscript plan of Harmony, Pennsylvania, in 1815, drawn by W. Weingartner in 1833.OEP

131. *Economy.* Plan of Economy, Pennsylvania, from Joseph A. Caldwell, *Caldwell's Illustrated, Historical Centennial Atlas of Beaver County, Pennsylvania.* Condit, Ohio, 1876.LC-M

132. *A Bird's Eye View of one of the New Communities at Harmony in the State of Indiana North America.* Undated view of New Harmony, Indiana, drawn by Stedman Whitwell, published by Ingrey & Madelly. London, ca. 1825.NYHS

133. *Plat of Zion City.* Manuscript plan of the ideal Mormon city, with descriptive text, drawn by Joseph Smith in 1833.HLDS

134. *Map of the City of Nauvoo.* Plan of Nauvoo, Illinois, drawn by Gustavus Hill's, printed by J. Childs. New York, ca. 1842. NY-M

135. *Bird's Eye View of Salt Lake City.* View of Salt Lake City, drawn and published by Augustus Koch. Chicago, 1870.LC-M

Explanation of Symbols

A	Author's Collection
AMCB	Archives of the Moravian Church, Bethlehem, Pennsylvania
BM	The British Museum, London, England
BN	Bibliothèque Nationale, Paris, France
CHS	Chicago Historical Society, Chicago, Illinois
CCI	Clark County, Indiana Official Records, Jeffersonville, Indiana
CU-DP	Cornell University, Department of City and Regional Planning, Ithaca, New York
CU-FA	Fine Arts Library, Cornell University, Ithaca, New York
CU-O	Olin Library, Cornell University, Ithaca, New York
CWML	College of William and Mary Library, Williamsburg, Virginia
DCL	Dartmouth College Library, Hanover, New Hampshire
DP-BC	Burton Historical Collection, Detroit Public Library, Detroit, Michigan
FCL	Filson Club Library, Louisville, Kentucky
HLDS	Church Historian, Church of Jesus Christ of Latter-Day Saints, Salt Lake City, Utah
ISL	Indiana State Library, Indianapolis, Indiana
JCB	John Carter Brown Library, Brown University, Providence, Rhode Island
LC-GC	Library of Congress, General Collection, Washington, D.C.

LC-M	Library of Congress, Division of Geography and Maps, Washington, D.C.
LC-MS	Library of Congress, Division of Manuscripts, Washington, D.C.
LC-P	Library of Congress, Division of Prints and Photographs, Washington, D.C.
McGL	McGill University Library, Montreal, Canada
MAWS	Moravian Archives, Winston-Salem, North Carolina
MHR	Maryland Hall of Records, Annapolis, Maryland
MHS	Missouri Historical Society, St. Louis, Missouri
NYHS	New-York Historical Society, New York, New York
NY-R	New York Public Library, Rare Books Division, New York, New York
NY-S	Stokes Collection, New York Public Library, New York, New York
OEP	Old Economy, Pennsylvania, Harmony Society Archives, Ambridge, Pennsylvania
PM	The Peale Museum, Baltimore, Maryland
SAS	State Archives of Sweden, Stockholm, Sweden
UC	University of California Library, General Collection, Berkeley, California
UC-BL	University of California Library, Bancroft Collection, Berkeley, California
VSL	Virginia State Library, Richmond, Virginia
WRHS	Western Reserve Historical Society, Cleveland, Ohio

Selected Bibliography

GENERAL WORKS

Beresford, Maurice, *New Towns of the Middle Ages*. New York: Frederick A. Praeger, 1967.

Bridenbaugh, Carl, *Cities in the Wilderness: The First Century of Urban Life in America, 1625-1742*. New York: The Ronald Press Co., 1938.

Brown, Ralph H., *Historical Geography of the United States*. New York: Harcourt, Brace and Co., 1948.

Glaab, Charles N. and A. Theodore Brown, *A History of Urban America*. New York: The Macmillan Company, 1967.

Green, Constance McLaughlin, *American Cities in the Growth of the Nation*. New York: John DeGraff, 1957.

Gutkind, Erwin A., *Urban Development in Southern Europe: Spain and Portugal*. New York: Free Press of Glencoe, 1967.

Reps, John W., *The Making of Urban America: A History of City Planning in the United States*. Princeton: Princeton University Press, 1965.

Stokes, I. N. Phelps, and D. C. Haskell (comps.), *American Historical Prints: Early Views of American Cities*. New York: New York Public Library, 1932.

Trewartha, Glenn T., "Types of Rural Settlement in Colonial America," *Geographical Review*, Vol. 36, No. 4 (October 1946), pp. 568-96.

Tunnard, Christopher, and Henry Hope Reed, *American Skyline: The Growth and Form of Our Cities and Towns*. Boston: Houghton Mifflin, 1955.

EUROPEAN PLANNING

Burke, Gerald L., *The Making of Dutch Towns: A Study in Urban Development from the Tenth to the Seventeenth Centuries*. London: Cleaver-Hume Press, 1956.

Camblin, Gilbert, *The Town in Ulster: An Account of the Origin and Building of the Towns of the Province and the Development of their Rural Setting*. Belfast: W. Mullan, 1951.

Gothein, Marie Louise, *A History of Garden Art*. 2 vols. Translated from the German by Mrs. Archer-Hind. Edited by Walter P. Wright. London: J. M. Dent and Sons, Ltd., 1928.

Hiorns, Frederick R., *Town-Building in History*. London: G. G. Harrap, 1956.

Lavedan, Pierre, *Histoire de l'Urbanisme*. 3 vols. Paris: H. Laurens, 1926-1952.

Mumford, Lewis, *The City in History: Its Origins, Its Transformation, and Its Prospects*. New York: Harcourt, Brace & World, 1961.

Rasmussen, Steen Eiler, *London: The Unique City*. New York: Macmillan Company, 1937.

Torres Balbas, Leopoldo, *Resumen Histórico del Urbanismo en España*. Madrid: Instituto de Estudios de Administración Local, 1954.

Zucker, Paul, *Town and Square from the Agora to the Village Green*. New York: Columbia University Press, 1959.

PUEBLO AND PRESIDIO:
SPANISH PLANNING IN COLONIAL AMERICA

Castañeda, Carlos E., *Our Catholic Heritage in Texas: 1519-1936,* Vol. ii, *The Mission Era: The Winning of Texas*. Austin: Von Boeckmann-Jones, 1936.

Chatelain, Verne Elmo, *The Defenses of Spanish Florida, 1565-1763*. Washington, D.C.: Carnegie Institution of Washington, 1941.

Hammond, George P., and Agapito Rey (eds. and trans.), *Don Juan de Oñate: Colonizer of New Mexico, 1595-1628*. 2 vols. Albuquerque: University of New Mexico Press, 1953.

Instituto de Estudios de Administración Local, *Planos de Ciudades Iberoamericanas y Filipinas Existentes en el Archivo de Indias*. 2 vols. Madrid: 1951.

Lowery, Woodbury, *The Spanish Settlements within the Present Limits of the United States: Florida, 1562-1574*. New York: G. P. Putnam's Sons, 1905.

Nuttall, Zelia, "Royal Ordinances Concerning the Laying Out of New Towns," *Hispanic American Historical Review*, Vol. 5 (1922), pp. 249-54.

Palm, Erwin Walter, *Les Monumentes Arquitecténices de la Española*, Vol. i. Ciudad Trujillo: Universidad de Santo Domingo, 1955.

Scott, Mellier Goodin, *The San Francisco Bay Area: A Metropolis in Perspective*. Berkeley: University of California Press, 1959.

Stanislawski, Dan, "Early Spanish Town Planning in the New World," *Geographical Review*, Vol. 37, No. 1 (January 1947), pp. 94-105.

THE CITIES OF NEW FRANCE

Belting, Natalia Maree, *Kaskaskia under the French Regime*. Urbana: University of Illinois Press, 1948.

Champlain, Samuel de., *The Works of Samuel de Champlain*. 6 vols. Reprinted, translated and annotated by six Canadian scholars under the general editorship of H. P. Biggar. Toronto: Champlain Society, 1922-1936.

Dollier de Casson, François, *A History of Montreal, 1640-1672*. Translated and edited by Ralph Flenley. London: J. M. Dent & Sons, 1928.

Douglas, James, *Old France in the New World: Quebec in the Seventeenth Century*. Cleveland: Burrows Brothers Company, 2nd edn., 1906.

Hamilton, Peter Joseph, *Colonial Mobile*. Boston: Houghton Mifflin Co., Rev. and enl. edn., 1910.

Peterson, Charles E., "Colonial Saint Louis," Missouri Historical Society, *Bulletin*, Vol. 3, No. 3 (April 1947), pp. 94-111.

Pickins, Buford L., "Early City Plans for Detroit, A Projected American Metropolis," *The Art Quarterly*, Vol. 6, No. 1 (Winter 1943), pp. 34-51.

TOWN PLANNING IN THE TIDEWATER COLONIES

Carson, Jane, *We Were There: Descriptions of Williamsburg, 1699-1859, Compiled from Contemporary Sources and Arranged Chronologically*. Williamsburg: Colonial Williamsburg, 1965.

Forman, Henry Chandlee, *Jamestown and St. Mary's, Buried Cities of Romance*. Baltimore: Johns Hopkins Press, 1938.

Goodwin, Rutherford, *A Brief & True Report Concerning Williamsburg in Virginia*. 3rd edn. Williamsburg: Colonial Williamsburg, 1941.

Hatch, Charles E., *Jamestown, Virginia: The Townsite and Its Story*. U.S. National Park Service Historical Handbook Series, No. 2. Washington: Government Printing Office, rev. edn., 1957.

Lorant, Stefan (ed.), *The New World*. New York: Duell, Sloan & Pearce, 1946.

Riley, Edward M., "The Town Acts of Colonial Virginia," *The Journal of Southern History*, Vol. 16, No. 3 (August 1950), pp. 306-23.

Shurcliff, Arthur A., "The Ancient Plan of Williamsburg," *Landscape Archi-tecture*, Vol. 28, No. 1 (January 1938), pp. 87-101.

Whiffen, Marcus, *The Public Buildings of Williamsburg*. Williamsburg: Co-lonial Williamsburg, 1958.

PILGRIMS AND PURITANS:
NEW TOWNS IN A NEW ENGLAND

Akagi, Roy Hidemichi, *The Town Proprietors of the New England Colonies: A Study of Their Development, Organization, Activities and Controversies, 1620-1770*. Philadelphia: University of Pennsylvania Press, 1924.

Andrews, Charles McLean, *The River Towns of Connecticut: A Study of Wethersfield, Hartford, and Windsor*. Baltimore: Publication Agency of Johns Hopkins University, 1889.

Egleston, Melville, *The Land System of the New England Colonies*. Baltimore: N. Murray, Publication Agent, Johns Hopkins University, 1886.

Garvan, Anthony W. B., *Architecture and Town Planning in Colonial Con-necticut*. New Haven: Yale University Press, 1951.

Maclear, Ann Bush, *Early New England Towns: A Comparative Study of Their Development*. New York: Longmans, Green & Co., 1908.

Scofield, Edna, "The Origin of Settlement Patterns in Rural New England," *Geographical Review*, Vol. 28, No. 4 (October 1938), pp. 652-63.

Whitehall, Walter Muir, *Boston, a Topographical History*. Cambridge: Belknap Press of Harvard University Press, 1959.

NEW AMSTERDAM, PHILADELPHIA,
AND TOWNS OF THE MIDDLE COLONIES

Board of Proprietors of the Eastern Division of New Jersey, *The Minutes of the Board . . . from 1685 to 1705*. Introductory Essay by George J. Miller. Perth Amboy: Board of Proprietors of the Eastern Division of New Jersey, 1949.

Elting, Irving, *Dutch Village Communities on the Hudson River*. Baltimore: W. Murray, 1886.

Johnson, Amandus, *The Swedish Settlements on the Delaware, 1638-1664*. 2 vols. Philadelphia: University of Pennsylvania, 1911.

Kouwenhoven, John A., *The Columbia Historical Portrait of New York*. New York: Doubleday & Co., 1953.

Lingelbach, William E., "William Penn and City Planning," *Pennsylvania Magazine of History and Biography*, Vol. 68, No. 4 (October 1944), pp. 398-418.

Miller, The Rev. John, *A Description of the Province and City of New York with Plans of the City and Several Ports as They Existed in the Year, 1695*. London: Thomas Rodd, 1843.

Roach, Hannah Benner, "The Planting of Philadelphia, a Seventeenth-Century Real Estate Development," *Pennsylvania Magazine of History and Biography*, Vol. 92, No. 1 (January 1968), pp. 3-47; No. 2 (April, 1968), pp. 143-94.

Stokes, I.N. Phelps, *The Iconography of Manhattan Island, 1498-1909*. 6 vols. New York: R. H. Dodd, 1915-1928.

Tatum, George B., *Penn's Great Town*. Philadelphia: University of Pennsylvania Press, 1961.

COLONIAL TOWN PLANNING
IN CAROLINA AND GEORGIA

Bannister, Turpin B., "Oglethorpe's Sources for the Savannah Plan," *Journal of the Society of Architectural Historians*, Vol. 20, No. 2 (May 1961), pp. 47-62.

Dill, Alonzo Thomas, *Governor Tryon and His Palace*. Chapel Hill: University of North Carolina Press, 1955.

Jones, Charles Colcock, *The Dead Towns of Georgia*. Georgia Historical Society, *Collections*, Vol. 4, Part 1. Savannah: Georgia Historical Society, 1878.

Mountgomery, Sir Robert, *A Discourse Concerning the Design'd Establishment of a New Colony to the South of Carolina in the Most Delightful Country of the Universe*. London, 1717. Reprinted. Washington: Peter Force, 1835.

Nichols, Frederick Doveton, *The Early Architecture of Georgia*. Chapel Hill: University of North Carolina Press, 1957.

Paul, Charles L., "Colonial Beaufort," *North Carolina Historical Review*, Vol. 42, No. 2 (Spring 1965), pp. 139-152.

Stevenson, Frederick R., and Carl Feiss, "Charleston and Savannah," *Journal of the Society of Architectural Historians*, Vol. 10, No. 4 (December 1951), pp. 3-9.

PIONEER CITIES OF THE OHIO VALLEY

Carmony, Donald F., "Genesis and Early History of the Indianapolis Fund, 1816-1826," *Indiana Magazine of History*, Vol. 38, No. 1 (March 1942), pp. 17-30.

Howe, Henry, *Historical Collections of Ohio*. 2 vols. Cincinnati: State of Ohio, 1900.

Lorant, Stefan, *Pittsburgh: The Story of an American City*. Garden City: Doubleday & Co., 1964.

Ranck, George Washington, *Boonesborough: Its Founding, Pioneer Struggles, Indian Experiences, Transylvania Days and Revolutionary Annals*. Louisville: J. P. Morton & Co., 1901.

Reps, John W., "Thomas Jefferson's Checkerboard Towns," *Journal of the Society of Architectural Historians*, Vol. 20, No. 3 (October 1961), pp. 108-14.

Reps, John W., "Urban Redevelopment in the Nineteenth Century: The Squaring of Circleville," *Journal of the Society of Architectural Historians*, Vol. 14, No. 4 (December 1955), pp. 23-26.

Wade, Richard C., *The Urban Frontier: The Rise of Western Cities, 1790-1830*. Cambridge: Harvard University Press, 1959.

Wright, Alfred J., "Joel Wright, City Planner," *Ohio Archaeological and Historical Quarterly*, Vol. 56, No. 3 (July 1947), pp. 287-94.

WASHINGTON: A NEW CAPITAL
FOR A NEW NATION

Bryan, Wilhelmus Bogart, *A History of the National Capital*. 2 vols. New York: The Macmillan Co., 1914-1916.

Caemmerer, H. Paul, *The Life of Pierre Charles L'Enfant, Planner of the City Beautiful, The City of Washington*. Washington: National Republic Publishing Company, 1950.

Kite, Elizabeth S., *L'Enfant and Washington, 1791-1792*. Baltimore: Johns Hopkins Press, 1929.

Padover, Saul K. (ed.), *Thomas Jefferson and the National Capital*. Washington: Government Printing Office, 1946.

Peets, Elbert W., "L'Enfant's Washington," *Town Planning Review*, Vol. 15, No. 3 (May 1933), pp. 155-64.

Peets, Elbert, *On the Art of Designing Cities*, edited by Paul D. Spreiregen. Cambridge, The M.I.T. Press, 1968.

Reps, John W., *Monumental Washington: The Planning and Development of the Capital Center*. Princeton: Princeton University Press, 1967.

U.S. Federal Writers' Project, Works Progress Administration, *Washington: City and Capital*. Washington: Government Printing Office, 1937.

URBAN PLANNING ON
THE GREAT LAKES FRONTIER

Bingham, Robert Warwick, *Cradle of the Queen City, a History of Buffalo to the Incorporation of the City*. Buffalo: Buffalo Historical Society, 1931.

Chapman, Edmund H., "City Planning Under Mercantile Expansion: The Case of Cleveland, Ohio," *Journal of the Society of Architectural Historians*, Vol. 10, No. 4 (December 1951), pp. 10-17.

Evans, Paul D., *The Holland Land Company*. Buffalo: Buffalo Historical Society, 1924.

Hatcher, Harlan, *The Western Reserve: The Story of New Connecticut in Ohio*. Indianapolis: Bobbs-Merrill Co., 1942.

Pierce, Bessie Louise, *A History of Chicago*. 3 vols. New York: A. A. Knopf, 1937-1957.

Reps, John W., "Planning in the Wilderness: Detroit, 1805-1830," *Town Planning Review*, Vol. 25, No. 4 (January 1955), pp. 240-50.

Woodford, Frank B., *Mr. Jefferson's Disciple: A Life of Justice Woodward*. East Lansing: Michigan State University Press, 1953.

CITIES OF ZION:
THE QUEST FOR UTOPIA

Arndt, Karl J. R., *George Rapp's Harmony Society*. Philadelphia: University of Pennsylvania Press, 1965.

Bennett, Charles E., *Laudonnière and Fort Caroline: History and Documents*. Gainesville: University of Florida Press, 1964.

Bestor, Arthur Eugene, *Backwoods Utopias: The Sectarian and Owenite Phases of Communitarian Socialism in America, 1663-1829*. Philadelphia: University of Pennsylvania Press, 1950.

Fries, Adelaide (ed.), *Records of the 'Moravians in North Carolina*. Vol. I. Raleigh: Edwards & Broughton Printing Co., 1922.

Holloway, Mark, *Heavens on Earth: Utopian Communities in America, 1680-1880*. London: Turnstile Press, 1951.

Levering, Joseph Mortimer, *A History of Bethlehem, Pennsylvania, 1741-1892, with Some Account of Its Founders and Their Early Activity in America*. Bethlehem: Times Publishing Co., 1903.

Murtagh, William J., *Moravian Architecture and Town Planning*. Chapel Hill: University of North Carolina Press, 1967.

Nelson, Lowry, *The Mormon Village: A Pattern and Technique of Land Settlement*. Salt Lake City: University of Utah Press, 1952.

Nordhoff, Charles, *The Communistic Societies of the United States*. New York: Harper & Brothers, 1875.

Sellers, Charles L., "Early Mormon Community Planning," *Journal of the American Institute of Planners*, Vol. 28, No. 1 (February 1962), pp. 24-30.

INDEX

Abercorn, Ga., 250

Akron, Ohio, 363

Alabama, French colonial town planning in, 95-98; single tax community founded at Fairhope, 410

Alamo, founded as Mission of San Antonio de Valero, 52

Alarcon, Martin de, founder of *presidio* at San Antonio, 52

Albany, N.Y., planned by Stuyvesant, 190; named changed from Beverwck, 191-93; dominant city of upper Hudson valley, 344, attracted Huguenots, 386

Alberti, Leon Battista, theories of city planning, 7; doctrines familiar to Spanish, 46

Alexandria, Va., plan of, 124; arrival of French settlers bound for Ohio, 289

Allegheny, Pa., plan of, 262-65; resemblance to New Haven, 265

Allentown, Pa., 222

Altruists, 420

Amana, Iowa, 420, 421

Amaurot, imaginary capital of More's *Utopia*, 12

Amsterdam, Holland, extension of in 17th century, 29-30; well planned, 256, 424

Andreae, Johann Valentin, ideal city of, 12

Andros, Edmund, 130

Annapolis, Md., planned by Nicholson, 129; named changed from Anne Arundel, 133; novel plan for, 133-36; radial street system, 133; public building sites, 135-36; Bloomsbury Square, 136; peculiar feature of radial streets, 136; character in 19th century, 137; part of American planning tradition, 223; temporary site of national capital, 305; planned on public land, 307; example of public initiative, 429

Anne Arundel, Md., renamed Annapolis, 133

Appalachian Mountains, barrier to settlement, 261

architecture, as vital ingredient of urban planning, 426

Ashley-Cooper, Lord Anthony, 225

Augusta, Ga., 247

Austin, Texas, state capital planned on public. land, 307

Avilés, Don Perdro Menéndez de, founded St. Augustine, 47

axial planning, at Annapolis, 136; at Williamsburg, 141-43; at

Washington, D.C., 323; at Buffalo, 351

Bacon, David, planner of Tallmadge, Ohio, 363

Bacon, Francis, 12

Baily, Francis, description of New Orleans, 101-102; description of land speculation techniques, 271-72; visited Louisville, 279; description of national capital, 332-33; comments on gridiron street plans, 427

Baltimore, Md., center of commerce and industry, 137; temporary site of national capital, 305

Bangor, Northern Ireland, 22

Barlow, Joel, 289

baroque planning principles, used at Annapolis, 133-35; used at Williamsburg, 141-43; not employed in New England, 154; applied by L'Enfant at national capital, 322; used at Esperanza, 345-47

bastide towns, in Europe, 13, 15; influence on Spanish Laws of the Indies, 46-47; first plan of Detroit similar to, 86

Bath, N.Y., land office opened, 348; planned by Charles Williamson, 348; decribed by Rochefoucauld,

planning in, 47-48; Spanish settlement at Pensacola, 56; Huguenot settlement at Fort Caroline, 383-85

Fort Caroline, 383
Fort Casimir, 204
Fort Christina, 203, 204
Fort Dearborn, 377
Fort Duquesne, 88, 260
Fort Louis, 95
Fort Pimitoui, 88
Fort Pitt, 261
Fort St. George, Maine, 145
fountains, proposed by L'Enfant for national capital, 320, 321
Fourier, Charles, 409
Franklinville, Ky., 269-71, 273, 275
Frederica, Ga., 247
Fredericksz, Cryn, 185
French colonization, attempted in Florida, 47; variety of settlement forms used, 70; early efforts, 70-74; in Canada, 74-85; in Michigan, 86; in Illinois, 88-89; in Missouri, 89-92; in Alabama, 95-98; in Louisiana, 98-101; remains of, 104; by Huguenots, 383-90
French settlers, at Gallopolis, 289-91

Gallatin, Albert, 377
Gallipolis, Ohio, planned, 289; primitive conditions in, 291
Galvez, La., 54-56
garden design, in Renaissance,

30-32; in France, 32-34; influence on American city planning, 34
Gates, Thomas, 109
geography, as factor in lack of towns in Virginia, 111; influences of in town location in North Carolina, 228-29
Georgetown, Md., 306; near site selected for national capital, 308; scene of meeting of Washington and land owners of capital site, 309-11
Georgia, proposed settlement in by Mountgomery, 235-38; towns planned in by Oglethorpe, 238-50; Brunswick, 258
Gloucester, Mass., 146
Gloucester, Va., courthouse square in, 127
Gnadenhutten, Ohio, 400
Goerck, Casimir, 196
Gorges, Ferdinando, 145
Gorham, Nathaniel, 348
Graffenried, Baron Christopher de, 230, 232
Granada, Spain, 19
Grand Circus, Detroit, 376
Granger, Gideon, 359
Grant Park, Chicago, 377
Gravesend, N.Y., 250
green, village or town, see public squares, common land
Greenfield, Mass., 173, 182
gridiron street plan, in *bastide* towns, 13; in towns of Northern Ireland, 20; proposed for London

by Knight, Hooke, and Newcourt, 22-24; in Paris, 29; prescribed by the Laws of the Indies, 43; use of in Virginia and Maryland, 118-22; at New Amsterdam, 185; early development in New York City, 194; adopted by street commissioners in 1811, 197; in New York City as model, 203; Philadelphia as model for, 221; good and bad features of, 221; advocated by Jefferson, 312-14; criticized by L'Enfant, 314-16; combination with radial system at Washington, 324; substituted at Detroit for radial system, 374-76; at Chicago, 381; at Harmony, 402; at Far West, 413-14; widespread use in America, 426-28; criticized by Baily, 427; wise use of, 428. *See also*, street systems
Grosvenor Square, London, 253
growth of towns, policy for in New England, 151-52
Guast, Pierre du, 71
gunpowder, effect of introduction in Europe on fortifications, 8-9
Gwathmey, John, 282

Hamburgh, Md., 309
Hamilton, Alexander, 306, 353
Hampstead, Ga., 250
Hampton, Va., 109, 111
Hanover, N.H., 162
Hanover Square, London, 253;

and Ellicott, 316; explained plan to Washington, 317-20; proposed land policy for capital, 320; revised plan, 320-22; trained in baroque planning techniques, 322-23; criticism of his plan, 323-25; concern for urban beauty, 325; opposed sale of lots in capital, 325-26; requested to arrange for printed plan of city, 326-27; difficulties with commissioners and property owners, 327; changes made in his design, 328; dismissed as planner of capital, 330; later years, 330; plan criticized by Latrobe, 338; vision ultimately justified, 343; friend of Woodward, 367

Le Nôtre, André, 32, 322
Leroy, Ohio, 363
Lexington, Ky., 269
Lincoln's Inn Fields, London, 212, 253
Lindstrom, Peter, 204
linear plan, at lower town of Quebec, 76; at Montreal, 80, 84; at St. Louis, 92; in New England villages, 168-73; at Gallipolis, 289; at New Rochelle, 387
Litchfield, Conn., 162
Lititz, Pa., 393, 394
Livingston, Edward, 345
Locke, John, 224
London, England, fire in 1666, 20; rebuilding plans for, 20-24; plan for by Newcourt as possible in-

fluence on design of Philadelphia, 212-13; squares in as possible source of Savannah plan, 253-55; plan of new portions of contrasted with that of Savannah, 424

London Company, responsible for Virginia colonization, 107, 113
Londonderry, Northern Ireland, 20; plan of known by Oglethorpe, 251
Long Wharf, Boston, 176
Los Angeles, Calif., order by de Neve establishing, 63; plan of, 65
Louisburg, Cape Breton Island, plan of, 78; similarity to French plans of Vauban, 80
Louisburg Square, Boston, 180
Louisiana, Spanish settlement at Galvez, 54-56; French settlement at New Orleans, 98-101
Louisiana Purchase, 92, 102
Louisville, Ky., first settled, 275; site moved, 276; planned by Clark, 276; later development, 276-79
Ludlow, Israel, 292, 294
Lystra, Ky., 269-71, 273, 275

Machiavelli, Niccolo, castremetation theories, 12; influence on Laws of the Indies, 46
Madison, James, 304
Madison, Ohio, 363
Maerschalck, Francis, 194

McCloskey, James, 373
McMillan, James, 343
Maine, French settlement at Isle de Sainte Croix, 72; English settlement at Fort St. George, 145
Mall, in Washington, D.C., 319-20, 321, 334, 339, 341, 372
Manakin, Va., Huguenot settlement at, 387; plan of, 388
Manhattan Island, 187, 203
Margravate of Azilia, plan for described by Mountgomery, 235-38; possible influence on plan of Savannah, 253
Marino, Hieronimo, plan for Vitry-le-François, 9
Marlborough, Va., plan of, 118
Marshall, Friedrich, instructions for planning Salem, 394-99
Martineau, Harriet, described land speculation in Chicago, 379-80
Martini, Francesco, 9
Maryland, settled under Lord Baltimore, 115; first town at St. Mary's, 115; new town legislation, 116-17; elementary forms used in town plans, 122; towns planned in 18th century, 124-27; Nicholson governor of, 131-33; new capital planned at Annapolis, 133-37
Massachusetts, early settlement in, 145-47; settlement policy of General Court, 151-52; chief town at Boston, 173-80; Huguenot settlement at Oxford, 386

Massachusetts Avenue, Washington, D.C., 328
Mathews, Maurice, description of Charleston, 225
Mayvil, N. Y., 353
Medford, Mass., 157
Michigan, French colonial town planning in, 86; development of Detroit, 367-76
migration, routes in U.S., 262, 344
military engineers of Renaissance, city planning theories, 8-9
Mills, Isaac, 364
Minuit, Peter, 203
missions, Spanish, 52, 54; in California, 61
Missouri, French colonial town planning in, 89-92; Mormon settlements in, 410-11, 413
Mobile, Ala., influence of topography on plan of, 82; founded, 95; planning of, 95-97; passed to English, 98
Monpazier, France, 13
Monterey, Calif., 61
Montreal, Canada, influence of topography on plan, 80; first plan for, 82; development of on linear pattern, 82-84; building regulations after fire, 84-85; continued growth of, 85; mentioned, 95, 104
monumentality, aimed for by L'Enfant in plan for national capital, 325

Moore, Francis, explanation of Savannah plan, 251-52
Moore, Thomas, poem describing national capital, 334
Moravians, origins, 390; at Bethlehem, 391-93; settlements of in North Carolina, 393-99; mission towns in Ohio, 399-400
More, Thomas, ideal city of, 12
Morfi, Father Juan Agustín, description of San Antonio, 54
Mormons, origins, 410; settlements in Missouri, 410-11; model town for prepared by Smith, 411-13; at Far West, 413-14; at Nauvoo, 414; in Nebraska, 416; planned Salt Lake City, 416; founded towns in Utah, 419; distinctive character of towns, 420
Morris, Gouverneur, 196
Morris, Robert, 348, 353
Mound Builders, effect of constructions, on plan of Marietta, 285-87; on plan of Circleville, 299
Mount Auburn Cemetery, Cambridge, 275
Mountgomery, Robert, granted land in Carolina, 235; description of proposed settlement unit, 235-38; failure to colonize, 238; possible influence on plan of Savannah, 253

Naarden, Holland, 19

Nancy, France, 16
national capital, one town on wheels and two sites proposed for, 305; Residence Act, 306; sites inspected by Washington, 306; site selected by Washington, 308; site surveyed and studied by Ellicott and L'Enfant, 308-309; land acquisition arranged by Washington, 309-11; L'Enfant appointed to plan, 312; plan for by Jefferson, 312-14; L'Enfant's plan for, 317-22; criticism of plan, 323-25; land policy in, 325-26; land sales, 326-27; changes in plan of, 328; described by Twining, 330-32; described by Baily, 332-33; described by Birkbeck, 333; derogatory comments about, 333-34; subject of poem by Moore, 334; admired by Frances Trollope, 334-36; description of by Smith, 336-37; plan and buildings analyzed by Latrobe, 338; improvements in, 339-41; railroad authorized on Mall, 341; replanning in 20th century, 343
National Cemetery, Arlington, Va., 330
National Road, 265
Nauvoo, Ill., Mormon settlement of, 414
Nazareth, Pa., 393
Nebraska, Mormon settlement in, 416

neighborhood unit, wards of Savannah similar to, 255

Neve, Philip de, governor of California, 63; founder of San José, 63; order establishing Los Angeles, 63-64

New Amsterdam, settled, 184-85; plan for, 185; plan ignored, 185-87; early building regulations in, 187-88; appearance and description at end of Dutch period, 188-90; renamed New York, 193; Huguenot settlement in, 385-86. *See also* New York City

Newark, Ohio, 294-95

New Bern, N.C., 229; planned by de Graffenried, 230; plan of, 230-32

New Bordeaux, S.C., 390

New Castle, Delaware, 204

Newcourt, Richard, plan for rebuilding London, 24; possible influence on plan of Philadelphia, 212

New Ebenezer, Ga., plan for, 245-47

New Elfsborg, 203

New England, heritage of planning in, 181-83; settlement patterns transplanted to Western Reserve, 355-59

New England land system, 147-49; at Plymouth, 145-46; general character, 147; similarity to Spanish pueblo communities,

149; Wethersfield as example, 149-51; methods of town growth under, 151-52; changes in 18th century, 152-53; changes in, 152-53; summarized, 153-55

New England village planning, green or common in, 154-55; variations in form, 157-59; irregular patterns, 167; linear patterns, 168-73

New Gothenburg, 203

New Hampshire, plan of Exeter, 164, 167

New Harmony, Ind., founded by Rapp, 402; sold to Robert Owen, 402, 406; proposed plan for, 406-409; utopian community, 409

New Haven, Conn., similarity of Eden to, 127; plan for, 159; possible influence on plan of Penn's agricultural villages, 183; part of American planning tradition, 223; similarity of Allegheny to, 265; open space in, 428

New Lanark, Scotland, 406

New Mexico, Spanish settlement at Santa Fé, 56-60

New Orleans, La., influence of topography on plan of, 82; rural land pattern near helped shape growth patterns, 86; founded by Bienville, 98; planned by Pauger, 99; described by Charlevoix, 99; plan of, 99-101; de-

scribed by Baily, 101-102; building in under Spanish rule, 102; boulevards built on fortifications, 102; development of, 102-104; repeating pattern of open squares, 104; preservation of old buildings in, 104-105

New Paltz, N.Y., 386

Newport, R.I., 162-64

New Rochelle, N.Y., Huguenot settlement, 386-87

new towns, in Renaissance Europe, 13-24; legislation for in Virginia and Maryland, 116-18; proposed in Britain by Owen, 406

New York City, abandonment of original settlement plan, 5; early development as New Amsterdam, 184-90; taken from Dutch by English, 193; growth under English rule, 193-94; land subdivision in, 194; became temporary capital of U.S., 194, 305; loss of open space in, 196; beginning of gridiron expansion, 196; plan in 1811 by street commissioners, 196-202; deficiencies in early 19th century planning, 202-203; population in 1830, 376

Nicholson, Francis, planner of Virginia and Maryland capitals, 129; early career, 130; colonial administrator in America, 130-31; assisted in founding College of William and Mary, 131; in

Public Garden, Boston, 180
public land acquisition, widely used for planning of new towns, 307-308
public ownership of land, made possible controlled growth of Savannah, 256
public squares, in Londonderry, 20; proposed in London rebuilding plans, 22-24; in Renaissance cities, 25-28; in Spanish colonial towns, 42-43; at San Antonio, 52-54; at Galvez, 54; at Santa Fé, 58-60; at Los Angeles, 64; at St. Louis, 92; at Mobile, 98; at New Orleans, 99; in later development of New Orleans, 104; at Charlestown, Maryland, 124; at Eden, 127; at Annapolis, 136; at Williamsburg, 141; in New England towns; 147, 154-55; at Cambridge, 157; at New Haven, 159; at Fairfield, 162; at Woodstock, 167; at Ipswich, 168; at Boston, 174, 176, 178; at Philadelphia, 209, 212, 213, 220; in Pennsylvania towns, 222; typical of midwestern towns, 222-23; at Charleston, 225-26; at Savannah, 245; at Darien, 247; similarity of Savannah's to that at Coleraine, 251; at Savannah modelled after those in Ireland and London, 253-55; at Pittsburgh, 262; at Allegheny, 262; at Beaver, 265; at Lexing-

ton, 269; at Franklinville and Lystra, 271; in speculative towns, 272; pattern of proposed by Jefferson, 280; at Jeffersonville, 282; at Marietta, 285; at Gallipolis, 289; at Indianapolis, 297; at Circleville, 301; proposed by L'Enfant for Washington, 320-21; at Hudson, 345; at Esperenza, 347; at Bath, 350; at Cleveland, 355; at Jefferson, 360; at Chardon, 360; at Elyria, 363; variety of shapes used for in Western Reserve towns, 363; at Tallmadge, 364; at Sandusky, 364; at Detroit, 370; at Manakin, 388; at Bethania and Bethabara, 394; at Salem, 398; at Harmony, 402; proposed by Robert Owen, 406; in Joseph Smith's City of Zion plat, 411; at Charleville, 423; comparison of those in London with Savannah's, 424. *See also* residential squares
pueblos, Spanish, 51; of San Fernando, 52; in California, 63-68; resemblance to New England towns, 68
Pulteney Purchase, 348
Puritans, settlers of Massachusetts Bay, 146; in Holland, 385
Putnam, Rufus, 283; laid out Marietta, 285; described Campus Martius at Marietta, 287; skillful planner, 288

Quakers, in settlement of Philadelphia, 206, 220
Quebec, Canada, 70; founded by Champlain, 74; plan of, 76; description of by Charlevoix, 76-78; buildings in, 78; mentioned, 80, 85, 104; plan compared to Charleville, 423

radial plan, at Detroit, 370, 372
railway, on Mall in Washington, D.C., 341
railways, Chicago as focal point for, 381
Raleigh, N.C., 222-23; state capital planned on public land, 307
Raleigh, Sir Walter, 106
Ralston, Alexander, 297, 299
Rapp, George, leader of Harmony Society, 400; planned Harmony and New Harmony, 402
Reading, Pa., 222
redevelopment, of Jeffersonville, 282; of Circleville, 301-303
Redick, David, 265
Red Lion Square, London, 253
Residence Act, passed, 306; Jefferson's views of implementation to establish capital city, 306-307; commissioners appointed to carry out, 308
residential squares, in Renaissance cities, 25; in London, 28-29; in Paris, 28; in London, 132; in Boston, 178-80; in New York City, 194, 196; in Savannah,

245, 253; at Hygeia, 273; those in London compared to Savannah's, 424. *See also* public squares
Reuter, Christian Gottlieb, 394
Rhode Island, compact plan of Newport, 162-64; plan of Providence, 171
Ribeaut, Jean, 383
Richelieu, Cardinal, 74
Richmond, Va., 144
Rio de Janeiro, Brazil, 383
Roanoke Island, North Carolina, attempted English settlement on, 106, 145
Rochefoucauld-Liancourt, Duke de La, description of Bath, 348-49
Rockefeller, John D. Jr., 144
Rocque, John, plan of London, 253
rural life, and American ideal, 425-26
Rutherford, John, 196

St. Augustine, Fla., founding, 48; plan of 48-51; combined three functions, 51; Spanish base for elimination of Huguenots, 385
St. Clair, Arthur, 292
St. James's Square, London, 253
St. Lawrence Seaway, 376
St. Louis, Mo., founded by Pierre Laclede, 91; described by Chouteau, 91; plan of, 92; described by Brackenridge, 94; later development, 94-95
St. Mary's, Md., first settlement in colony, 115; replaced as capital by Annapolis, 133
St. Petersburg (Leningrad), U.S.S.R., 324
St. Simons Island, Ga., 247
Ste. Croix Island, Maine, Huguenot settlement, 385
Ste. Geneviève, Mo., 89
Salem, Mass., settled, 146; plan of, 155-57, 174
Salem, N.C., planned by Reuter, 394; instructions for planning of, 394-99
Salisbury, England, 15
Salisbury, N.C., 235
Salzburgers, settled in Georgia, 245-47
San Antonio, Texas, *presidio* at, 52; missions near, 52; plan of, 52; description by Morfi, 54
San Diego, Calif., 61
Sandusky, Ohio, 364-67
San Francisco, Calif., 61; Burnham plan for, 71
San José, Calif., founded by de Neve, 63; plan of, 64
Santa Barbara, Calif., 61
Santa Fé, N.M., founded, 56; described by Dominguez, 58-60
Santa Fé, Spain, 16-19, 46
Santayana, George, 422
Santo Domingo, planned by Ovando, 36; described by Oviedo y Valdés, 36-37; plan of, 37-38
Sauthier, C.J., plans drawn by, 230, 232
Savannah, Ga., plan compared to Williamsburg, 141; part of American planning tradition, 223; site selected, 239; described by Oglethorpe, 239-40; early building described, 240; plan of by Oglethorpe, 240-45; conveyance of land in, 241-42; common land, 242; system of streets and open spaces, 242-45; growth described, 245; villages near, 250; source of design for, 250-55; explanation of plan by Moore, 251-52; common land made possible control of development, 256; planned growth, 256-58; described by Buckingham, 258; lack of influence on subsequent planning in America, 258-60; plan for contrasted with West End in London, 424; squares in, 428
Scamozzi, Vincenzo, plan for Palma Nova, 9
Schenck, William, 294
Schoenbrunn, Ohio, 399-400
Scioto Company, formed, 283; efforts to attract settlers, 288-89
Separatists of Zoar, 420
Shakers, 420
Sharon Center, Ohio, 363
Shepherd, Alexander, 341
Smith, John, description of Henrico, 109-111
Smith, John Cotton, views on national capital, 336-37

wrote to Jefferson about land acquisition, 309-11; appointed L'Enfant to plan capital, 312; received report from L'Enfant, 314-16; visited site for capital, 316; described preliminary plan, 317; received memorandum from L'Enfant, 317; disagreed with L'Enfant's proposed land policy, 326; appointed Ellicott to prepare engraving of town plan of Washington, 327; dismissed L'Enfant, 330; artistic sense criticized by Latrobe, 338

Waterbury, Conn., 182

Watertown, Mass., 157

water transportation, important in French colonial towns, 85-86; importance in Virginia, 111-13

Weld, Isaac, description of Bethlehem, 391-93

West, John Jr., 124

Western Reserve, of Connecticut in Ohio, 353-54

West India Company, 184, 185, 385

Wethersfield, Conn., founded, 149; plan of, 149-51

Whitwell, Stedman, 407

Wilkinson, James, 294

Willemstad, Holland, 19

William and Mary, College of, founded, 131; building for probably designed in office of Christopher Wren, 132; at Middle Plantation, 139

Williamsburg, Va., planned by Nicholson, 129; replaced Jamestown as colonial capital, 137-39; legislation governing planning of, 139-40; main street in named for Duke of Gloucester, 139; first plan incorporated cypher, 140; plan for described by Robert Beverley, 140; described by Hugh Jones, 140-41; first plan revised, 141; plan analyzed, 141-43; axial planning in, 143; small size, 143; capital moved from, 144; restored in modern era, 144; part of American planning tradition, 223; planned on public land, 307; unique three-dimensional plan, 426

Williamson, Charles, land agent in Pulteney Purchase, 348; planned Bath, 348; plan for Bath, 349-50

Wilmington, N.C., plan of, 229-30

Wiltwyck., renamed Kingston, 190

Winchelsea, England, 15

Windsor, Conn., 152, 181

Winter Quarters, Neb., 416

Winthrop, John, 173

Wisconsin, towns planned in, 380

Woodstock, Vt., 164-67

Woodward, Augustus Brevoort, appointed judge of Michigan Territory, 367; prepared plan for Detroit following fire, 368; his plan for the city, 368-72; opposed by Hull, 373; plan for Detroit revised in his absence, 374; vision of, 376

Woodward Avenue, Detroit, 374

Wren, Christopher, plan for rebuilding London, 22; possible influence on Francis Nicholson, 132, 135

Wright, Joel, 295

Yeamans, John, 225

York, Pa., 222, 305

Yorktown, Va., plan of, 118

Young, Brigham, 416, 419

Zane, Ebenezer, 294

Zanesville, Ohio, 294

Zeisberger, David, 399-400

Zinzendorf, Count, 390

Zoar, Ohio, 421

French

New England

New York

Georgia
    Savannah
       plan dev by
James Oglethorpe
held to –